David Toop is a musician, author and music curator. His first book, *Rap Attack*, is now in its third edition. Since the publication of *Ocean of Sound* in 1995 he has recorded four solo albums, including *Screen Ceremonies, Pink Noir* and *Spirit World*. He lives in London with his daughter, Juliette.

Also by David Toop and published by Serpent's Tail

Rap Attack #3
Ocean of Sound

exotica

fabricated soundscapes in a real world

david toop

Library of Congress Catalog Card Number: 98–89855

A catalogue record for this book is available from the
British Library on request

The right of David Toop to be identified as the author
of this work has been asserted by him in accordance with
the Copyright, Designs and Patents Act 1988

Copyright © David Toop 1999

First published in 1999 by
Serpent's Tail, 4 Blackstock Mews, London N4

Website: www.serpentstail.com

Phototypeset in Sabon by Intype London Ltd
Printed in Great Britain by Mackays of Chatham plc

10 9 8 7 6 5 4 3 2 1

exotica
a dream
colonisation
a bizarre image
an image of paradise
mutual misunderstanding
an imagined quality of elsewhere
a projection from the unconscious
a conjured place, person or atmosphere
erotic desire synthesised with asexual phenomena
constructs of the imagination, essences of difference
that which is remote, other, unusual, unfamiliar, obscure
a fantasy of alien culture, behaviour, appearance, environment

exotica

Exotica is the art of ruins, the ruined world of enchantment laid waste in fervid imagination, the paradox of an imperial paradise liberated from colonial intervention, a golden age recreated through the lurid colours of a cocktail glass, illusory and remote zones of pleasure and peace dreamed after the bomb. Nothing is left, except for beaches, palm trees, tourist sites with their moss-covered monuments, shops stocked with native art made for the invaders, beachcomber bars and an absurd perception of what may once have been.

Just ruins and a spell, repeated endlessly to provoke fading memories: lust and terror, chainsaw bikers, sultry tropical airs, Aztec spells, x-ray eyes and hot pants, sunken cities, lost cities, singing sea shells, electric frogs, bustin' bongos, wild stuffed bikinis, jungle jazz, sacred idols, space escapades, switchblade sisters, pits and pendulums, tabu, taboo, tabuh, tamboo, taboo, tabuh, tamboo, tabuh-tabuhan.

contents

exotica

part 4 ● pink noir: adventures in paradise

introduction

● the archive

Swimming after death, I floundered in deep water, waves of word-less anguish flooding through me. Sobs were shaken from my closed mouth. I saw my own pain transforming into bubbles, mocking the cold touch of grief. Solid and supernatural, a liquid casket, the water offered me my own death. At that moment of panic I decided I could no longer put aside the opening of the tea chest filled with my travel diaries.

Since the suicide of my wife I had been engulfed by a rich diversity of agonies. The cataloguing of these travel notes had seemed urgent before the event, irrelevant after. I left the archive in storage, in disorder, in seclusion at the museum and forgot about it. I believe the archive forgot about me.

But memory grows potent in the wake of catastrophe, acquiring magical force, the power to derange and transfix. Personal history becomes a maze. I felt myself lured by flickering candlelight along serpentine alleys and dank gothic tunnels, then silently pushed from behind into a graveyard of buried stories, all demanding emotional resolution.

Sound was the medium that pulled me. I had curated sound for most of my working life yet music was degraded for me, an irritant now. Recapturing the significance that music had played in my life before this pivotal event seemed impossible. Now I was interested in death and life. Some might have seen this as pretentious and in a sense they were right. My tolerance for trivia had narrowed sharply.

But sound still held a key. I might describe a sense impression visually; the sirenic call flickered in my peripheral vision: a snapshot of a ghost. But I was struggling to give form to forces that were aether. Like sound, they were elusive wraiths, moving through zones that could not be isolated: body, emotion, intellect, chemistry, sexuality, spirit, memory. By moving so fluidly, with so little regard for the classifications of human society, the wraiths reconstructed my being; sound also possessed that capacity.

To be honest, I had no idea how some of these archived texts had come into being. Whole sections appeared to be suctioned out of the future or constructed from events of which I had no recall. People I had never met spoke to me. Places I had never visited seemed too vivid to be fictions. Even the incidents I remembered had taken on an ambiguous cast. I began to believe that suppressed dreams were infiltrating the record of past life that this tea chest and its mysterious contents represented. In this aspect, the notes acted as a reprimand. How many lives can be lived, or should be lived, within one lifetime?

Yet there was a curious element. An occult element that could prickle my skin at dead of night. Maybe my actions with regard to The Book were responsible for this disturbing aspect of the diaries.

I had stolen The Book from an obscure museum – prudence dictates that I keep secret the name of both museum and book. Youthful, inexperienced, hungry for knowledge, I had no intimation of the consequences of this act.

So I came to the event that may have changed my life.

The nature of The Book was arcane: a thorough cataloguing of Tibetan demons. Some years after publication, the author had died in an accident; not because he had catalogued the demons, authorities claimed, but because he had made them appear so boring. Why did I want The Book? Because of its obscurity, I suppose, and a fascination with the fearsome things of our own psychology ... and, to be truthful, because a tedious study of demons and spirits might function as a campfire to keep those fearsome things at the dark outer edges of the self.

For my crime, I exploited the undignified, chaotic depths of a man's bereavement (again, caution prevents me from revealing the full details), using deception to steal The Book and placing guilt for its disappearance on the shoulders of this drunken sufferer, a man who had lost his wife and perhaps, for the first time in his life, was blind to the responsibilities of his job. So The Book sat on my shelves for years, black-bound, heavy and thick with pages. Too exhaustively boring to read, the object proved too seductive, too powerful to discard.

Then my own tragedy fell out of the sky, its mysteries as impossible to unravel as any other event of its kind. At times, when my feelings were exhausted and rationality demonstrated its limits, I blamed The Book. Actually, I blamed the army of demons catalogued within. Their names – unpronounceable and as harsh in their sound as exploding logs on a fire – reminded me of Joseph Conrad, writing in *The Rescue*: '. . . she was appalled to find she was unable to connect these names with any human appearance. They stood out alone, as if written on the night; they took on a symbolic shape; they imposed themselves upon her senses. She whispered as if pondering: "Belarab, Daman, Ningrat," and these barbarous sounds seemed to possess an exceptional energy, a fatal aspect, the savour of madness.'

So it was with me. *Tsi'u dmar po, bDud btsan, Khrag btsan dmar po, Grib btsan*; all of them were furious, no doubt. Made dull as a shopping list through the bloodless process of schematisation, then scorned at a point when they might become better appreciated, they had decided to punish me in a manner appropriate to the original theft. If I survived the initial shock, then they might drown me at a later date, either in chlorinated water or alcohol.

The self-aggrandising exoticism of my superstition was abhorrent yet grief is fierce and clings to the unconscious. As James Hillman wrote in *The Dream and the Underworld*: 'There is an opening downward within each moment, an unconscious reverberation, like the thin thread of the dream that we awaken with in our hands each morning leading back and down into the images of the dark.'

Frozen in deep water with inner pain and tension, I concluded that a thorough perusal and documentation of my own archives might help me to locate a safe path leading out of this labyrinth of dark memory.

This was a matter of identity, besides, since any certainties of self-image that survive life's accumulated experiences can be shattered by trauma. As it emerges, like Frankenstein's creation, the renewed body is sensitive to all questions of identity. Life had become exotic, even though this word – exotic – was pungent, not only with Conrad's exceptional energy, but with his fatal aspect, his 'savour of madness'.

● a cartographic anomaly

For two months the tea chest sat in one corner of the room, looking like the kind of box that goes straight into storage in the loft of a newly bought house and stays there, undisturbed, until the next change of address. While my daughter slept upstairs, I busied myself with Booty Shaker videos, sumo tournaments, X-rated *manga*, Tony Little fitness product infomercials, Tamagotchi web sites, Ringo Lam films from Hong Kong. Exploding heads, bodies like tropical fruits, beings that sprouted tentacles, self-evolving non-human entities, cities on fire. I had heard Ringo Lam describe the process of making his films in a terse formula: no money, no time; just do it. That was the kind of art I liked, the kind of art that fed my very private despair.

Then I remembered the story of the cartographers' nightmare. For years a new world map had been in preparation. All major floodings, earthquakes, erosions and volcanic eruptions were monitored. Every new state, devolved territory and fissured country had been accounted for. Every dictator's ruling on name changes and boundary claims had been evaluated. Where possible, the outcome of guerrilla wars had been determined by secret organisations in order to comply with the shape of the map.

The map was published to huge acclaim, its detail and accuracy outstanding, its beauty breathtaking. Less than one year after publication, a new island appeared in the Indian Ocean. Roughly the size of Madagascar, the island lay to the south of Sumatra. There were people living on the island; culturally, they seemed uninteresting to the world. There was little chance of Steven Spielberg rushing to film them. Anthropologists who specialised in South-East Asian studies were excited, however, since the kinship system they discovered was minutely yet significantly different from anything previously encountered.

The same was true of flora and fauna: no lost-world dinosaurs or man-eating plants but a fabulous range of growing and creeping things that were just different enough to attract armies of ecstatic specialists in botany, lepidoptery, mycology, ornithology and other interests too obscure to name. In the battle for rights to name the island, the governments of Indonesia and Australia reached a dangerous level of hostility. Proposals for names such as Sambir, Typee or Tsalal were rejected for their vestigial allusions to colonial history, albeit the sector of that history belonging to the imagination. Even before a decision could be reached, news editors tired of the story. Public interest waned. Speculation ceased. Beyond the infrequently consulted pages of academic journals, the island became just another remote plot of land where there were no film stars, no computer networks and, for the time being, no tourist hotels.

Then, suddenly, the island vanished. No earthquake tremors were reported, no UFOs had been sighted. Satellite photography proved its disappearance without giving any clue to the cause. The media treatment of the event was structured according to the response apparatus activated by a sudden, catastrophic and totally inexplicable plane crash – the type of crash when a jumbo jet full of children, pregnant women, honeymooners and at least one sports star plummets into the sea, leaving only a black box that records the final words of the captain as he screams, 'Aah, shit, we're gonna die . . .' Rolling news reports were illustrated by pictures of nothing in particular, followed sharply by analysis, blame, exoneration, the hard news rounded off by human interest stories questioning the value of counselling, the wisdom of foreign travel, the madness of science.

Inevitably, the island's retreat back into its oceanic source led to eventual indifference. Perhaps the entire incident had been a fantasy, a media fabrication, an elaborate diversion from something malign taking place on the other side of the world. Only conspiracy theorists, grieving academics, Atlanteans and professional treasure hunters from Florida maintained an interest. Of course, the cartographers could hardly forget. In a collective death pact reminiscent of posthuman Webcults they committed suicide.

This story of the cartographic anomaly vibrated in my skull with the profound resonance of a Japanese temple bell. By an oblique route, which is how the best stories work, it had revealed the danger into which I had fallen. For years I had been industriously, pointlessly mapping a world that lacked sense or shape. This was how I finally came to open the tea chest, to discover if my archive of travel notes, meetings, letters and diaries contained more effective maps than the ones I had drawn in the past.

A matter of survival, then, and fuck anybody who failed to see the point. Those touched by suicide become wary, as if stalked by an invisible predator. I had to create my own sense, my own soul even, out of remote exotic zones that came and went of their own unpredictable volition. Either that or drown.

● a history of the marvellous

I had a friend who described herself with typical student humour as a reverse hypnopaediatrician; that is to say, somebody who learns from sleeping people. Personally, I felt the title made her sound like a medical crank who practised hypnosis on children. A rather unworldly perpetual research student, she recorded words spoken by volunteer subjects during sleep. She would say that they bubbled out of the unconscious as word shards or chips of sound. Despite her dedication to the study, she believed that these unguarded utterances possessed a similar illusory meaning to the movements of flying birds or the sounds of a waterfall. In other words, none (or that was what I thought when she told me about the happy progress of her latest research grants).

Of course, Taoist monks and poets found plenty of meaning in such phenomena. To give one example, they made associations between writing, sound and the movements of clouds. Inspired by cloud formations, Taoist calligraphers used Cloud Script to speak with the spirits that lived in mist. A similar script – Sound of Jade – notated music and the sound of natural phenomena such as waterfalls, since sound, vaporous yet potent, could interpenetrate the aethereal environment of the spirits. A long history had attached itself to the idea that spontaneous or naturally occurring phenomena were possessed with a kind of truth, a direct route to the mumblings and scribbles of God.

With a frisson of dread, I thought of my Tibetan demons and

the trance oracles who dredged messages from extrahuman worlds. In his Surrealist Manifesto of 1924, André Breton documented his own experience of thoughts that can appear, fully formed, during that period of half-sleep we call hypnagogic. In fact, he defined surrealism as 'pure psychic automatism'. This process, he claimed, was an expression of 'the true function of thought'.

We can return to this history later, since there are interesting connections between surrealism's assault on bourgeois logic and the spontaneous utterances of the 'voiceless' poor through speaking in tongues and similar uncontrolled speech mechanisms. For now, I can only say that the healing services of American devil-destroyers such as Benny Hinn proved as amusing during my period of ennui as all the other pornographic cable fare. This odious arch-manipulator of impressionable crowds seemed capable of firing Uzi bursts of glossolalia out of the sick and crippled, zapping them repeatedly on the forehead with God's power, leering as they fell like babbling puppets.

In the present context, what I have been learning from my friend the hypnopaediatrician is the necessity of allowing these word shards to emerge from sleep. I could have been looking for an equivalent of Breton's 'true function of thought' but besides being a little high-flown for me, the premise seemed dubious. Is there really a single authentic function of thought? For years I had been collecting stories from narrators in many different countries. Like Benny Hinn, I had made their tongues into my story. Call that imperialism, if you like; the imagination does it anyway. I had also sought out a certain kind of specialised experience in order to define my notion of the marvellous, the exotic.

1

neo-noir

1
the vending machines

◆◆◆◆◆◆◆◆◆◆◆◆◆◆◆◆◆◆

The French author and translator, Arthur Mangin, published a romantic study of wilderness in 1872. *The Desert World* defined its subject as 'all the regions where man has not planted his regular communities or permanent abodes; where earth has never been appropriated, tilled, and subjected to cultivation; where Nature has maintained her inviolability against the encroachments of human industry'.

This may have been true in the nineteenth century, particularly for Mangin, who promoted the colonial view, the 'one incontestable fact, the superiority of those races that have acquired civilisation over those which are incapable of so grand a work'; in our time, wilderness is a place where the grand works of the civilised races have done their worst. I found myself in such a wilderness, stumbling into a central encampment during the dry season. Was encampment the word? I don't think so. This was a city, but a city like none I had ever seen. Loud, complex, fluid, terrifying; a city of extraordinary possibilities. Before entering the inner walls, I took my bearings. In one direction, the suburbs, surrounded by whipping fences armed with deadly voltage. Blackened animals sat at electrical throwing distance from these banshee defences and wondered why they had died.

In another direction, sand without boundaries, chaotic with strange life forms. There were legends of a subsonic boom that paralysed sidewinder snakes as it rolled across the dunes, hurling trapdoor spiders out of their burrows and high into the air and causing instantaneous diarrhoea in all two- or four-legged creatures unlucky enough to be caught without nappies.

In the encampment, pornographic raconteurs delivered circadian monologues from open-fronted shops, thin plastic microphones held delicately between thumbs and forefingers in the manner of lounge singers. Speaking quickly, without pause, in disconnected fragments, they described colourful incidents of bestiality, torture, exotic autoerotic devices, industrial accidents, the histories of dismemberment and cannibalism. Their listeners – children and old people, dogs and empty chairs – accumulated a mass of dismembered knowledge. Their dreams were disturbed by the arcana of the raconteurs, a rich brew of sexual fantasy fortified by references to Samoyed hand-cutting spirits, Mayan priests playing flutes and rattles to decapitated heads resting in pots, the bat god Tlacatzinacantli with his skulls and gourd rattles, itinerant Tantrics conversing with the dead through skull drums.

As the monologues droned on past the witching hour, nocturnal cult ceremonies weaved through the streets, faces of the initiates hidden behind masks beaten from obsolete household labour-saving devices. These were known variously as the Flashing Night Spirits, the Society of Faces, the Spore Diviners, the Boneless. Their secret speech mixed borrowed expressions from so many different languages, all transformed through partial understanding, that even the cult leaders found themselves lost in a sea of alien tongues.

I had arrived, I discovered, at the moment preceding a burial rite. No child was exempt from the forage during these rites. More than fifty cavity beetles had to be collected. Their mating song was unique. They would burrow backwards into the sand until vertical, then open their abnormally wide mouths and wait for the wind to catch the edges of their jaws.

For those few travellers who had heard it, the sound was said to be as haunting as a wolf howl. I was reminded of the potoo or wood nightjar, an ugly bird cursed with a body like a fungus and a gaping mouth like a surgical operation. Found in the West Indies, Haiti and South America, the potoo has contributed to local mythology and spirit lore. In Trinidad, for example, its eerie cries are said to be the carriers of criminal souls.

I imagine something similar must have occurred with the cavity beetles. For the burial, they were mounted in fishbone glue, upright and separated according to sex. Hidden behind a screen, their eerie singing was interpreted by non-initiates as the sound of spirits caught in string-woven ghostcatchers as they tried to break through into the world of humans.

My isolated arrival preceded a wave of refugee offcomers. City life was transformed when the new guests arrived. Confronted by the vending walls they discarded their shyness with the speed of new lovers in the heat of sex. On-line celebrities, all cut-price grunts of narrowband culture and none of them known to the strangers, beckoned them forward, offering change tokens in exchange for cash or credit.

To one side, security personnel chewed coca leaves, stroking the heads of fighting dogs and closely watching each transaction between human and automatic dispenser. The colour and luminosity of these machines reminded the exhausted strangers of toucan beaks, bird of paradise feathers, beetle carapaces, rainforest flower petals. Eagerly, they exchanged the meagre hard currency they had been given before their long journey, then watched in amazement as beer cans, magazines, condoms, lunch boxes, chocolate ice cream bars, cassette tapes and other essentials tumbled from tarnished openings. Some spent their entire allowance on self-portraits taken in the photo booths, unconcerned about the privations they might face in the coming days.

During the day I observed the offcomers as they adapted the environment to suit themselves. Three ancient singers and their apprentices gathered under the stained awning of a Roti Hut. Without rain, they could only clutch at inspiration together. Across the empty road, an old woman was resting in front of House of Pies. Eyes sheltering deep in a face darkened to the colour of scorched wood, she stared at food through plate glass without seeing. Resigned to being moved on, she leaned into her supermarket trolley after a few moments and set it rolling. The detritus piled into her mobile home, the heaped clothing tied and taped around a body of unknown shape and size, the parched and broken texture of her skin all merged into one creature. From a distance, the steel framework of her trolley might have been antlers trained into exotic grid formations.

As she shuffled away a moth hovered over her mouldy possessions, searching for an entrance. One of the young apprentices heard wing beats. Pointing across the road to the source of the sound, he looked down at the pavement to avoid seeming presumptuous. The three singers sucked their teeth, the eldest of them waving her arms at the boy in supple movements intended to symbolise the flow of energy from one human to another. He pulled out a notebook that had grown fatter from continual use.

Waiting at such an intolerably dry spot had proved to be a positive idea. In the parched silence, a song could now be composed. By this time, the old woman was a dark smudge vanishing into the rubbish of the streets. She had received three transmissions today. The messengers could be so active and yet they would take care to speak slowly to her, knowing that her senses were dulled by years of constant movement.

Once I had gained their confidence, the ancient singers told me stories after sunset. Neon had been appropriated for poetic diversions by the goddess of light, they said. She wrote impenetrable haiku in drunken scrawling worms across the skies. Her hero was the calligrapher Bosai, who once signed a folding screen thus: 'Written by old man Bosai, totally drunk.' The god of sound blasted his own terse and enigmatic comments through Tannoy systems in rail and air terminals. After dark, the shapeshifters climbed onto high bridges to swing their bullroarers until dawn. They hoped to appease these capricious, mystifying beings but the gods were enthralled and appalled by the multitude of echoing, metallic musics that rose through the night air.

They related their curious story of the spider-robots: dysfunctional and abandoned mechanical creatures that scratched calligraphic inscriptions in the salt caves. In the far distance, a generator throbbed. Once in every hundred years, a blind worm would be caught by a spider claw and dragged across the salt. The unexpected thickness of the line was aesthetically pleasing to the spiders.

In general, the spiders were bored with their own creations.

Consequently, they would try to entice more worms into their orbit with hypnotic high-frequency signals. The results were never as they hoped, for these high tones generated strange heterodyning swirls when crossed by the ultrasonic patterns of bat cries. Huge insects, even tiny oilbirds, would drop dead onto the floor if they passed through this crossfire. In unlucky cases, a bird would fall into the middle of an inscription, destroying centuries of work in one ugly explosion of white powder. At times such as this, the spiders questioned the value and meaning of their efforts.

When the monsoon came, the encampment ecology mutated. Rotten fruits glowed in the trees, phosphorescent, radioactive, explosive. Shaken by the vibration of howler monkey calls, the branches released their volatile decorations. Each soft luminous fruit startled the more timid animals as it smashed on the forest floor. After decay came dust, the ink of the ants and other small insects, who wrote intricate essays on the history of movement and complexity. If the wind was strong enough to suck nasal moans from woodpecker holes, then the essays revealed their impermanence.

For three months, rain misted the sky. Deep fungal growths filled every crevice. Walls shaded from white into Egyptian umber, the colour of hot sand soaked in blood. Rain-sodden, the plaster had cracked, breaking into stigmata and open sores. Soft moss rounded harsh angles and a once pristine surface trembled with slow life. Touching became an adventure. Dry had become damp. The cool shining skin of our shelter, like chrome at its peak, now grew fur. Microscopic tentacles waved in each minor breeze and hues that had once seemed organic, subtle, natural were overtaken by the livid smears of true nature. Overhead, MeteoSat predicted more rain.

By this time, I had found a friend. She had taken a job at the aquarium, feeding sharks and barracudas in the deep pool. The job requirements insisted that she swim naked, with no breathing apparatus or defensive weapons. Every day I watched her work, convinced that each time would prove fatal. Later, she would whisper details of the day's work, though every day seemed much as the last. Exactly poised in the chaotic boundary between one medium and the other, she would lose all orientation. From below, the world was a silvered melting blur; from above, the reflections of foliage and sky were overlaid with such photographic precision that a third zone emerged in the intermingling of shape and colour. She could see this world but, holding it, she saw it fracture into droplets and fall away.

This was a game circumscribed by strict time limits. After less than a minute, microscopic points of light darted in her eyes. Her chest tightened and then she would be forced to plunge back into olive darkness, gulping water as she dived. This giddy feeling induced a brief state of bliss during which she was convinced she heard the spiralling melismatic songs of Bearded Seals as they hunted under the winter ice.

Submarine light cast shadows over the winding trails of slugs, urchins, brittle stars and rabbit-eared cucumbers. Some were estimated to date back three hundred years or more. Some were moving now, imperceptibly extending their length into the darkness of the simulated ocean trench. Lined up at the port panel of the immersion gallery, every observer experienced an ignorance of distance which held them in suspended animation for a moment. The sound of heavy-duty Ultrashock fencing collapsing across thousands of miles of desert in a graceful wave rang in their ears.

My friend had been forced into this dangerous work by the marginalisation of some speculative research that obsessed her and a group of young colleagues. Media pundits tagged them as the New Pharaohs, but amongst themselves they were the Nu-Bi-an Alchemists. Surrounded by stuffed crocodiles, the tusks of marine mammals, poppy seeds and belladonna, dogfish bones, frame drums and other traditional arcana that reminded me of my visit to the Museo Storico dell'Arte Sanataria in Rome, they claimed to be guided by oracular pronouncements from Nu and the Chaos-gods.

Researching mummification, they sought a substance they called the Dream Fluid. This fluid, once isolated from the corporeal body, could be analysed for its structure and reconstituted in any form: aural, plastic, olfactory, tactile, theatrical, interactive and so on. One day, archives would be richly stocked with Dream Fluid samples, or so they believed. Future generations would be able to replay the unknown and buried dreams of peoples whose thoughts, beliefs and visions would have otherwise passed from the earth with negligible impact. At this point, the technology of the Nu-Bi-an Alchemists was slow to reveal this wonderful potential.

Realising I needed to exorcise certain hauntings within myself, my friend suggested a number of possibilities. None of these were considered to be respectable, or even sanctioned, yet I felt compelled to sample their clandestine diversions. Concerned for my safety, the Alchemists would solemnly deliver lectures, intended to arm me against the dangerous world I was entering.

I listened in silence, unable to perceive any clear method for converting their esoteric information into practical knowledge. Many years after, I discovered in the tea chest a number of letters that I had posted to the Alchemists during this period. Some were written with care, enlivened with detail; some were breathless and sparse. All of them had been returned to sender, address unknown.

● ceremony viewed through iron slit

Exploring diversions, I found a starless place, dark as the weather described by Conrad in *The Shadow Line* and *Typhoon*, where 'it was as if the masked lights of the world had been turned down'. A place so dark that beyond the darkness the sea might be solid.

Moving with the deliberation of a blind man, I groped through a hidden opening in the wall. False Faces blocked my way; pierced men weighed down by metal discs. Baboon masks, they called themselves, and they dressed as demon primates. Well aware of my needs, they gave me access to the iron slit. Squatting down on my haunches and peering through, I saw six creatures sitting in a circle, features barely visible. A candle flame moved with their movement, their breath. They passed a container round, refilling it and drinking more, groaning as the liquid spilled from the corners of their mouths, running like blood in the gloom, soaking their naked torsos, darkening the floor in spreading stains.

One of them retched, shooting a spray into the centre of the circle. Saturated, unable to speak, the leader gestured for them to start. They picked up a broad, heavy wooden disc. Kneeling, they leaned forward, pushing its thick edges into their diaphragms.

Mouths stretched open into abyssal trapdoors, they began a complex rhythmic hammering on the disc, like hail on a tin roof, toads in distant marshes, swans duelling in drifting fog.

Minutes passed, the vibrations convulsing the bodies I watched. Even from my vantage point I could sense a cold, still atmosphere collecting in the room. The floor was now alive with crawling things. Thick worms with helpless legs, frilled lizards with blazing red eyes, spiders that moved in erratic sideways leaps. Like a great sunken wood bell tolling under water, the sound boomed, drawing out this demon's menagerie. Rising above it came the rasp of breath, the sparking of electricity. I had seen enough and I rose to leave but, again, False Faces blocked my way. Then I understood my responsibility. The disc would be sounded without me, yet if I chose to witness the ceremony then I must accept my role and stay until the conclusion, whatever the outcome.

2

neo-noir

◆◆◆◆◆◆◆◆◆◆◆◆◆◆◆◆◆◆

For a time, I lived a nomadic life. I understood desert nomadism, the landscape in constant flux, yet always staying the same. Memories are buried or swept away; nothing is fixed, only landmarks, myths, ceremonies, songs, the significance of sounds. I wanted to live on water, to feel movement at all times.

By day we slept under nets, hot breezes thick with the perfume of crocodile kill, stagnant water and rotting flowers. Our becalmed raft rocked gently, green lake slap-slapping beneath us in an occult language taught to amphibians by fish but kept secret from humans. Woken by sharply falling night, we lay in stupor and gazed upwards, watching satellites track their way through the white star shower. Bats jerked and wheeled in the ultrasonic hunt. By the edge of the lake, a gulping percussive web of frog signals threaded into such unpredictable complexity that we felt ourselves sucked into depths of electronic interference, imagining we were inverted, suspended in space, looking down into a vast bowl of seething abstract life.

In another region, on land . . . neon and shadow, oil lamps, shredded posters, crackling electricity, the sizzle of ghee and chilli, chattering digital drums and the roll of bass. The city coiled itself. Stretched violins shuddered and soared over the blare of traffic. Piloted at a malevolent serpent crawl, the limousines of neo-soap stars nosed out fleeting gaps between ox carts and buses, bicycles and mopeds, their smoked windows blind to limbless beggars.

Distant sirens made us nostalgic for the harsh crying beauty of Ramnaryan's sarangi.

Hearing the faint clang of industrial metal turned our thoughts to the aether ring of santoor, Pandit Shivkumar Sharma dragging beaters across the strings in a shiver of silver. Scanning across temporal frequencies with our most powerful receiver we picked up an ancient All India Radio broadcast . . . flute scientist Pannalal Ghosh exploring the serene evening mood of Raag Yaman, soft notes of wood and breath melting into the drone, the occasional glitches of time-zone slippage adding to our sense of awe.

As always we began our evening on the water with biomechanics, chanting and clapping drum rhythms with our bodies. Loose, fluid, our throats open, we moved on to our living history, opening a precious page in the digital archive, leaning forward at the centre of the raft to hear transcriptions from interviews with great film directors from the past.

I read aloud Bhaskar Chandavarkar's comments on Ritwik Ghatak:

> He was of the view that the whole sound track, flowing alongside the visual track, must be treated as the music track. He believed in, and worked towards, the goal of fortifying this music track with 'music'. We had heard about his making the track literally 'thick' at a mixing and recording session in a Calcutta studio.
>
> While mixing, he heard the whine of a projector leaking in from the projection room. Obviously, the glass plane on the projection window was missing. A live track was also being fed into the mixer from the studio. Ritwikda heard the whine awhile and then advised the recordist to leave it as it was. 'Let the window remain open,' he said. 'The sound of the projector mixed with these others is lending the track an added and effective perspective . . . I prefer it that way.' He had the knack of incorporating the uninvited or the most accidental of sounds to enrich his sound track.

Some felt that he gave excessive prominence to certain sounds, such as the crackling of rice as it boils in the pot. He was accused of indulging in melodrama. 'Son of a pig,' he answered. 'It is the right and privilege of an artist to take the leap from the ridiculous to the sublime. That's what I have done and I am sure I have succeeded.'

Veena took over the reading by describing the work of film sound designer B.V. Karanth. He used recordings of children making sounds with pencils and matchboxes. 'In *Rishyashringa* he used four tanpuras with loosened strings,' she read, 'to evoke arid, dry landscape and the threat of famine on the horizon. For Mrinal Sen's *Parshuram* he used masons' and builders' tools and implements to make up his musical score.' She quoted Karanth himself, discussing the sound design for *Choma's Drum*: 'I used varieties of chirping sparrows as background sound for different characters in the movie. I recorded the croaking of frogs. It was as though they were responding to my instructions – as if I were conducting a chorus of frogs with a baton in my hands.'

Paddling to the centre of the lake where we felt the highest margin of safety from water pirates and cops, predators and spy-eyes, we hooked into the satellite and clicked on our call sign. Let the window remain open.

3

look up, is that the moon we see?

◆◆◆◆◆◆◆◆◆◆◆◆◆◆◆◆◆

I recalled a European journey. Majel was driving after midnight from Nijmegan to Rotterdam and composer Huib Emmer slid his new Jeff Mills album into the car's tape player. For a moment I thought, Do I want to hear techno from Detroit? Then as genteel Nijmegan vanished into history, we fed onto the motorway and the lights flicked by, metronomically in time with a rushing of hi-hats, bass and snare drum, staccato chords, churning bass. This sensation of rapid forward movement through a regulated landscape of lights, signs, crash barriers, bordered by an outer darkness of utter mystery, is the enclosed, nomadic condition in which techno finds its meaning.

In reverse, we were repeating a journey made earlier in the day, a drive in weak sunlight made interminable by Holland's agricultural pancake landscape of fields, canals, cows, crops, regulated tree lines, the car slowed by the smell of fertiliser. 'This music makes us go faster,' I said. 'Yes, we'll be there in no time,' replied Huib. Tunnelling into the void, sprayed by oncoming headlights, we raced past a Cadillac, a chrome-tailfin, whitewalled, baby-blue rocket built for the age of rock'n'roll, an aerodynamic turtle of a thing, serenely glamorous, sailing along the centre lane at a leisurely pace. 'They must be listening to Ricky Nelson,' Huib said.

'It's late, we gotta get on home,' I hear. Faint thirty-five year echoes from my sister's collection of 45rpm singles still linger in my memory, an audition room full of quiffed, greased, lip-tremblers, sheathed in gold lamé and leopardskin, tattooed with money, sticky with sperm. One after another, 45s wobble, slap down onto the turntable, the heavy arm moves through its laborious routine, descends, cruel needle burrowing into the groove, crackling with anticipation. Stories that document journeys real and imagined, infidelities, frustrated desires, leisure pursuits, parental tyranny, items of novelty clothing, physical symptoms, exotic locales, the sliding of rough hands over silk underwear. 'It's late, we been gone too long . . . hope this won't be our last date.'

'Look up, is that the moon we see? Can't be, looks like the sun to me.' Gone too long, no need to rush, what's the hurry? For us, many reasons to move, move fast, though not a single one that could be specified or justified. The music, compulsion its nature, turned the wheels, increased the power of our ordinary engine, lightened the load of Huib's Juno 106. As we floated through the outskirts of Rotterdam, industrial illuminations clustering, I could make out a halo in the distance, not knowing what it was yet, seeing a mist of light blurring the outline of its sharp curves and spines and suspecting that, whatever this manifestation might be, the secret purpose of its erection was to make sense of music like this Jeff Mills tape.

Now I could see that the halo was a bridge, so new that the landscape was still in a rejection phase. Then the strangest thing happened, a *Fortean Times* moment; as Majel peeled off from the motorway, turning into the Rotterdam exit, slowing sharply on the downward slope into a maze of signs and looping concrete, so the music slowed, chugging to a halt. The strongest drug any of us had taken all evening was Belgian beer, a glass or two of wine, yet this pleasurable sensation of collusion between the three of us in the car, the arc of the journey, Mills and his taped machine music, synchronised so strongly that something mystical seemed to have happened. Of course, we all laughed at the ridiculous shock of it.

Somewhere we lost ourselves in the loops and signs, doubling back, folding over, for a moment driving upside down, screaming, ecstatic. Back on the motorway, Mills was speeding up again, the cassette stretching to accommodate this unexpected twist in the journey. Majel eased off on the accelerator as we approached a destination board, the music dropping from 130 beats per minute to 116–118.

ROTTERDAM 20, the sign informed us so we pushed forward through resistant air, overtaking the same American love boat as it weaved from side to side, tail bumping obscenely like a sex-crazed mule. Sadly, the big ole' Caddy had lost its sugar-frosted charm, though whitewall tyres still flashed in the night, kustom kar dragon's breath rippling over the crimson hood, licking the main beam. As we overtook, steering wide of their driver's erratic flight path, I fancied I could hear the choppy funk of Mandrill's 'Fencewalk' trailing in the slipstream.

The drive settled into a hypnotic trance, Mills locked onto a steady, shuffling, train-time 130bpm. This strip of motorway took us ten minutes, maybe ten decades. The Cadillac was ahead of us once more, sprayed white now, raised, double-glazed, radiating heat haze. They rolled at a steady 100, Tupac Shakur booming from underslung bass bins that rippled the road like a tidal wave, knocking cows to their knees, shaking dead birds from the trees, flushing water from the dark canals. Snare cracks split the sky with fork lightning at 95 beats every 60 seconds, a hammer of the gods that punched smoking craters into the blacktop.

We weaved and waited, hanging back, inching close to the deadly Shaolin boom zone. Timing her passing manoeuvre with the finesse of Ayrton Senna, Majel slipped into the 0.6315789th second gap between snare drops. Thrown into a spin by the sub-bass of the kick drum she grazed the hard shoulder, fighting the wheel, pulling ahead. The misted bridge was visible once again. Jeff Mills had wound up the beats to 135 and we took the Rotterdam exit for the second time, braking hard as the motorway ended, the music squealing down through the gears until it glided on a beatless plateau. Hair white, eyebrows scorched, we all laughed, shaking off the terror, flooded with panic and exhilaration, the shock of outrunning time.

4

word sticks

◆◆◆◆◆◆◆◆◆◆◆◆◆◆◆◆◆◆

On a filthy November night of floods and fork lightning some years ago, I found myself drawn into conversation with one of the more troublesome curators at the museum. Resigned to sleeping with the fetishes because of the weather, Mathers had begun an intensive study of the Glenfiddich bottle and was clearly on his way to a revelation of some sort. In normal circumstances, we avoided each other as far as possible. I disliked the man's pedantry, the sour mood that overtook him when whisky spirits were summoned, his taste for violent pornography; I disliked the barking shorthand he used as a substitute for communication; particularly, I disliked his shoes.

Yet we were incarcerated until the morning so I resolved to make an effort. We ruminated for a while on the subject of pagan survivals, those ancient practices that had overlapped with the industrial age and beyond. I told him about the Cornish frame drum that I had once seen in the Boscastle Museum of Witchcraft. Used by a witch for divination, the drum was still in use in the era of photography and the motor car. I found this astonishing, since it suggested a uniformity of shamanistic paraphernalia that stretched through Tibet, the Soviet Republics, North America, Scandinavia and England, surviving religious persecution, Marxist-Leninist ideology and the industrial revolution. He listened politely enough, then delivered the kind of staccato lecture that made him so unpopular.

'Oceania, Amazonas, Central Africa, Korea, China, North Devon, possibly other locations. Serrated sticks, notched and decorated,' he croaked. I had no idea what he was talking about. 'Reconstruction, of course. Abrasions and tonal variations suggest that string had been wound around the notched end of each stick. Traces of decorative designs survive in some cases.'

As I understood his gist, the sticks were akin to a musical instrument, yet something else entirely. Until recently, these rare objects had been grouped in most museum collections alongside either tally sticks, bullroarers or magical pointing sticks. The discovery of an unpublished manuscript written by the recently deceased explorer and amateur ethnologist Sir Lewis Farmarkham (1903–1994) suggested an alternative function. Travelling among remote communities in the New Guinea Highlands shortly before World War II, Sir Lewis encountered magical practices that shared many of the characteristics of classic shamanism as defined by the pioneering authority, Mircea Eliade. To communicate with the spirit world, the shaman deployed two notched sticks, connected to stridulating spikes with woven fibres. He would place the end of each stick against opposite ears, according to Sir Lewis's informants, and an assistant would scrape along the serrations with the spikes.

Customarily used in conjunction with sensory deprivation techniques and the ingestion of hallucinogenic plants, the sticks were said to produce actual words pronounced by spirits. Were these words always the same or did the shaman's trance imbue the sounds with fresh meanings during each successive seance? Sir Lewis did not say, apparently, or perhaps his informants were reluctant to impart the information. But these shamans insisted that the polarity, so to speak, of the sticks should not be reversed. If the wrong stick was placed in the wrong ear then the recipient might suffer from persistent lapses into psychosis or even fatal illness (making interesting parallels with the pointing sticks and *Kurdaitcha* shoes once used in magical killing by indigenous Australian shamans).

Clearly, the sticks could not be classified as a musical instrument. The respected American professor of acoustical arcana, Dr Warren Mumputt, has suggested, controversially, that the sticks represent the first example of recording technology in human culture. Dr Mumputt has made claims that similar objects unearthed in parts of Asia, Africa, the Amazon rainforest and the English west country all served a similar purpose.

There was a pause after Mathers finished his monologue. 'So what you are saying,' I offered cautiously, 'is that the New Guinea shamans had stumbled upon an instrument that predicted both the telephone and the record player?'

Mathers looked up from his whisky tumbler. 'Evolutionism?' he murmured. Then came the more familiar bark. 'New category of magico-acoustic technology. Further research may shed a most revealing light on the development of sound storage in material culture. All we can say.' With that, he fell asleep where he sat.

5

the barkless dog

◆◆◆◆◆◆◆◆◆◆◆◆◆◆◆◆◆◆

Wanting to vanish into the strangeness of old television, I watched an episode of *Lassie*. A TV series featuring a dog in the starring role enforced an unusual regime upon its makers. Dialogue was absent for long periods of screen time, or substituted by barks, growls and other animal sounds. Narrative drama could only be constructed from shots of the dog (ignorant of its role in a story) running or barking, so laying bare the construction of narrative coherence through editing. Directed only in the broadest sense, the coherence of that drama, along with its emotional impact, necessitated an unusually heavy dependence on music. *Lassie* swung wildly between elegiac pastoralism undermined by the constant threat of ominous events about to transpire. Nostalgia conflicts with an unstable future. To watch is to learn a relatively sophisticated, though necessarily limited, language of suggestive sound.

This strangely anxious language corrupts our ability to hear clearly, since once the language is learned then its symbolism is imprinted. A cultural conditioning takes place, just like Hollywood's depictions of specific exoticas such as Japan, Mexico, the South Pacific or Hawaii through the scales or rhythms that we can all identify, despite their tenuous connection to the appropriate local music. Certain chords, whatever their innocence, convey certain expectations. *Lassie* was fascinating to me, not only because of its absurd formal demands and constraints but because excessive musical elaboration creates expectations that are frustrated before they can develop. The music shouts: 'Look out! Bad things on the way! Right now!' More often than not, the scene then switches to an inert landscape or a tepid verbal exchange between two humans. Made to feel anxious about events in which I have no interest, I feel deflated. I need to be picked right up by the next scene.

Like the symphonic music from which it derives, schlock TV and film scoring has the capacity to signify minute and specific changes of mood. Yet the flexibility becomes a burden in this context, as we neurotically interpret every shift in key, every discordant note, every quickening rhythm. Reading a vacuous canine drama through adult eyes and ears becomes an exhausting exercise in second-guessing the future. *Lassie* is a template, albeit extreme, of cinematic structuring in the commercial domain, whereby the nineteenth- and early twentieth-century European approach to symphonic musical structure, an endpoint in a particular history, has come to dominate one aspect of a far more modern medium in the late twentieth century.

The alternative approach is to exploit well-known pop songs as self-contained narratives and emotional triggers. Through this device, a peculiar echo of opera, musicals, the pop portmanteaus of the rock'n'roll era and Kenneth Anger's *Scorpio Rising*, pop songs throw a hiatus into narrative drive, a glitch into celluloid reality, a package of stylistic or historical associations to supplement the design scheme.

Through this pairing of pop song and moving pictures, film can disrupt the agreement between director and audience of where the focal point of reality lies. In *Chungking Express*, Wong Kar-Wai obsessively deployed 'California Dreaming' as soundtrack, *mise-en-scène* and barometer of private aspirations. A literal time-dreaming, the device was a knowing approach to the problems of matching sound and image in an age when every sound comes equipped with its own stereotypical image and every musical gesture automatically formulates mental pictures, emotional tripwires and psychological states, altered or otherwise.

In Martin Scorcese's *Casino*, music scrolls through time. Characters speak – voluble, loud, like gunshots, or quietly, their secrets, in the head – while their actions betray their words; the music – hyper, trashy, ecstatic, sentimental, violent, incoherent – belongs to this shadow world of half-understood action. In David Lynch's *Lost Highway* the technique loses its potency. A terrifying aphasia afflicts the central characters; like Lady Asaji in Akira Kurosawa's *Throne of Blood*, they are sucked into apertures and hallways of gloom, reappearing after their brief encounter with hell's waiting room. In previous Lynch films, dark inner lives or concealed worlds were colourised by songs; in *Lost Highway*, the songs are redundant, shining searchlights into a darkness that has been revealed more effectively by abstractions: the texture of a wall, the void of a corridor, finally plummeting into witless cliché with the aural threat of a synthesiser drone.

If film is a kind of actualised dreaming, a passively collective vision of the possible or improbable, a twentieth-century electro-mechanical (now digital) screen ceremony, then the dislocated relationship of sound and image is unsurprising. Dreams are notoriously a visually prejudiced form of imagination. As James Hillman wrote in *The Dream and The Underworld*: 'Only rarely do we hear, touch or taste in dreams, and, rarest of all, do we use the sense of smell.' Surrealist, traveller, curator and ethnographer Michel Leiris dreamed of 'A Scotsman with puffed-out cheeks' blowing into a bagpipe shaped like a gigantic bloated man, but he made no comment (in *Nights as Day, Days as Nights*) on the sound of this anthropomorphic instrument. William Burroughs writes (in *My Education*) that he heard distant airport sounds in a dream – 'blurred, incomprehensible' – then loud and clear announcements fading into static, all familiar characteristics of the airport environment, a place of temporary states possessed by the quality of dreams. He also heard a humming sound, as the room 'communicates a silent menace', which reminds me of Lynch's *Lost Highway* or the eerie noise of chthonic plumbing that swirls around Gary Oldman in Francis Ford Coppola's *Dracula*. Of course, we all hear bangs in our sleep: the mysterious bang without cause that wakes us in the middle of the night. Leiris heard gunshots; Burroughs saw guns and gunshot wounds in sufficient detail to be able to specify the calibre of weapon. Did he hear them?

But Burroughs pinpointed the boredom that disarms most dreams when they are related in the light of day. Their lack of context makes them like a 'stuffed animal set on the floor of a bank'. Similarly, the music of consumer-age rites has been split off from its context and reduced to trivia. At this transition point of communications and media, all art forms aspire to the conditions of other art forms. There is a feeling of exhaustion in established art media, yet for the moment, at least, new multimedia and interactive forms have little to say.

Intimately linked with these developments is the speculative area of unknown psychological conditions as humans adapt to dramatic changes in communication, trading, political geography, the very nature of things. In a saturated, often intangible environment, perceptions must change, also. The relationship of seeing to hearing and hearing to seeing has an unknown destination. Film currently provides very few maps. As in *Lassie*, the barking of music is our only guide.

6

squat low to the ground

◆◆◆◆◆◆◆◆◆◆◆◆◆◆◆◆◆

Not a huge amount of time elapsed after the invention of the cine camera before somebody conceived the notion of documenting sexual activity and selling it. Uses of early audio recording technology were a little less worldly: give a man a microphone and one of his first thoughts was to point it at the birds, mating or not.

With the advent of the digital sampler and its operator, the human audio sponges known as DJs or record producers, documentary records have become highly regarded food supplements in the daily diet of music professionals: how to incorporate *The Exciting Sounds of Grand Prix* or 'Gang Fight' from *Street and Gangland Rhythms Beats and Improvisations of Six Boys in Trouble* into the virtual mix?

Published music becomes less and less a record (performance captured in real time) and more a process of layering, revision, recycling, shifting perception. When the idea of recording was still enthralling for its own sake, all records were, as their name suggests, a documentary. In New York City, Moses Asch's Folkways label pursued this didactic programme to its logical conclusion. Asch saw his goal as the distribution of a total sound world, unbounded by profit-oriented categorisations of music and dismissive of the niche marketing approach typified by the selling of so-called Race Records to the African-American market.

The son of a Yiddish writer, Moses Asch grew up in Paris and

New York. According to Anthony Seeger, current curator of the
Smithsonian Folkways recordings, Asch's philosophy was confirmed and consolidated by a meeting with Albert Einstein. 'That's
the reported story,' says Seeger. 'He was recording an interview
between his father and Einstein. Apparently at some point he told
Einstein he wanted to record all the sounds of the world. Einstein
said, "That's a good idea, young man," and got him started.
He was an interesting and complex person. He came up with a
philosophy for a record label that didn't confront the major labels
on any turf but put out lots and lots of things that they weren't
interested in doing. He said he could put out almost anything.'

Apocalypse culture before their time, LPs such as *Sounds of
the Junkyard*, *Sounds of Medicine – Operation and Stethoscope
Sounds*, *Voices of the Satellites* and *Urban Holiness Services*, along
with hallucinogenic mushroom ceremonies, conversations with
dolphins, unknown sounds collected from 2,000 fathoms down
in the Pacific Ocean and even a whole album of vocal sounds
produced without the aid of a larynx, all floated at the edges of
ethnomusicology and bioacoustic documentation.

'I think there's exotic and exotica,' says Seeger. 'Different
people were interested in different things. A number of the Folkways recordings that look exotic on the outside were prepared by
people who had something else in mind for them. Like speaking
without your larynx, I think they hoped to sell a whole bunch to
hospitals that were doing the operation. And a lot of the folklore
things were actually done by scholars who wanted to get their
scholarship to a broader audience. They weren't told to clean up
their ceremonies for the recording.'

These records also redefined the outer limits of the audio
spectrum, the relationship of signal to noise, the boundaries of
the pleasure principle. Who, other than an auto-surgeon, would
find entertainment in a track entitled 'Sounds of the Bowels – A
Normal Hungry Man Smoking a Cigarette Before Dinner', or one
whole side of an LP devoted to conversation conducted during an
operation on a small boy with a cyst on his neck? Beyond scientism, the upward curve of an academic career, the liberal education
of the great masses, there lay voyeurism, the fascination of the
unknown, the vinyl frontier.

● a dog's life

In 1889, an eight-year-old sound recordist named Ludwig Koch recorded the song of an Indian shama thrush. More than a hundred years later, the technology has evolved from wax cylinder and wire recording into the digital domain, yet this urge to document and enjoy non-human music has grown into a fascinating minor industry. Is this evidence of technology's role in the synthetic reproduction of nature, purchased to compensate for the loss of wild places, the systematic reduction of biodiversity?

I asked Lassie.

'Within the New Age or Spoken Word sections of music hypermarkets,' she barked, 'you can find a growing number of environment, relaxation and bioacoustic CDs: tropical rainforests, dolphins, howling wolves, primates, seashore and country garden, rainfall and thunderstorms. Extracts can be sampled on the in-store touch'n'listen displays, demonstrating that this is an impulse shopper niche. Superficially, this is a slice of the stressbuster market: a pair of headphones, a sixty-minute recording of waves rolling gently onto a beach, a subtle underpinning of digital synthesiser drones and the urban info-warrior is fortified for the next battle.'

'Good girl,' I said.

Clearly piqued by my patronising address, she fixed me with one of those dog stares that precedes a bite. 'The history of wildlife and environment recording,' she continued, 'adds another aspect to this demotion of whalesong CDs to the level of goldfish videos, hypnosis cassettes and do-it-yourself meditation manuals. Like television and photography, sound recording is an unstable mixture of documentation and entertainment. Tape recorders have proved to be a vital tool for bioacousticians investigating the mechanics and meaning of animal vocalisation. Many early commercial discs of animal and bird sound were structured to appeal to a market of amateur scientists. So species would be introduced by a suitably sober narrator, Latin names would be given, habitats described.'

I recalled a personal favourite in my own collection. A 1957 Folkways album – *Sounds of North American Frogs* – was narrated in an unwittingly comical, frog-like voice by amphibian specialist Charles M. Bogert. Bogert's croak may lack the surreal dimension at the outer limits of the Folkways catalogue but his album typifies the humour that lurks wherever bioacoustic sound is emitted. For the ultimate in scientific endeavour collapsing into hysteria I listen to a 1968 LP – *Sounds in the Sea* – produced by the Electro-Marine Sciences Division of Marine Resources Inc. Following recordings of sperm whales, drum fish, sonar signals, torpedo launches and an unidentified *boing* comes a recording of Commander Scott Carpenter and his crew singing 'Goodnight Irene' 250 feet below the surface in Sea Lab II, their voices Smurfed into the stratosphere by helium.

As if it were a favourite slipper, Lassie tugged the conversation back to her favourite subject. 'As television co-opted this audience of wildlife enthusiasts with its exotic journeys of zoological voyeurism,' she growled, 'so the scientific narration guiding them through animal sound albums took on a travelogue feel. By aspiring to the condition of TV they moved towards the current idea of soundscape as virtual environment. But do we need a Crocodile Dundee in the wilderness if we're sitting in an armchair in the suburbs?'

'Ah, the armchair traveller,' I interjected. 'Some discs began to acknowledge that there are two kinds of traveller: the guided tourist and the free spirit. *The Swamp in June*, produced in 1964 by Droll Yankees Inc., gave you one side with narration, complete with "comments on swamp life", and a reverse side of uninterrupted flies, frogs, birds and beavers. You could just feel yourself being bitten by the mosquitoes. Others followed, like the Saydisc label's *Antarctica*, with its fabulously flatulent Weddell seal recordings and creaking ice floes, but the major breakthroughs were Dr Roger S. Payne's *Songs of the Humpback Whale*, released by Capitol at the beginning of the 1970s, and Syntonic Research Inc.'s *Environments* series.

'The prominent trademark symbol appended to the title of this series suggests that Syntonic Research Inc. (whatever syntonic means) knew they were on to a moneyspinner with their soothing nature backgrounds. "Turn your hi-fi into a psychoacoustic device," they instructed on the cover alongside endorsements from psychiatric technicians and songwriters. The success of these two American projects – serious science and pseudo-science overlapping the psychedelic diaspora – was linked to a growing environmental movement.'

'So who, or what, got the royalties?' snarled my canine friend.

'Fair point,' I agreed. 'Particularly from your perspective. In the laudable case of Payne's recordings, the creatures themselves, since his intention was to create whale awareness and fund research and conservation projects from the massive sales of the two whale records. Elsewhere the profit margins were huge, relatively speaking.

'But the ecology movement was descended from a spiritual hunger that had been expressed in very different ways by Henry David Thoreau, Jack Kerouac and Jimi Hendrix. Immune to the lure of post-hippie psychobabble, some recordists stuck to the idea of birdsong as music, a notion that is surely as old as music itself. In France, the records in Jean C. Roché's *L'Oiseau Musicien* series were presented as continuous concerts, beautifully recorded and edited. The standard is maintained with his current Sitelle series of *Natural Concerts*. This is a world of rich, strange sounds – a voyeuristic plunge into the intimacies of potoos, peppershrikes, lemurs, bearded seals and belugas.'

Lassie had fallen asleep, I noticed. Undeterred, I continued. 'By 1973 Roché was abandoning the concept of sound guide for some discs, instead evoking the atmosphere of remote environments. With the advent of digital compact discs, this concept of the wilderness packaged into substitute environment, sonic therapy or complex sound field was matched by the appropriate technology. No more confusion between vinyl imperfections and the high frequencies of insect stridulation; no more mix-ups between turntable noise and the low rumbles of marine mammals; no need to get up and turn the record over. Just lie back and be transported.

'Inevitably, this evolved into abominations: float-tank soporifics and whale banalities. Mysteries – or, at the very least, gastric rumbles – once conveyed by humpback whale songs have been drastically cheapened by anthropomorphism and overexposure. This new age notion that nature is all beauty and peace is nonsense. Listen to the screaming racket that seabirds make; the crackle of Alaskan krill; the harsh signals of insects such as the Gratte-Coui locust from Guadeloupe; the noisemaking birds – the mangrove cuckoo, the Lesser Antillean grackle, the giant coua of Madagascar, the black-headed oriole, the trumpeter hornbill, the black-winged stilt. All of them sound like cogs and scrapers pulled from a Futurist noise machine.

'We only need one major earthquake or typhoon to remind us that wilderness is not a benign, shock-free backdrop that decorates earth solely for the benefit of alienated humans. The best atmosphere CDs acknowledge this. Rykodisc's *Thunderstorms* even comes with a safety warning: "If you feel your skin tingle or your hair stand on end, squat low to the ground on the balls of your feet." '

Crocodilian in her sudden menace, Lassie opened one eye in response to this human-centred assumption that all feet have balls. 'Interestingly,' she growled, 'a bitch might argue that bioacoustic recordings anticipated the pathetic human obsession with alien kidnappings.'

'Are you familiar,' I asked, ignoring the provocation, 'with music that manipulates bioacoustic sounds? Graeme Revell's *The Insect Musicians*, for example? "And perhaps the ultimate horizon of technology is nature itself," Revell wrote. Does that fit your theory . . . the idea that nature is an extraordinarily complex, unknown world, an alien world in fact, and technology can only aspire to that complexity?'

'I can't listen to that stuff,' groaned Lassie. 'It hurts my ears.'

'Tough being a dog,' I rallied. 'In my opinion, Revell undermined his project by using insectile sounds to play melodies that were distressingly human. The true fascination of these signals is not just the sound quality or what they may communicate, but their alien structure. The best description of these patterns I have come across is outlined by an anthropologist and musician named Steven Feld. In *Music Grooves*, a book he co-wrote with another musicologist, Charles Keil, Steve illuminates the possible meanings of lift-up-over-sounding, an awkward yet remarkably resonant phrase used by the Kaluli people who live in the tropical rainforest of Papua New Guinea's Southern Highlands. "For me, intuitively," Steve writes, "lift-up-over-sounding creates a feeling of continuous layers, sequential but not linear; nongapped multiple presences and densities; overlapping chunks without internal breaks; a spiraling, arching motion tumbling slightly forward, thinning, then thickening again." '

Lassie cocked her head on one side, one ear bent, a quizzical look in her eyes. I pressed on with my main theme. 'For many years I've been fascinated by the unusual rhythmic, seemingly random relationships that can be heard in call-and-response duets sung by African bou-bou shrikes and trumpeter swans, a chorus of tree frogs, or from the ensemble flute playing of Amazonas, Central Africa Republic, Ethiopia and Papua New Guinea. There are similarities to hocketing – the medieval music hiccup – or church bell change ringing, though these are predictable, systematised forms. It's something to do with wind, breath, unpredictable complexity, though bird duets can be remarkably precise in their timing. Sometimes two birds take one of the parts, creating a three-part duet; in a pair, after one bird dies, the surviving partner continues to sing both parts of the duet. I've tried to duplicate the effect in the studio with some success, using randomised overdubbing, but the sustained interest comes from listening to a group performance in which the component parts sound totally integrated yet perpetually out of synch.

'Feld describes the essence of lift-up-over-sounding as "part relations that are *in synchrony while out of phase*". For the Kaluli people of New Guinea, unisons are anathema; interest comes from staggered entries or multiple densities. "Part of the stylistic core of lift-up-over-sounding," Feld explains, "is found in nuances of textural densification – of attacks and final sounds; decays and fades; changes in intensity, depth and presence; voice coloration and grain; interaction of patterned and random sounds; playful accelerations, lengthenings and shortenings; and the fission and fusion of sound shapes and phrases into what electroacoustic composer Edgard Varèse called the 'shingling' of sound layers across pitch space."

'Do you get it now?'

'Does he object to you quoting these meaty chunks of his work?' asked Lassie. 'Where can I hear his stuff?'

'These are important ideas,' I blustered. 'What Feld and Keil call fat thoughts. Listen to the CD he recorded – *Voices of the Rainforest*. Interestingly enough, Steve's personal stash of music tapes didn't crank the handle for his New Guinea hosts when he was living with them. The exception was *Nefertiti*, by the Miles Davis Quintet. The subtle textural shifts and staggered, overlapping echoes of the Quintet "made sense to Kaluli because it *sounds* like their kind of groove". Imagine what might grow out of these ideas: textural and rhythmic microworlds elevated to their rightful place in our aesthetic value system; we might even discover a more grounded awareness of our own insecure place in the thick, exotic rainforest of mediated, marketed, MIDI music. Among the Kaluli, Feld had discovered a way of classifying the world that was totally different from ours. Think of it; a taxonomy based on sound.'

Lassie sniffed the air. A long pause followed. Faintly, from a distant ranch I heard the self-pitying lament of Don Gibson's 'Sea of Heartbreak', or was it La Monte Young singing a never-ending cowboy song to the cicadas? I saw a shadow in the trees, maybe a man from the city, armed with a gun. 'So what you're saying,' said Lassie, a sly look in her eye, aware of the shadow long before I was, 'is that I'm more in tune with this subject than you are.'

My throat tightened, dry as a sand lizard's belly.

2

the beast within

7

hot pants idol

◆◆◆◆◆◆◆◆◆◆◆◆◆◆◆◆◆

Deep into that darkness peering, long I stood there, wondering,
fearing, doubting, dreaming dreams no mortal ever dared to
dream before.

Edgar Allan Poe, *The Raven*

Fasting in the Sonora Desert, I dreamed a vision of a
different America. Gliding north on the air currents of a hissing
seedpod rattle, I looked down at Southern California. Spread
below me, the swimming pools of the rich and famous gleamed
like shards of a Mayan mask, broken into neat rectangles of
turquoise jade, then tossed into the wilderness.

No longer the slim, handsome young man with the Robert
Mitchum chin, slick sweep of blond hair aerodynamically super-
charged for the space age, Les Baxter eased the bulk of old age
into a lounger by the pool and slid into reverie. He was sitting in
an old theatre, completely alone. Stravinsky's *Firebird* was playing,
yet the orchestra pit was empty. Painted backdrops were carried
onstage by men dressed in black, like the puppeteers in Japanese
bunraku. They showed river scenes, a yellow slick threading
through arboreal overhang. Just as soon as a backdrop was
erected, so it was taken down and replaced by another. He saw
paintings by Gauguin, Picasso, Rousseau, Paul Klee, followed by
images of masks, totems, sacred animals, sacrifice; they came and
went so quickly, making him aware of his slowing senses. Drums

throbbed, a voodoo incantation, the sound of a journey upriver, into the unknown.

A woman walked to the centre of the stage, wearing a zebra-stripe dress cut low in the bust and skin-tight. She reminded Les of the voluptuous June Wilkinson. Featured on *The Spike Jones Show*, back in the early sixties, Wilkinson would bend forward, one hand on her thigh, the other on her hip, and lower her cleavage onto the faces of the audience as they ate their TV dinners. Spike would stand there holding a couple of big round maracas, ear-to-ear grimace stretching his ugly face. Then there was Sandy Warner, black-haired model who posed for Martin Denny covers. Same kind of big soft bosom as June Wilkinson, not like the concrete outcrops every girl's hauling around on her chest these days. All that stuff, nothing compared to what you see now, what your dollar can buy, and even then, way before then, you had the smokers with their Joan Crawford clones sucking on some guy's woody woodpecker, but in their time they were hot, those valleys of lust.

The woman stared into the darkness of the stalls and Les felt as if his mind had been split open, probed with a rubber glove, scooped out. Then she did that June Wilkinson thing, leaning forward, hands in just the right places, and with the voice of a demon, she began to recite '. . . dust and terror, chainsaw bikers, sultry tropical airs, Aztec spells, x-ray eyes and hot pants, sunken cities, lost cities, singing sea shells, electric frogs, bustin' bongos, wild stuffed bikinis, jungle jazz, sacred idols, space escapades, switchblade sisters, pits and pendulums, tabu, taboo, tabuh, tamboo, taboo, tabuh, tamboo, tabuh-tabuhan . . .' As the bathetic riches of the spell resonated in his head, throbbing with the mantric bamboo power of *Gamelan Jejog*, Les knew he was falling into the long sleep. His power gone, he faded from sight.

● the surrealist map of the world

I had read somewhere that Les Baxter wrote the *Lassie* theme. Was this true? I never find his name on *Lassie* credits. Too late to enquire in person. Described by *Baby Boomer Collectibles* magazine as 'One of the [Space Age Bachelor Pad] genre's coolest cross-referential masters', Les Baxter died of a heart attack in Newport Beach, Southern California, in January 1996. Of course, winter in Newport Beach is not like a frozen January in New York City or Europe. For Baxter the audio world was an environment in which a season might be suspended indefinitely. Throughout the 1950s he offered package tours in sound, running excursions for sedentary tourists who wanted to stroll around some taboo urges before lunch, view a pagan ceremony through gaps in the bamboo, go wild in the sun or conjure a demon, all without leaving home stereo comforts in the whitebread suburbs.

Ports of Pleasure, one Les Baxter album was titled, a concentrated suggestion of exotica, cruising, nomadism, sexual orifices, indulgence without commitment. By contrast, the music itself was innocent, innocuous, touristic, at times mediocre. But Baxter had strange, inventive ideas that could lift risible arrangements and melodic schlock into a realm of warm leatherette enchantment. Of all the American exotica musicians who recorded during the fifties and early sixties – Martin Denny, Arthur Lyman, Esquivel, Yma Sumac the Inca princess, Eden Ahbez, Korla Pandit the turbaned organist, Elisabeth Waldo and a host of one-shot bandwagon jumpers – Baxter was the most sophisticated in his fabrications.

Baxter's music was visionary without being revolutionary. Odd pre-echoes of more respected musical celebrities emerge from time to time, as if he had consciously seeded the future with daring ideas disguised as cocktail froth: parts of 'Sunken City' could be a precursor of Robert Fripp's looped guitar Frippertronics; 'Jungle River Boat' on *The Ritual of the Savage* could be Steve Reich in a Happy Hour mood. The best of Baxter's recordings are interesting predominantly as arranger's music. Solos were rare, often undistinguished, unless a Plas Johnson or Larry Bunker was booked for the session; improvisation was strictly controlled; compositions came second to their ornamentation. The surface of the music still sounds ornate, shimmering. It holds the listener at arm's length, away from the heart of the music. Listen to Baxter as background music, a prospect he abhorred, and his work can sound cheap and superficial. Listen with more attention and the emotion of the music, a deep longing for the sensuous, fabulous, even mythical, is entrapped, as a ghost in a web, within the details of sound.

As is the case with many musicians whose commercial instincts do daily battle with an innocent need to be regarded as serious, his work was a crucible for unique skills, fabulous inventions and chronic lapses of judgement. Baxter synthesised many exoticas rich in their own troubled histories – Afro-Cuban, Polynesian, South-East Asian, Japanese and Chinese, African, Brazilian, Central and South American, Caribbean – channelling them through a typically cool-school jazz schizophrenia of exquisitely sensitive textural detail undermined or flattened by brashness. The synthesis culminated in a fabricated exotica without boundaries or sovereignty, a place where hybridisation met its final destiny as pure fantasy.

Yet there were times when Baxter could be enchanting, spellbinding, truly magical. Like a languid dawn, 'Mozambique', recorded in 1955, opens with congas, bongos, harp, tambourine, celeste, serpentine alto flute, a single xylophone key struck like a Korean stone chime.

Noise for the machine age mixed with echoes of magical rites and ancient court ceremonies. Alongside the futurism of electronics, percussion emerged from centuries of intellectual purdah as a major new multiple instrument for the first half of the century. The newly invented jazz drum kit took its place alongside ritual drums of Cuba, Africa, Haiti and Brazil, shakers and rattles of Central and South America, scrapers from Mexico, gongs from Burma, woodblocks from China, bells from Japan, xylophones and marimbas from Africa, tuned percussion from Bali and Java. Then there were the unique creations of numerous instrument inventors: Harry Partch and his Spoils of War, Zymo-Xyl and Mazda Marimba; Luigi Russolo and his Intonarumori; Harry Bertoia's Sonambient gongs and metal rods; the Baschet Brothers and their chronophagic Structures Sonores – the Cristal, the Glasshorn, the Tubes Graves, the Grille a Écho.

● moon moods

Like the surrealist map of the world, exotica contrived a view of global culture that was so distorted, so outlandish, so dismissive of reality, as to be both surreal and absurd. 'No longer can rhetorical figures of the "primitive" or the "exotic" be used with impunity,' wrote Michael M. J. Fischer in *Writing Culture*. 'Audiences have become multiple.' This truth is more acutely felt in Los Angeles than in any other city on earth.

Back in the early 1950s, jumping LA rhythm & blues at its peak and rock'n'roll but a few moments away, it is hard to imagine that the African-American record buyers of Watts were fired up by Hollywood junglist fantasies like Baxter's 'Zambezi'; harder still to imagine that the Mexican-Americans of East LA, zoot suit riots still fresh in their minds, experienced the slightest exotic tremble if they happened to hear 'High Priest of the Aztecs' or 'Pyramid of the Sun'.

There was one exception, at least, and that was the bandleader from Saturn, Sun Ra, living in his own sun belt in Chicago. According to Ra biographer John F. Szwed, Sun Ra was uninterested in the big postwar jazz bands. Instead, he was inspired by the lush mood music of David Rose, Walter Schumann, Martin Denny and Les Baxter. 'Sonny first heard Baxter on *Perfume Set to Music* and *Music Out of the Moon*,' writes Szwed, 'two albums built around melodies for theremin performed by Dr. Samuel Hoffman, a Los Angeles podiatrist who had played on the soundtracks of *Spellbound* and *The Lost Weekend*.'

These 78rpm albums were collaborations featuring the themes of pop and film composer Harry Revel with Baxter arranging and conducting the orchestra and chorus. 'Moon Moods' is a good example of the strange parallel: a doo-doo-dah wordless vocal crooned over eerie theremin, teeming harp and 'jungle' rhythms, the track sounds like a cover version of one of Sun Ra's semi-comic vocal pieces of the early sixties. 'Everybody bought it,' Baxter told James Call and Peter Huestis for *Hypno* magazine. 'I had some interesting experiences with the wide range. Somebody at Capitol told me – it was very surprising – he said this *Music Out of the Moon*, which was theremin and choir – it had a little jazzy feel in a couple of places – he said this is selling in South-Central LA. So anyway we could never figure anything out.'

Harry Revel was something of an exoticist himself. Born in London in 1905, he had toured Europe as a teenager with an ersatz Hawaiian band; composed American songs such as 'I'm Going Back to Old Nebraska' *before* his emigration to America in 1929; composed music for an all-black stage show – *Fast and Furious* – in 1930; co-composed 'Down Argentine Way' and 'I Yi, Yi, Yi, Yi (I Like You Very Much)' for the exotica star of the forties, Carmen Miranda; written 'Under the Harlem Moon' for Fletcher Henderson; and produced albums such as *Music for Peace of Mind*, a pre-New Age record that offered 'music that has a message to give, *if you will open your hearts and minds to receive it*. Turn down the lights, relax in an easy chair and listen. Then, for a few stolen hours, perhaps you will warm to happy memories and blissful hopes: Yours, for as long as you may hold it, will be *peace of mind*.'

● tupperware futurism

Sun Ra was familiar with Revel's more conventional compositions, particularly since he had worked with Fletcher Henderson in 1947 and maintained an interest in Henderson's music throughout his life. Music created to evoke the aroma of perfume, fabricate lunar sound or promise peace of mind must have struck deeper chords, as well as alerting him to Baxter's unusual approach. As a striking illustration of the link between these two mavericks of American music, compare Baxter's 'Brazilian Bash', released in 1956 on *Skins! A Bongo Party with Les Baxter*, with Sun Ra recordings from the late fifties and early sixties. Tracks such as 'Solar Drums', 'Solar Symbols', 'Friendly Galaxy' and 'Angels and Demons at Play' feature a similar blend of exoticas: either echo-saturated Asian percussion meditations or Afro-Latin rhythms, mysterious flute melodies and glistening keyboard ostinatos. Even their song titles seemed to be borrowed from each other's exotic aesthetic: Baxter recording 'Saturday Night on Saturn' and 'Blue Jungle'; Sun Ra recording 'Space Mates', 'Kosmos in Blue', 'Tiny Pyramids' and 'Watusa'.

For both Ra and Baxter, the exoticisms were a part of a broader picture. Sound, particularly electronically generated or mutated sound, was a highly evocative medium for depicting vivid unknown worlds, utopias implied by America's postwar Tupperware futurism yet repressed by cold war paranoia, the conservatism of the suburbs and racial division. Though there were some small similarities in their aims and methods, the real world in which they lived and worked divided them so totally, they may as well have been creatures from two different planets. While Sun Ra was defining a New World Afrocentric identity, Baxter confirmed the imperialist fantasies of the old world, now indulged in tourist escapades as well as military expeditions.

Ultimately, Baxter was a professional in Hollywood. How seriously he took his role as a sonic conjurer of vicarious experience is unclear.

Back in the days when celluloid sex and horror were still soft core, titillation and unfulfilled promises were an accepted element in the selling of forbidden pleasures. 'They weren't up to my strangeness,' he told Call and Huestis.

Baxter was born in Mexia, Texas, in 1922. Trained as a concert pianist, he moved on to tenor saxophone, performing in LA clubs in the forties. As a singer he joined the Velvet Fog – Mel Tormé – in 1947 to become a Mel-Tone; later he worked in comedy, as a musical director for the Bob Hope and Abbott and Costello radio shows.

In 1950 he conducted his own orchestra, accompanying Nat 'King' Cole's rendition of 'Mona Lisa', a song that languished on the shelf until picked as a B-side for a lesser track. The episode is typical of Baxter's career. As a house arranger and conductor for Capitol Records, Baxter's orchestra backed Cole on two hugely popular records: 'Mona Lisa' and 'Too Young'. Characterised by their contrast of a single instrument – piano and Spanish guitar respectively – against a vortex of strings, they established Cole as a balladeer. It was the young arranger, Nelson Riddle, however, who was declared the discovery of these sessions. Riddle's orchestra went on to greater successes with Frank Sinatra, also recording a less imaginative exotica than Baxter with albums such as *Sea of Dreams* and *Love Tide*.

Joseph Lanza compares Riddle's brief aquatic obsession with Baxter's in *Elevator Music*, his survey of Muzak, easy listening and the Space Age Bachelor Pad genre: 'But unlike the turbulent orchestrals on Les Baxter's album *Midnight on the Cliffs* (where the suggested clangor of waves summons cliff dwellers to their doom), Riddle's music is more focused on the calm before the storm. This is music in suspension, where drowning is only a sensual slumber.' Though the moods they conjure are different enough, the most striking divergence lies in the materials they used and the way in which they structured them. Baxter's *Jewels of the Sea* album was equally immersed in suburbanised oceanic myths of sea nymphs, sunken cities, singing sea shells and ancient galleons, yet into the ebb and surge of his characteristically melodramatic themes, Baxter splashes colour in dislocated spasms. Like other film composers, such as John Barry or Ennio Morricone, the attraction of such sensual depths of sound – in this case electronic keyboards and organ, samba rhythms and shimmering percussive effects – outweighs any populist urges to tether listeners in the shallows of melody.

● in my room

Welcome to *Music of the Sixties*. I'm Les Baxter and this is my chorus and orchestra. The show is live with the emphasis on the sound of music, featuring new arrangements of some of the current songs and some of your old favourites. The atmosphere tonight was set by our first arrangement – 'It's a Big Wide Wonderful World' – so let's go on a musical trip around the world tonight for a little diversion from horse operas, private eyes, seductive ladies and gunslingers. Our seductive ladies will be the violins. Notice the similarity in shape and sound . . .

Les Baxter, *The Lost Episode of Les Baxter*, Dionysus Records

'Les Baxter is a great traveller, chiefly with the object of studying the music and instruments of foreign countries,' claimed the sleeve notes of *Baxter Style*. 'He is something of an expert on African music, for example, and incorporates his discoveries into his orchestral arrangements whenever possible.'

In his interview with V. Vale in *Incredibly Strange Music Volume II*, Jello Biafra gleefully accuses Baxter of never having left Hollywood at all, let alone studied exotic instruments. This unkind cut was not absolutely true. In *Soundtrack* magazine, Baxter reminisced about a trip to Mexico. 'When I went there to score *The Sacred Idol* in 1959,' he said, 'I was flown in, ensconced in a hotel room and, without any piano or instrument whatsoever, I sat down and wrote the whole score just sitting at a desk.' So Baxter *had* travelled, though in the surrealist manner of writer Raymond Roussell, never leaving his hotel room. Some (including Baxter himself) have said he was an ethnomusicologist, he had studied Balinese gamelan and Chinese music, travelled to Cuba and heard ritual drums. How completely irrelevant. To justify his music with bogus scientism undermines Baxter as a fabulist.

In fact, Baxter was in on this joke himself. 'I don't think I got any further than Glendale,' he told Call and Huestis. 'No, it's not true. I hadn't been to South America or Cuba or anyplace when I did my exotic stuff. It just came out of nowhere. Later on I went to Cuba . . . I heard carnival in Rio too.'

Stereo hi-fidelity was a new technology in the 1950s. As the name suggests, hi-fi promised the cinematic authenticity of being there, in imaginary and acoustic space. The exotica composers shared an obsession with space. Juan Garcia Esquivel, a Mexican arranger and bandleader, explored the hallucinatory possibilities of stereo by recording sections of his orchestra in separate studios to achieve an exaggerated spatial image. As the sleeve notes of Esquivel's *Latin-esque* explained: 'the orchestra was separated into two parts – half in Studio 1 and the other half in Studio 2, almost a city block down the long corridor of the RCA building in Hollywood. Through an intricate system of intercommunication by headphones, the musicians were able to hear each other and play together just as if they were all in the same room. The effects are startling, the arrangements are daring, and when an image moves from side to side it can literally be said that the motion is almost a block long!'

The opening track of this 1962 album is typical: a rasping *güiro* scraper floats from left to right, followed by an arrangement that would be imbecilic were it not so economic, so skilful.

Throughout the tracks that follow, grand pianos drift from one side of the room to the other. They are bookended by two relentlessly bright though forever divided worlds of Hawaiian steel guitars, accordions, happy brass, trilling xylophones, rattling snare drums, claves, vocal choruses, boobams, electronic keyboards, whistling and every inane possibility of the orchestrator's art. Unlike most recordings, there is no attempt to cement the right and left loudspeaker channels into a cohesive (if virtual) whole; for Esquivel, the space between loudspeakers was an empty vessel through which normally immovable instruments roamed, sometimes hovering in the air or darting back and forth like hummingbirds. Crude as the sound magic is, the illusionism has parallels both with the Kinetic painting and sculpture of Bridget Riley and Pol Bury or with the surreal imagistic dislocations of Salvador Dali and Rene Magritte.

Another strong presence echoing in Esquivel recordings is Spike Jones, percussionist, arranger and satirist bandleader of the City Slickers. Known as the 'King of Corn', a murderer of the classics, Jones first formed a band in 1923 at the age of twelve; his final appearance, shortly before his death, was at Harrah's, Lake Tahoe, in 1965. Jones specialised in highly controlled chaos, interrupting romanticism or seriousness with rapid montages of idiocy and noise. Trumpeter George Rock gives a flavour of the humour in Jordan R. Young's biography, *Spike Jones and his City Slickers - the untold story*: 'Then we had a midget in Hawaii [Tony Boris] who looked like he was ninety years old; he always smoked cigars. In "Laura" he was the pair of pants that came running across stage. He was always afraid he was going to miss his cue. We'd look over and he'd be sitting in the wings, in the pants, with the fly open, with a cigar. Just a pair of trousers smoking a cigar.'

As Young points out, music made with a battery of bird calls, dustbins, flatulent brass, gunshots, sneezes and snores was nothing new: 'Musical instruments were being abused with humorous intent – and sounds not unlike Spike's – as early as 1909.' He lists characters such as Freddie Fischer, leader of the Schickelfritzers, and Paul 'Hezzie' Trietsch, inventor of the Wabash Washboard, 'an ordinary galvanised washboard flanked by tuned auto horns, pie pans, garbage can lids, a slide whistle and other noisemakers.'

Jones claimed other influences, including a Shrine Auditorium performance of *The Firebird*, conducted by Igor Stravinsky himself. According to Jones, Stravinsky was wearing new patent leather shoes that squeaked every time he went up on his toes. 'He should have worn a pair of sneakers,' said Jones. 'And the pseudos who went down to see the ballet, they didn't know what they were looking at anyway. They thought, Stravinsky's done it again. New percussive effects. I was hysterical. I was sitting real close and I could see and hear the shoes. When I left, driving home, I got to thinking if you made planned mistakes in musical arrangements and took the place of regular notes in well-known tunes with sound effects, there might be some fun in it.'

Although there were strong similarities between Spike Jones and Esquivel, the difference, listening in the present, is kinder to Esquivel's vintage of fun. Jones's taste in humour and music now sounds dated, whereas Esquivel's experiments with electronics and the illusory space of audio recording are coated with the synthetic sheen of fifties modernity.

● now voyager

A California orchestral violinist named Elisabeth Waldo also explored pictorial stereo, though her landscapes added a mythical dimension. Her *Rites of the Pagan: Mystic Realm of the Ancient Americas* album was a more studious form of exotica than Esquivel's. Alongside Apache and Pueblo instruments, the liner notes list a battery of pre-Columbian instruments – the *omitzicahuastli* or human bone rasp, the *teponaxtle* or sacred slit drum, deer hooves, obsidian stone and so on.

Waldo's late fifties music is quite as Hollywood bonkers as the Bollywood bonkers film music of Rahul Dev Burman, but cranked even higher on the crazyometer by her agenda to rescue 'the musical values of the Ancient Americas' and unveil 'the mysteries of a vast North-American Empire, silent for centuries'. As Dean Wallace wrote in a concert review for the *San Francisco Chronicle*: 'The effect was slightly devastating.' What it sounds like, more than four decades on, is the kind of music you might expect Charlotte Vale (Bette Davis) to write, had she been a composer, after her trip to South America in *Now Voyager*. Though rhythmically banal, Waldo's fabrications of Aztec sacrifices and animistic chants are compelling for the sincerity of their fictions, the oddity of their sound world. Reminiscent of Baxter's work with Yma Sumac, Waldo's fantasy of pre-Columbian America creates bizarre juxtapositions of plodding 'exotic' rhythms, bird and insect imitations played on the 'authentic pre-Columbian musical instruments', duets for alto flute and conch shell trumpet, and rhapsodic Jewish melodies played on the violin.

● lost world

Reconstructions were not unknown to ethnomusicologists. A two-LP set released on Folkways documented the individual sounds of eighty-nine pre-Columbian musical instruments, each played in isolation with traffic noise clearly audible in the background. Field recordings of Vietnamese Mnong Gar music, recorded in 1958 and 1966, released by the French Ocora label in their *Collection Musée de l'Homme*, were augmented by a performance on a lithophone discovered in northern Vietnam. 'The Mnong Gar, the present occupants of the site,' wrote recordist Georges Condominas, 'didn't know of this instrument's existence so no one has any idea of how it was played. It would however be a pity if these stones with their beautiful sound were to remain silent forever ... We should point out again that there is no attempt whatever to recreate "prehistoric" music, but simply an attempt to hear these stones, exceptional not only in their form, but also in their musicality.'

● house of bamboo

In *Elevator Music*, Joseph Lanza describes Les Baxter's *Tamboo!* as 'incontrovertible evidence that this is a genuine imitation of a previously fabricated wilderness'. So Baxter provides classic postmodern source material: when the soundtrack work dwindled to virtually nothing in the early eighties he wrote music for theme

parks and sea worlds, surely the ultimate pomo job. N
ently, Lanza notes that Baxter and the other professional E.
represented a 'celebration of America's power to mola
unknown in the image of reconstructed psychosexual fantasies o
G.I.s who had been stationed in the islands during World War II'.

Some sense of this new world of titillation for the conquering
heroes, stationed in Japan and Pearl Harbour, is visible in films
such as Sam Fuller's *House of Bamboo*. Released in 1955 and set
in postwar Tokyo, *House of Bamboo* was a gangster/stool pigeon
vehicle for Robert Ryan and Robert Stack. Also featuring Hollywood's resident Japanese actor, Sessue Hayakawa, the film gives
subversive glimpses into the tensions of occupation and the fascinations (or tedium, for some) of exotic culture to the conquerors.

In hindsight, one of the attractions of exotica from this period
is our perception of its pivotal position between the immediate
past and the possible future. War in the Pacific had introduced a
new set of cultural parameters to America. In the postwar period,
suburbanisation and technology were suggesting a future that
combined refuge with expansion. So exotica was a sexy stereo
soundtrack for tropical explorers who moved no further from the
'burb than a polyvinyl lounger poised in the epicentre of two
hi-fi speakers.

The innate surrealism of these records comes from the naive
but very professional way in which they overlaid easy listening
renditions of standard tunes with strange instrumentation, stereo
effects and exotic backgrounds. Travel was the coming thing, yet
fear of the unknown, the other, still festered. Maybe it seemed
very sophisticated, cosmopolitan even, to listen to 'Softly, as in a
Morning Sunrise' played on *shamisen* and celeste. The same desire
to throw in a touch of highbrow coloration was transforming
country music in roughly the same era, as hard drinking, rough-
edged country was dragged out of the honkytonks and sweetened
with strings and choirs.

Although the GI theory offers some explanation of the fad for
tiki bars and Afro-Hawaiian light jazz with bird calls, the cultural
embedding of exotica – the appeal and influence of barely understood foreign cultures – had been well established as a global
trend since the nineteenth century. Les Baxter's Latinisms, for

example, formed a relatively insignificant contribution to a fading boom that had its roots in the impact on America of Cuban and Mexican music in the nineteenth century, Argentinian tango and Guatemalan marimba bands in the early twentieth.

'The music of the early marimba groups,' writes John Storm Roberts in *The Latin Tinge*, 'was yet another illustration of a highly important point about the interrelationship of Latin and American music. Despite what one might expect, this does not proceed from the importation of something fairly genuine through a progressive watering-down. The early stages involve highly diluted Latinisms. Then, as Latin music and its various substyles have become familiar, they have become stronger – not necessarily moving toward "authenticity" in terms of their origins, though that has frequently happened, but establishing themselves as healthy U.S.-Latin forms.'

Baxter's music was an odd tributary of this evolutionary movement. The impulse to fabricate and exploit, whatever the source (skimpy Baxter biographies and interviews give us few clues), led him into regions that challenged notions of authenticity. An example from a later era was Baxter's venture into synthetic folk, a response to the growing appeal of a perennially rediscovered folk music. As Dave Laing wrote in *The Electric Muse*: 'Most of the seminal figures in rock over the past decade served their apprenticeships in the coffeehouses and on the campuses of the folk revival: Bob Dylan, Stephen Stills, John Sebastian, Neil Young, Roger McGuinn, David Crosby, Joni Mitchell, John Phillips, Jackson Browne – the list could go on and on. What these performers and others brought into rock was not just different sounds and musical styles, but a set of habits and attitudes which proved to be crucial in the expansion of rock's horizon in the late Sixties.'

In response to the folk revival, Baxter formed the Les Baxter Balladeers. Included in the membership were Bobby Ingram and, before him, David Crosby's older brother, Ethan. 'The lines were drawn between commercial and ethnic folk,' recalls Ingram in David Crosby's autobiography, *Long Time Gone*. 'I remember we recorded a track one time and Les Baxter dubbed drums on it. I was furious. One didn't use drums. And he had. He was an ethnomusicologist. He knew everything there was to know.'

Baxter and Ingram would go to see Babatunde Olatunji perform at the Troubadour, Les telling Ingram which rhythms were West African, Kenyan or Ugandan. Then a former stripper, a thirties legend named Sally Rand, came to hear the Balladeers play. With her Appalachian background, Rand was able to tell the Balladeers exactly why they weren't folksingers. 'Well, shit,' says Ingram, 'we knew we weren't folksingers.'

Ethan Crosby harboured no illusions about authenticity either. He remembers his debut with Les Baxter's Balladeers at the Desert Inn in Las Vegas, 'wearing scarlet bellboy jackets and faggot boots and doing the whole number and Vegas is the sleaziest place I have ever been'. Back in LA, Ethan persuaded Baxter to sack the other singers and hire Ingram and (predating the Byrds, Crosby, Stills and Nash, and celebrity drug dependency) his 'scuzzbut kid brother', David Crosby. Looking neutered in their pencil ties, transitional haircuts and matching jackets with no lapels, they are captured for posterity and their own embarrassment in a posed photograph now lodged in the Michael Ochs archives, three acoustic guitarists and a double bass player in the wrong place at the wrong time. The Les Baxter Balladeers' record released on Frank Sinatra's Liberty label was a resounding failure. 'David Crosby,' chided Baxter's daughter, Leslie, in the liner notes of *The Exotic Moods of Les Baxter*, 'you didn't say thank you.'

8

tabu

◆◆◆◆◆◆◆◆◆◆◆◆◆◆◆◆

an imperial interlude

After I left Gondar, I had various chance encounters with Somali girls in the native quarter of Djibouti; yet these *amours*, however absurd and unfortunate, have left me with an impression of Paradise.

In 1933 I returned, having killed at least one myth: that of travel as a means of escape. I have subsequently gone back to therapy twice, once for only a brief amount of time. The chief thing I have learned from it is that, even in what appears to be the most heterogeneous manifestations, one always finds that one is oneself, that there is a unity in life, and that everything leads back, whatever one does, to a specific constellation of things which one tends to reproduce, under various forms, an unlimited number of times.

Michel Leiris, *Manhood*, 1946

The Crosby family held another significance for Les Baxter. In 1953, Baxter set sail for uncharted lands, scoring his first of many low-budget film soundtracks: a sailboat travelogue called *Tanga Tika*. The filmmaker is unknown. Could the contact between Baxter and this unknown director have come from David and Ethan Crosby's father, Floyd? Floyd Crosby was a cinematographer who had sailed to Haiti in the twenties, then joined photographic and film expeditions to Tahiti, the Brazilian rainforest, Honduras and Greece. 'Why did the son of the treasurer of the Union Pacific Railroad go to such exotic locales?' asked his son, David. 'Because he wanted to and because he had already tried it the straight way.'

Glowing with filial pride, Crosby lists the adventures of his father's exotic life. He had shot underwater film with William Beebe, Brooklyn-born developer of the bathysphere, director of the department of tropical research at the New York Zoological Society, author of *High Jungle*, *Half Mile Down*, *Zaca Venture* and *Book of Bays*. Beebe was a lyrical writer, committed to technology and biodiversity. *High Jungle*, published in 1950, is filled with heady descriptions of jungle atmospheres and sounds. 'The rain loves our unfinished castle of Rancho Grande,' he wrote, 'for it can throb and beat out rhythms and measures never achieved elsewhere. It falls through open and half-closed roofs, down three stories with musical obstacles at varying heights, landing at last on cement or water or hollow tiles in half-finished rooms, whose crazy angles provide unheard of acoustics.'

Perhaps as a projection, David Crosby perceives his father's immersion in this world of exotic sense impressions as a rejection of bourgeois values. After a short period in Hollywood, Floyd teamed up with Robert Flaherty, a documentary filmmaker who had made *Nanook of the North* at the beginning of the twenties. Flaherty himself was an interesting case. A gold prospector's son born in Iron Mountain, Michigan, Flaherty came into contact with many ethnic groups, as well as indigenous Native Americans, during his childhood in the prospecting camps. He accidentally set fire to the negative of his first documentary on Eskimo life, then lost the work print. For his next venture he was more careful not to smoke while editing.

Often described as the first ethnographic documentary film, *Nanook of the North* was distributed to cinemas by Pathé. Despite the industry's view that there was no audience for this kind of film, *Nanook of the North* became a global success. Flaherty was then commissioned to travel to Polynesia to film a South Seas sequel: *Moana*. He is photographed in Samoa during this period, on one knee like a supplicant, his arm around a laughing child. He is smiling at a group of three Samoans and one American to his left: a mature woman sitting, a young woman standing behind her, a man on one knee, like Flaherty; at the far edge of the group, shy and smiling, gaze averted from the sun and the lens, sits Flaherty's wife, Frances, who assisted him in the making of *Moana*, *Man of Aran* and *Louisiana Story*. The scene is idyllic, the South Seas as any fantasist might imagine them: lush vegetation, bright sun, bare-breasted women, bare-torsoed men, happy children, all adorned with flowers in their hair.

The essence of this paradise image was potent for David Crosby's generation; potent for his father's also. Flaherty took Floyd Crosby to the Pacific to assist with *White Shadows in the South Seas*, an exotic melodrama for MGM that inspired South Seas yearnings in unlikely places. Although Flaherty was unhappy with the experience, the film was a logical extension of his documentary style. 'A film is always a construction,' wrote Asen Balikci in *Principles of Visual Anthropology*. 'Anthropological films are no exception . . . the anthropological film becomes an admittedly personal interpretation of the local culture. With this in mind, Flaherty developed a specific method for constructing (and reconstructing) cultures on film.' Describing one of Flaherty's favourite themes as 'the continuously heroic struggle of total, primordial man against infinitely powerful and hostile elements', Balikci quotes anthropologist John C. Messenger's comments on another Flaherty film: *Man of Aran*. 'Flaherty was so deeply influenced by primitivism and his philosophy of esthetics,' wrote Messenger, 'that he created new customs, such as shark fishing – a central theme of the work, and seriously distorted numerous indigenous ones in order to make the "man of Aran" fit his preconceptions and titillate his camera.'

In the service of an idealised image of the savage, Flaherty's populist, though not always popular, docudramas flickered in an ambiguous imaginative space that was memoir, theory, document, deception and fiction. *White Shadows in the South Seas* told the story of an alcoholic doctor who falls in love with a Tahitian woman, finally meeting his demise at the hands of white colonials. Stripped to bare bones, the plot resembles one of Joseph Conrad's South-East Asian tragedies of white men meeting bad ends – *An Outcast of the Islands* or *Almayer's Folly* – endings whose degradation was particularly colourful when erotic desire transgressed taboo.

After abandoning a project involving Pueblo Indians, Flaherty joined with F.W. Murnau in a partnership. German born but working in Hollywood by 1927, Murnau had directed a silent version of *Nosferatu the Vampire*, the most chilling, visually disturbing film interpretation of Bram Stoker's *Dracula*. The first and only film to come out of the partnership with Flaherty was *Tabu*. Photographed by Floyd Crosby in Tahiti in 1929 (his work on this project was nominated for an Academy Award), *Tabu* became a focal point for irreconcilable differences between the two directors. Murnau bought Flaherty out of the deal and finished the film, though he never lived to see the première. As the gossip in Kenneth Anger's *Hollywood Babylon* whispers, Murnau was breaking taboos himself when he died in a car crash: 'Murnau had hired as valet a handsome fourteen-year-old Filipino boy named Garcia Stevenson. The boy was at the wheel of the Packard when the fatal accident occurred. The Hollywood *méchantes langues* reported that Murnau was going down on Garcia when the car leaped off the road.'

● the first taboo . . . the last taboo

Taboo; the word has a long and interesting history. Captain James Cook introduced the word to Europe in 1784, describing his third voyage around the world. He used the word in connection with religious practices in Atui, one of the Sandwich Islands, and Tahiti. After Cook was killed in Polynesia, his successor – James King – attempted to be more specific about the occasions and meanings of taboo. 'Mention hath been already made,' he wrote, 'that women are always *tabooed*, or forbidden to eat certain kinds of meats. We also frequently saw several at their meals, who had the meat put into their mouths by others; and on our asking the reason of this singularity were told they were *tabooed*, or forbidden, to feed themselves . . . This word is also used to express anything sacred, or eminent, or devoted.'

In his book, *Taboo*, anthropologist Franz Steiner underlined the significance of the journals of Cook and King in the European imagination: '[T]hey are the classic passages from which the word "taboo" became known to Europeans. It soon became the property of the educated, particularly in Britain where Cook was widely read: he was, after all, the last of the great navigators, the last person to sail around the globe in the grand manner *and* discover new and inhabited land; his writings showed him to be a man of genius and his death was an event of the mythical order.'

Steiner went on to examine the subtle interpretations of taboo and its causes, critically analysing two famous landmarks in the establishment of this concept in modern thought: the first published essay on taboo – Sir James Frazer's 'Taboo', printed in the 1875 edition of the *Encyclopedia Britannica*, and Sigmund Freud's *Totem and Taboo*, published in 1950. As the writings of Frazer and Freud filtered into popular consciousness during the twentieth century, via literature, film, pop psychology, pornographic magazines and the neon signs over strip club doorways, the meaning of taboo narrowed to a more straightforward signification: erotic desire, prohibited yet indulged.

● a dream text

Tropicana is localized outside the town. It is a sylvan cabaret . . . every square yard is overgrown with trees and bushes and lianas and *epiphytes* which Mrs. Campbell insisted were orchids, and classical statues and fountains with running water, everywhere, and spotlights with occult colors . . . Then the two women come in, severely naked. They go to bed together and compromise themselves in some really unhealthy gymnastics, which are indecent and completely unhygienic. At the climax, the lights flash on and off and the couple becomes a single woman, screaming, because such cries are the most common form of expression in Cuba . . .

G. Cabrere Infante, *Three Trapped Tigers*, 1980

In 1935, the Lecuona Cuban Boys, an exotic rumba band led by Cuban composer Ernesto Lecuona, recorded the first version of 'Tabou'. Lecuona's band became hugely popular in Europe after the runaway success of 'Peanut Vendor', recorded by Don Azpiazú. 'In 1931, Queen Mary included the song in the music for the first Buckingham Palace ball since 1924,' wrote John Storm Roberts in *The Latin Tinge*, 'and Marion Sunshine sang it at a Royal

Command Performance.' From this regal enthusiasm for an American hit record composed by a Cuban, enthusiasm for the rumba spread to continental Europe.

To judge from recordings and photographs of their performances, the Lecuona Cuban Boys were more than just a rumba band. Their touring embraced Biarritz, Paris, Athens, London and Istanbul, where they presented a Latin revue of comedy and exotic tableaux, spiced with a peculiarly eclectic version of Cuban idioms and 'jungle' music. In 1936 they participated in a package tour with dancer and vocalist Josephine Baker, the woman whose charisma and presence burned a myth-image of erotic exoticism into the fantasies of Europeans.

'Tabou' was co-composed by Ernesto's niece, the mezzo-soprano vocalist Margarita. The recording begins with 'native' drums, followed by a serpentine 'Egyptian' theme played on the clarinet. A photograph of the band onstage shows a *conguero* and clarinettist wearing fezzes, charming a string of sausages out of a basket. Other band members, wearing turbans, clown around them, one of them waving a large fan of peacock feathers. Perhaps this was the routine that accompanied 'Tabou'. The international flavour of their repertoire between 1935 and 1937 is evident from song titles: 'Hindou', 'La Cucaracha', 'Canto Indio', 'Panama', 'International Rumba' and 'Antillana', whose intro has an uncanny similarity to 'The James Bond Theme'.

Twenty-one years later, Les Baxter recorded his own version of Lecuona's 'Tabou'. With a new spelling – 'Taboo' – and an additional songwriter credit given to Bob Russell, the song was included on the *Caribbean Moonlight* album, alongside Ernesto Lecuona's 'The Breeze and I' and Xavier Cugat's 'Nightingale'. Prefaced by harp, eerie strings and chiming piano, the melody is introduced by alto flute (played with so little vibrato that it sounds electronic) then echoed by Baxter's trademark sweep of lush violins. The bass line (maybe Bob Russell's contribution) is bold, stately, almost funky, and Baxter plays down the exotic snake-charmer kitsch of the melody in favour of languid mystery.

A confused, hybrid exotica evolved as the century progressed. Although Baxter was careful to theme his territories and highlight individual cultural mysteries (a different paradise, a different sales pitch for each album), the music layered dislocated fantasy on dislocated fantasy. Recorded in a period when a variety of Latin rhythms were making inroads into American music, Baxter's 'Taboo' was more Cuban than the Lecuona Cuban Boys original, yet clearly influenced by contemporary Latin-tinged R&B, jazz and the LA-based crossover Latin-pop of Perez Prado. 'I used colors that the average arranger was not using at the time,' he told David Kraft and Ronald Bohn of *Soundtrack!* magazine. 'Also, I introduced Latin rhythms, African drums or Afro-Cuban drums to concert composing. When I went into a studio, everyone would say, "Well, it's Les's usual combination – a cello and 12 drummers!" '

The mambo, the *chachachá* and the Brazilian *baião* were igniting dance crazes and restructuring jazz. As for Margarita Lecuona's Egyptian theme, Baxter had air-freighted it to a verdant rainforest in the Amazon; a *Green Mansions* scene, a white man, peering through dense foliage at the totemic exotica fantasy, a native girl, swimming naked in a lake.

● babu-english

And yet the very density of the network of global communication, the very accessibility of foreign lands, directly or indirectly, intensified the confrontation and the intermingling of the western and exotic worlds.

E.J. Hobsbawm, *The Age of Empire*, 1987

With a disregard for specifics, exotic musics were delineating a false ethnographic map of the world, as if Sir James Frazer had written *The Golden Bough* as a dream text, even a deliberate deception. Fake exotics emerged – a phoney Canadian Indian called Grey Owl or T. Lobsang Rampa, the mystic Tibetan who turned out to be a Devonshire plumber named Cyril Henry Hoskins. More down to earth in his adoption of an exotic identity was the London-born Hawaiian guitarist Kealoha Life. In an interview with slide guitarist and exotica researcher Mike Cooper, Life claimed that his love affair with Pacific culture hit him as a six-year-old boy in the cinema, watching *White Shadows of the South Seas*, the first film to feature the Hawaiian guitar. These were people too ordinary for their own liking, reinventing themselves as characters in a parallel universe.

The process had begun properly in the nineteenth century, at its sublime height with Joseph Conrad and Rudyard Kipling, at less demanding altitudes with the imperial literature of H. Rider Haggard and then in 1912, Edgar Rice Burroughs with the first of his Tarzan novels.

'Increasingly the exotic became part of everyday education,' wrote E.J. Hobsbawm in *The Age of Empire*, 'as in the enormously successful boys' novels of Karl May (1842–1912), whose imaginary German hero ranged through the Wild West and the Islamic east, with excursions into black Africa and Latin America; in the thrillers, whose villains now included inscrutable and all-powerful orientals like Sax Rohmer's Dr Fu Manchu; in the pulp-magazine school stories for British boys, which now included a rich Hindu speaking the baroque Babu-English of the expected stereotype.'

America's fascination with exotica has reflected the fantasies and desires of a country built on extraordinary social and ethnic diversity: immigrants from every part of the world, the legacy of slavery, the genocide of the Indians, the annexation of Mexican land. Music could express the unthinkable, which meant that black and white hybrids such as Western Swing, rockabilly and rock'n'roll could exist before civil rights.

Postwar, the references from stage, film and television were rich in disinformation: the Bob Hope, Bing Crosby, Dorothy Lamour series of *Road* films (*Road to Singapore, Road to Morocco, Road to Zanzibar, Road to Bali* and so on), the exotic films featuring singer and wearer of exotic fruits, Carmen Miranda (*Down Argentina Way, That Night in Rio, Weekend in Havana*), and the exotic musicals written by Rodgers and Hammerstein – *Flower Drum Song, The King and I* and *South Pacific*.

'Carmen Miranda was the fantasy of some impotent executive who called himself a movie mogul,' wrote Felipe Luciano in his sleeve notes for *Latin Roots*, a compilation of Cuban recordings from 1946 to 1956. 'She writhed, she danced, she pouted and pranced to the erotic rhythms of jungle drums, bananas on her head and thoughts of sweaty passion on her brain. Then came Desi Arnez Ba-Ba-looing his way from a Florida nightclub to a syndicated T.V. program with a redhead who was as dumb as he was diluted. And Des Moines, Iowa howled at his antics and wondered why all those Cuban Commies couldn't be as nice as Lucy's husband.'

Luciano's righteous swatting of Miranda, the 'brandy-peach of Brazil', as a synthetic construction raises problems in its harsh polarisation of the authentic and the fabricated, the pure and the manipulated. Later research on Carmen Miranda suggests that her notorious costume, the banana hat (apparently so kitsch, so insultingly stereotypical), was an adaptation of the hats that Bahian fruit sellers balanced on their head. Miranda first wore this seemingly bizarre, though actually practical, headgear for her Rio de Janeiro performance debut in 1939. From a tip-off, she was spotted there by the Broadway impresario Lee Schubert and offered work in his New York show, *The Streets of Paris*.

Born in a small Portuguese village, she emigrated to Brazil as a child. Later, she collaborated with Brazilian samba composers such as Laurindo Almeida and Synval Silva, becoming a success by singing Argentinian tangos and Brazilian sambas. With her arrival in New York, she found her speech, accent and mannerisms turned into idiocies by the American media. The American public (and Wittgenstein) loved her for her fractured accent and odd expressions, the inter-language of her songs and high-speed repartee, part-English, part-Portuguese, part-monkey cries and sound poetry. Men, of course, lusted after her exotic exuberance or, lusting after other men, they dressed in Carmen Miranda outfits. Though puzzled by the inexplicable, unexpected foolishness of it all, Miranda turned both the misunderstanding and the lust into a potent, ultimately tragic trademark: the firebrand exotic, inarticulate in speech, virtuoso in the body, in pre-rational utterance. 'They don't understand the slightest thing I sing,' said Miranda, 'but they say I'm the most sensational foreign performer to ever perform here.'

With a move to Hollywood, where she enlivened dumb but lucrative musical films with her vivacity and energy, her turbans and platforms, she became the highest paid female entertainer in America. For this Americanisation, Miranda was rejected by her Brazilian fans. Embroiled in wartime propaganda, the image of Latin America with which she colluded generated increasing hostility in Argentina and Brazil. 'Our greatest star has been conquered by a foreign power,' wrote one Brazilian journalist. Locked into the studio system with Twentieth Century Fox, she was unable to escape the treadmill of escapist fun. The fruit baskets were piled higher, the bananas grew longer and fatter, until with Busby Berkeley's extraordinary dance routines in *The Gang's All Here* – gigantic swollen bananas swooping down over supine women who opened their legs to receive them – the underlying message was driven home.

Already demoralised by her unhappy marriage, Miranda was broken by the relentless pace of work. In the face of intolerable pressures to conform to her tutti-frutti image she bought a personally expensive way out of her studio contract. Addiction to uppers and downers followed. Suffering acute anxiety and depression she finally made a temporary return to Brazil, where frequent electric shock treatment was administered, as was customary at the time in cases of nervous breakdown. In 1946, after returning to Hollywood and its hectic schedules, she collapsed on Jimmy Durante's TV show and died of a heart attack that night. She was forty-six years old.

Half a century later, she is hardwired into the lexicon of Latin larks: at screenings of Disney's *Flubber* in 1998, none of the children, few of their parents even, would have the slightest idea of who this Carmen Miranda was, yet inevitably, a fruit basket hat appears during the Latin dance scene, a Hollywood valentine for a torched *amour*.

● an exotic e-mail

hi david . . .
        did i tell you about Tao Moe (you know who he is right? the
hawaiian steel player . . . when he was in india with his family . . .
they got stuck there durin the war when they were on tour and the
japanese bombed pearl harbour . . . they stayed in india for a long

time playing . . . in order to stay up to date with the current musical trends he used to go to the cinema and watch carmen miranda films . . . he would sit in the dark with a pencil and paper and write the tunes down (notate them note by note) . . . he went back several times until he got them all note perfect . . . then they would learn them . . . they were very versatile performers . . . they still live in hawaii . . . him and his wife are in their eighties and his son and daughter in their sixties . . . The tao moe family . . .

Terry Zwigov (cant spell hs name) made a great film about them but has never edited it for showing. ive seen bits of it . . . its incredible . . . Tao used to make super eight films of them . . . and he still has them all . . . and the most amazing scrap book as well . . . right from back in the twenties when they started playing . . . they were on the road for 29 years!!

● ciao for now . . . *mike cooper*

● special hopes, special dreams

Planning the music of *The King and I*, composer Richard Rodgers had to consider just how much exotica a mainstream audience could stomach. 'Rodgers was convinced,' wrote Stanley Green in *The Rodgers and Hammerstein Story*, 'that an evening of tinkling bells and gongs – even if he could write that kind of music – would drive the people into the street long before the final curtain went down.' Rodgers worked out a strategy that, in its rationale, encapsulated the arrogant self-deceptions of exotica. 'The composer has compared his approach,' Green explained, 'to the way the American artist Grant Wood might paint a series of scenes in Bangkok, the capital of Siam. His paintings of the people and buildings would certainly be accurate, but they would also look as if they had been seen through the eyes of a man whose roots went deep into American soil.'

There were none of the disruptions or dialogues of surrealism here. As Rodgers was aware, his solution to the problem of depicting otherness to an audience hungry for stereotypes was informed by pre-modernist Orientalist painting. The theatrical realism of nineteenth-century painters such as Hans Makart and Jean-Léon Gérôme served to intensify the erotic voyeurism into which the observer is seduced.

Between 1949 and 1958, Rodgers and Hammerstein wrote three orientalist musicals: *South Pacific*, *The King and I* and *Flower Drum Song*.

If any musical event of the fifties proves a connection between exotica and the Pacific campaigns of World War II, or better illustrates the notion of exotica as a painted backdrop for the important deeds and forbidden romances of white Americans, then it must be *South Pacific*. Based on *Tales of the South Pacific*, a James Michener book of short stories about the Pacific war, the stage musical actually began its five-year Broadway run in 1949. The luridly photographed film followed in 1958. Rodgers and Hammerstein's most exotic song for the show was 'Bali Ha'i', its ethereal melody reportedly composed by Richard Rodgers in five minutes during dinner. 'Specifically,' wrote Stanley Green, 'it is about the island called Bali Ha'i, the one special island for everyone's special hopes and special dreams.'

● gutter cats . . . the sound of light

These 'faraway' places frequently came to exert a mysterious fascination. I would argue that they were truly sacred places, but in modern guise. Whereas sacred places in traditional culture seem to have been created *ex nihilo*, to have existed always, these new places can be seen in a process of creation, fulfilment and decline. In them we can trace how a geographical location becomes transformed into a sacred place. They offer a unique opportunity to follow the relationship between cultural imagination, physical landscape and the sense of the sacred. They are windows into the changing spiritual aspirations, the soul, of modern Europe.

Peter Bishop, *The Myth of Shangri-La*, 1989

'Bali Ha'i' is a strange song. The island that may call at any time of night or day, come to me, come to me, like the summoning of death. By summoning a number of influential travellers, writers, artists, filmmakers and opinion shapers (some of them to their death), the supposed paradise of Polynesia was imagined into a powerful sacred place, a totem of European, American and Japanese fantasy and nostalgia.

Herman Melville's first book, a bestseller called *Typee*, was a blend of fiction, borrowed knowledge and chronicle. Including rhapsodic descriptions of his romance with a tattooed 'child of nature', Fayaway, the story was based on Melville's one-month stay on the Marquesas Islands in 1842 after he and another sailor had deserted their whaling ship. 'They stayed in idyllic peace for four months,' wrote David Howarth, author of *Tahiti: A Paradise Lost*, 'but they never thought of staying forever. It was partly the restlessness which afflicts most sophisticated people when they try to live a simple life . . .'

Blind to the possibility of restlessness, others followed in search of utopia. After a winter of freezing temperatures in New York State, Robert Louis Stevenson sailed to Polynesia and settled in Samoa for the sake of his failing health. While living in Edinburgh he had heard a New Zealander tell South Seas stories until he had been made 'sick with desire to go there; beautiful places, green for ever; perfect climate, perfect shapes of men and women with red flowers in their hair; and nothing to do but study oratory and etiquette, sit in the sun and pick up the fruits as they fall'. Though Stevenson was happier and healthier in Samoa, paradise was not quite as indolent as he had imagined. Having exiled himself to the island of his own special dreams he wrote compulsively and nostalgically about Scotland, overworking, dying in Samoa in 1894 after a brain haemorrhage.

One of the most popular travel writers of the late nineteenth century was a French sailor, painter and acrobat who had reinvented himself as Pierre Loti and travelled extensively through exotic regions such as the Pacific islands. Exotic books such as *The Marriage of Loti*, *Madame Chrysanthème*, *Un Pélerin d'Angkor* and *Le Désert* proved irresistible to modish *fin de siècle* tastes, making Loti a celebrity in Europe. In his biography of Gauguin – *Paul Gauguin: A Complete Life* – David Sweetman describes Loti, or Julien Viaud in his previous incarnation, as 'a frail, dreamy young man of twenty-one who kept a cat, a tortoise and a monkey in his cabin along with his paints and sketchbooks . . . a decade hence, under his *nom de plume* Pierre Loti, he would be considered the most flamboyantly adventurous

Frenchman of his time, one of the most famous men of the century.'

Ambiguous in his own sexuality, Loti cultivated an ambiguity in the nature of his books. Some were frankly escapist novels, some were travel journals; the former mixed Loti's travel experiences in amongst his narrative fictions, the latter chronicled journeys notable for the unreliability of their observations.

'His writing shows a gross misunderstanding of the Arab cultures he encountered,' wrote Peter Wild in *Arid Lands Newsletter*, 'but art isn't often a true reflection of reality, and Loti's *The Desert*, for all the blithe liberties it takes with the facts, is an accomplished effervescence.' Consumed in small doses, Loti's writing, a haze of sense impressions that float above the ground, delivers a piquant flavour of French Decadent obsessions. 'In the cool, quiet morning at sunrise,' he writes in *The Desert*, 'when I open my tent, the outside air carries a whiff of perfume, so that it seems as if someone has broken a vial of aromatics in front of my door. And all this forlorn valley of granite is also perfumed, as if it were an oriental temple. Its few little pale plants, held back by drought, have awakened because of the night's deluge and waft their odors like countless incense burners. You could say that the air is ripe with benjamin, citronella, geranium, and myrrh . . .'

Like Melville before him, Loti pursued a theme that would continue to haunt the imaginations of European and American men. *The Marriage of Loti* tells the story of his marriage to a fourteen-year-old Tahitian girl named Rarahu. A featherweight narrative is peppered with observations that seem repugnant now. Loti's perception of Rarahu is cool and controlling. He seems to see her as a kind of animal-child, a creature of few qualities other than beauty and sweetness. He is indifferent to the fate of Rarahu after he has left Tahiti.

A description of Chinese opera performed in San Francisco in 1873 reveals prejudice in the face of unfamiliarity. Even Loti admits his anecdote is gratuitous: 'A grotesque reminiscence which has nothing to do with what has gone before, and still less with what is to follow; which has, indeed, no connection with my story but that of date . . . The actors, dressed in the costumes of departed dynasties, gave vent to the most astonishing and incredible yells in voices for all the world like cats in a gutter; the orchestra, consisting of gongs and banjos, performed in outrageous discord – or undreamed-of harmonies.'

Compare this with Antonin Artaud's description of Balinese music, heard at the Paris Exposition of 1931: 'Beside the booming, pounding musical rhythm – there is a sustained hesitating fragile music which seems to grind the most precious metals, where springs of water bubble up as in a state of nature, where columns of insects march through the plants, where the sound of light itself appears to have been picked up, where the sounds of deep solitudes seem distilled into crystal swarms.'

Yet despite Loti's distortions and hatreds (which can, after all, be found as frequently in Conrad, though expressed with more detachment), the seductive force of these floating worlds that he conjured can be imagined still; a relentless intoxication of scents, sounds, beauty and languor, discovered in strange places that the majority of his readers would never see.

Paul Gauguin was inspired by *The Marriage of Loti*. 'Because he is now a minor figure in the history of French literature,' writes David Sweetman, 'it is essential to see Loti in his place as a commanding influence on late nineteenth-century thought. While he may not have intended it, his books were a crucial part of the process of convincing the French people that their future lay as much in far distant places as it did in the farms and cities of France itself. And, yearning for an unspoiled Eden, the inhabitants of those overcrowded, smoky cities had no wish to be told that such a paradise did not exist – least of all a fantasist like Paul Gauguin, who read Loti and through him came to see in the colonial romance a solution to all his troubles, both financial and artistic.'

In fact, Loti, in his previous life as Julien Viaud, midshipman, had served with Gauguin on the same ship during the Franco-Prussian war. Fired with enthusiasm for exotic salvation by his old comrade's writings, Gauguin made an ill-fated trip to Panama, where he found chaos and disease in amongst the disastrous French effort to build a canal; then on to Martinique, where sickness and poverty mixed with disillusionment forced him back to Paris. True paradise, even before mass tourism, was a vaporous

romance. Finally he sailed to Tahiti to create the pa.
have etched an image of erotic, magical paradise into the
tieth-century imagination.

● village global

... Miami Beach, 1992, a ferret on a lead ... Soho, New York
City, 1997, two ferrets on leads, walked by woman wearing fur
coat ...

Anticipating Picasso and the Surrealists, Gauguin had been
intrigued by exhibits in the new Musée d'Ethnographie de Paris.
According to David Sweetman, he was drawn compulsively to a
Peruvian trepanned mummy from the Urubamba Valley. '[T]he
sight of so much strange beauty was enough to awaken his desire
to travel,' writes Sweetman. 'Matching these fantasies about
faraway places was another new fashion: the postcard, the ubiqui-
tous souvenir of the day.' Gauguin was also a keen visitor to
the Parisian Great Exhibitions, those turn-of-the-century imperial
showcases and markets that revealed spoils and curiosities of
colonialism alongside new technologies of photography and film.
Specially built colonial villages – the *villages indigènes* – titillated
urban Europeans with a simulacrum of life in a variety of exotic
locales.

At the Centenaire in Paris, he sketched Khmer sculptures and
visited the Javanese village. 'This was a simple affair of bamboo
and thatch,' writes Sweetman, 'with a chief's stilt house and
various huts.' The villages offered voyeurism, exotic diversion in
a compacted Darwinian ideology, 'generally reinforcing the sense
of superiority of the "civilised" over the "primitive",' as
Hobsbawm has written. They were also a conduit for promotion,
in a form that we would recognise only too quickly today. In
anticipation of beer sponsorship for world music, the Javanese
village was sponsored by Dutch businessmen, who offered Van
Houten Cocoa and Lucas Bols Spirits to footsore, thirsty Parisians
in one of the huts.

Sweetman speculates on another aspect of these human zoos:
erotic desire projected onto the village inhabitants. Performances
of dances, just the sort of spectacles that impressed themselves so

deeply on Claude Debussy at the Exposition of 1889 or Antonin Artaud in 1931, were given by a troupe of Javanese temple dancers, girls aged between twelve and sixteen. The convergence of exotic culture, paedophilia and colonial produce, comparable commodities without conscience, is striking. Maybe even Gauguin found the Javanese girls out of bounds; he embarked on a short affair with a woman from the Caribbean. Again, Sweetman speculates – 'one wonders if he took her with him on one of several visits he made to the Porte des Ternes to see Buffalo Bill Cody in his Wild West Show' – and in its parodic postmodernism, this concocted image appeals to 'an englobing appetite for the irony of apparently incongruous cultural syntheses', as described in Charles Stewart and Rosalind Shaw's *Syncretism/Anti-Syncretism*.

All of the colonial exhibitions between the 1880s and the Second World War, mounted on a grand scale and with huge popular appeal in Europe, America and many of the colonies, mixed a confusion of intentions. 'The great exhibitions . . . offer the most striking examples of both conscious and unconscious approaches to imperial propaganda,' wrote John M. MacKenzie in his book, *Propaganda and Empire*.

In Britain, showman Imre Kiralfy had mounted epic fantasy pageants – precursors of Cecil B. DeMille's exotic quasi-historic orgies for the cinema – such as *Nero, or, The Destruction of Rome*; the exhibitions offered opportunities to use authentic actors in similar theatrical productions. MacKenzie documents the extraordinary *tour de force* of Kiralfy's Greater Britain Exhibition of 1899, held at London's Earls Court. Among orientalist palaces, a Cairo street and re-enactments of the Matabele War was set a 'Kaffir Krall', organised in Natal by circus entrepreneur Frank Fillis and populated by '174 Africans, Zulus, Basuto, Matabele, and Swazi in four villages, infested apparently by strutting cranes and giant tortoises'. A thread of pragmatism hung off the showmanship. 'Once in London,' Ben Shephard writes in 'Showbiz Imperialism', 'Fillis solved the sensitive question of accommodation for his troupe by putting them on display, at sixpence a look, in an expensive replica of a "Kaffir Krall", thus continuing what was by 1899 a long tradition of putting "savages" on display in England.' Even Charles Dickens had been scandalised by a Zulu display in mid-nineteenth-century London. No more measured than his literary inferior, Pierre Loti, he dismissed Zulu music, dance and speech in a venomous outburst against 'the howling, whistling, clucking, stamping, jumping, tearing savage'.

Links between the husbandry of exotic animals and displays of exotic culture are strong. The Zoological Society of London was organised in its earliest stages by Sir Stamford Raffles, naturalist and lieutenant-governor of Java. It was Raffles who had written captivatingly about Javanese gamelan music at the beginning of the nineteenth century and who was the first Englishman to bring gamelan sets from Java. A polymath collector, Raffles attempted to make sense of the East with his shiploads of Hindu deities, Burmese figures, Javanese weapons and dance masks, dried plants, shells, rocks, insects, musical instruments and paintings. He even transported live animals. 'When the ship on which he was sailing back to England burned at sea,' wrote Harriet Ritvo in *The Animal Estate: The English and Other Creatures in the Victorian Age*, 'he lost his raw material – "a living tapir, a new species of tiger, splendid pheasants, &c., domesticated for the voyage," along with all his preserved specimens.'

'Zoo pets represented not Britain,' wrote Ritvo, 'but their native territories, which were invariably British colonies in Africa and Asia, and never colonies which, like Canada and Australia, had significant European populations. It is probably no accident that they were often accompanied by exotic human attendants who ... were presented in the press as equally curious if not equally loveable.' Ritvo argues that exotic animals were displayed as symbols of political submission: 'not just as a popular symbol of human domination, but also as a more precise and elaborate figuration of England's imperial enterprise'. MacKenzie draws similar conclusions about the 'Kaffir Kraal' and 'Savage South Africa' displays at Earls Court: 'The displays reflect a striking topicality, a powerful application of Social Darwinism to entertainment, and an extraordinary illustration of the imperial exhibition's capacity to chain and tame people who a mere three years earlier had been enemies, now sadly acting out their former resistance.'

Here began the global village.

9
the spell

♦♦♦♦♦♦♦♦♦♦♦♦♦♦♦♦♦♦♦

I had no *aku-aku*.

Thor Heyerdahl, *Aku-Aku*, 1958

bamboo . . . tamboo . . . tambuh-tabuhan . . .
taboo . . . tiki . . . Kon-Tiki . . . aku-aku . . .

On the west coast of the New World, fifty years into
the twentieth century, words drummed out a percussive sound
poetry of orientalist mystique, the incantations of strange gods,
the rumble and hiss of Polynesian surf, the polyrhythms of clashing
metal harmonics and gulping bamboo. Saucers landed, food was
faster, finned ultracars cruised the freeways, men traversed the
ocean on balsa rafts, lived as fish. 'Like many others I do not feel
in perfect harmony with our age,' wrote Philippe Diolé in *The
Undersea Adventure*, 'and the solitude of diving lulls and stays a
deep-rooted dissatisfaction. Down below, where dream and action
move silently forward through the dense waters, side by side, man
feels for a moment in tune with life . . . Could submarine landscapes constitute a revelation analogous to that of the East under
the brush of Delacroix?'

By 1960, when Les Baxter's subaqua-themed *Jewels of the Sea*
album was recorded, satellites were in orbit. *Jewels of the Sea* lured
the buyer with 'titillating orchestrations for listening and loving'
and a photograph of a submerged waterbabe, apparently naked,

Orientalist eyeliner, lipstick and hair intact, jewellery not yet
rusted. In its appeal to devotees of piscine sex, the effect recalls
underwater dancers performing as mermaids in Florida's roadside
tourist attractions.

Other Baxter covers revealed the sexual fantasies of the
American fifties, oceanic, primitivist, taboo. For *Ritual of the
Savage*, also known as *Le Sacre du Sauvage*, a painting depicts a
shadowed, moustached Lothario in his middle years, a Burt Reyn-
olds type. He appears to simultaneously entreat and ravish a Latin
beauty, Jane Russell in essence, who tosses her head, parts her lips
and averts her eyes in protest, rapture and erotic agony. One hand
pushes away, the other pulls forward. One half of her body is
washed in light; the other half shrouded in darkness. These lovers,
or fighters, merge into the bush, framed and dominated by a
crudely sketched museum tableau of carvings and masks, an
approximation of tourist pieces from Central Africa. In the distance, the silhouette of a tree or rock formation suggests the form
of a tapir – an animal renowned for its symbolism as avaricious
sexual seducer in South American mythology – about to crest the
hill. The setting could capture a moment of passion during a
ballroom dance contest, Latin section, held in the Disney Museum
of Fetish and Ancestral Worship. Wilson Bryan Key, author of
Subliminal Seduction, a 1973 analysis of 'the secret ways ad-
men arouse your desires – to sell their products', would find
the embedded symbolism – an open, raised, red-lipsticked female
mouth in juxtaposition with pubic undergrowth, penile silhouettes
and phallic ritual objects – too blatant to unmask.

The Soul of the Drums is similarly stage-set, this time photo-
graphically: drums from Cuba, India, Haiti, West Africa, stacked
alongside Melanesian masks and African carved figures; behind
them, misted, as if by a translucent shower curtain, a naked
woman, arms aloft, either dancing or throwing a bath towel in
the air. 'A decisive turning point is thus reached,' wrote Manfred
Schneckenburger in *World Cultures and Modern Art*, 'when the
twentieth century grants a multiplicity of superhuman beings –
demons, idols, totems, fetishes, according to the designation the
artists chooses – pictorial or plastic form.'

Schneckenburger suggests Goya and Fuseli as the precursors

of this trend. 'However, the breakthrough did not come until the twentieth century,' he continued, 'under the influence of new impulses from the realm of pre-history and ethnography: idols, totems, fetishes become the subjects of modern art, at the latest from the time of the Surrealist manifesto. Psychoanalysis provided a scientific explanation of the horrific creations of the subconscious without diminishing their menace. It assured them complete psychic reality.'

The Passions, Baxter's collaboration with Philadelphia vocalist Bas Sheva – 'a voice whose vivid colorations range from the guttural snarl of savagery to a delicate and lyric beauty' – represents the convergence of pop psychoanalysis (the fetish of the unconscious) with audio technology (the fetish of the machine). The cover simply showed a woman on the edge of nervous breakdown, one hand tearing at her hair, her mouth hanging open. Drowning in shadow, oppressed by the camera, trapped against a red background, this woman could be the threatening, threatened female of *film noir*, the screamingly distressed damsel of fifties creature-features or a TV soap housewife whose husband has elected to wash the dishes. The emotions portrayed by Bas Sheva and Baxter are despair, ecstasy, hate, lust, terror, jealousy, joy and passion, lust being depicted with a vocal performance of 'such violence that the threshold of distortion is nearly reached. The raw realism of these vocal effects is truly startling. In their harshness they are deceptively similar to distorted sounds.'

The Passions may have been described on the front cover as 'a HIGH FIDELITY adventure' but in the liner notes, the technicalities of Baxter's arrangements and instrumentation, the nature of the sound balance and other, doubtless masculine points of serious interest in a 'high fidelity critique' were elucidated in great detail (and, if nothing else, prove Baxter's seriousness and precision as an arranger). Protectively padded by quotes from Shakespeare, the album was described as 'a picture of woman's passion', but the subtext stroked ruffled male egos. A failure to understand the extreme emotions of women could be amply compensated by a den equipped with a well-balanced hi-fi system.

But behind the shotgun symbolism of jungle and aqua sex deployed by record company art departments, Baxter clearly enjoyed working with powerful and unusual female vocalists. Bas Sheva's vocalisations are extreme, considering the market and the genre. Though softened in the selling by a gimmicky dramatic theme and a pitch at hi-fi buffs, she anticipates the niche allowed for (or taken by) experimentally inclined female vocalists such as Patti Waters, Yoko Ono and Diamanda Galas. On *The Lost Episode*, a recovered tape from a Baxter television special, Baxter speaks as master of ceremonies, introducing the 'theremin voiced Beverly Ford' (as tape archaeologist and Baxter fan Skip Heller describes her), substituting for a harmonica part. 'I *think* you'll find it interesting,' Baxter speculates.

● goomba goomba

More interesting even than Ford's eerie soprano siren or the expressive psycho-abstractions of Bas Sheva was the fruity vocal swoop of Yma Sumac. Produced by her then husband, bandleader and songwriter Moises Vivanco, Sumac recorded music influenced by the fashions of the moment, ranging from mambos to psychedelic exotica, but the tracks that retain an impressive sense of otherworldly kitsch, a fully evoked vision of an imaginary world, are the songs she recorded in collaboration with Les Baxter as *Voice of the Xtabay* and subsequent recordings with Vivanco, produced in the Baxter exotica style.

Judging by later comments made by Sumac and Baxter, the *Xtabay* sessions must have been a war of the egos. 'When I was working with Yma Sumac,' Baxter told James Call and Peter Huestis, 'she had an absolutely insane husband who was a pain in the butt. He called himself the "Gershwin of South America". And he always had arthritis when it came time to play the guitar. He had no ability whatever, in anything. One day he said, "You stole from me." And I said, "How did I steal from you?" He said, "Well you stole my note, B flat." That's an honest to god true story. "You stole my note." '

Voice of the Xtabay was released by Capitol in 1950 as a 10-inch album of eight tracks. Melodramatic tone poems, they trade shamelessly upon the ignorance of record buyers by mixing Baxter's atmospherics – chiming percussion and piano, trembling flutes, shivering strings – with Hollywood Afro-Cubanismo, either quasi-ritualistic or cha-cha-cha. Nothing musical can be traced to South America, despite the vivid sleeve-note descriptions of Incan hymns, Andean mountain grandeur, Peruvian monkey calls and Aztec princes. Yma Sumac's exact origins are still in doubt, muddied by claims that she was an Incan princess, a descendent of Atahualpa, who was killed by the Spanish in 1527. This dubious legend was matched by counterclaims that she was Amy Camus from Brooklyn. Now there seems agreement that she was born in Lima, Peru, either in 1923 or 1927, recorded in Argentina with Moises Vivanco in the Inca Taqui Trio, then moved to the United States in 1947. The trio toured the US to little effect, but after Sumac was 'discovered' at the Blue Angel in New York, she signed to Capitol Records, recorded in Los Angeles and sold over half a million copies of her American debut, *Voice of the Xtabay*.

'She was definitely an Inca princess,' Baxter told Call and Huestis. 'And quite a remarkable person with a remarkable voice. But she was South American, plus Inca, you know, mestizo. Unfortunately, that made for a very volatile person, very temperamental, very fiery. One moment she was, "I love you, you are marvellous, I kill you!" All in one paragraph. And she really did say, "I kill you!" I thought I was going to die right then. But she was a marvellous talent. I think she's really mad at me but I don't know why.'

Only a few singers possess the freakish, multiple octave quality of Sumac's voice. Sixties soul man Joe Hinton and the late Minnie Riperton were notable for acrobatic ballad renditions that hovered on the edge of self-parody, but for Sumac, working in a fabricated soundworld, her elastic range, power and purity of tone conjured startling images, as garish and hot as the early twentieth-century primitivism of painters such as Ernst Ludwig Kirchner or Franz Marc, their exotic, sexualised figures stage-set in front of torrid backgrounds. The ambiguous nature of her South American ancestry, hyped by Los Angeles publicists to a credulous audience, reinforces the musical effect. A generic jungle landscape is conjured, interspersed with magisterial orchestral climaxes, presumably suggestive of pyramids, citadels and sun temples rising out of the forest.

' "My scores were *Petrouchka*," ' Baxter told R.J. Smith, ' "Stravinsky, Ravel. Other people's scores were movie music." It was a puzzling thing to hear. And then Les did something that was even more puzzling. He got up, walked over to his German grand piano, and sight-read Ravel's fluid, mercurial *Jeux d'eau*, a lyric piece by the man sometimes pegged as the father of exotica. But he didn't stop there; slowly, the Ravel transformed itself, and melted into a piano version of "Quiet Village". He'd made his argument, and there wasn't anything else to say' (sleeve notes of *The Exotic Moods of Les Baxter*).

Baxter draws on his love of Maurice Ravel's sensual exoticism for the Yma Sumac arrangements. Though Ravel's exotica was inspired by slightly less remote sources, his attachment to artificial otherness can be likened to Baxter's. Ravel described *Daphnis and Chloë*, commissioned for ballet by Diaghilev in 1909, as 'a broad musical fresco, less concerned with archaic fidelity than with loyalty to the Greece of my dreams, which in many ways resembled that imagined and depicted by the French artists of the latter part of the 18th century'. Like Debussy, he had been struck by the performance of Javanese gamelan at the Paris international exposition of 1889; his composing absorbed elements of Spanish music, jazz, Greek folk melodies and popular dance rhythms; his subject matter embraced pagodas and enchanted flutes. Sensitive and in poor health, Ravel surrounded himself with plants and sculptures, a Japanese garden, mechanical birds and music boxes, Japanese prints, an enclosure for the dreamworld that sound could conjure.

The Voice of the Xtabay is so clearly odd, a kitsch eccentricity that nevertheless endures through its originality, that the question of authenticity refuses to be heard. The music depicts a mystery that archaeology and other sciences of disinterment can only spoil. As Werner Schmalenbach wrote about Paul Gauguin, 'He is actually concerned with an ideal that he does not actually want to see in reality, but wants to invoke as a hidden mystery, a dream. He can only experience it as a mystery so that all obscurities, however much he suffers from them, serve to enhance the magic power of his vision. An identification with the primitive world would revoke its ideality and destroy rather than fulfil his dream; and his art would lose its actual source of energy.'

And in a subtle, closely argued investigation of the appropriation of Central African pygmy music and sound by Euro-American jazz and pop musicians, Steven Feld asks, 'Yet what of this diverse musical invention forms the basis of its global pop representation? In the most popular instances it is a single untexted vocalization or falsetto yodel, often hunting cries rather than songs or musical pieces. This is the sonic cartoon of the diminutive person, the simple, intuitively vocal and essentially non-linguistic child. Why, in the face of such a varied and complex corpus of musical practices, does global pygmy pop reproduce the most caricatured image of its origin?'

As for Sumac, like the parabola of her voice – its low moans and masculine gutteral, the musical saw of her upper registers – she floats between identities, wrapped in the image manufacturing of Hollywood and her self-created ambiguities. As her voice climbs through the earth's atmosphere, an operatic vibrato emerges. This stratospheric wobble was a throwback to an era of mannered popular singing epitomised by the now high-camp duets of Nelson Eddy and Jeanette McDonald in the late thirties, or the similarly virtuous, precisely enunciated quiver of Adriana Caselotti's 'I'm Wishing', featured in Disney's *Snow White and the Seven Dwarfs*. Although Sumac captured the exotic fantasies of the moment, the drama of her technique had been displaced by a more relaxed, conversational style epitomised by artists such as Frank Sinatra, Peggy Lee and Nat 'King' Cole.

Baxter claimed he had edited Yma Sumac's phrasing, splicing magnetic tape with the same painstaking precision as John Cage, working in 1952 with Louis and Bebe Barron, David Tudor and Earle Brown on pieces such as *Williams Mix*. 'Speaking of where to put it,' Baxter told Call and Huestis, 'I was very particular and we were into cutting tape then. It was before we had all the buttons we have now. So we could edit. We simply had her do her phrases until we got one we liked, and then we had a phrase going up high, and then we had her rest, had her sit down, "hit a high F," and when she finally hit the high F we'd paste it in on the end of the progression. So she's pasted together a lot.'

Mistress of melodrama, all eyebrows, eyelashes and curled lip, Yma Sumac mimed 'Taita Inty' to the studio recording in a 1954

Technicolor adventure film, *Secret of the Incas*, starring Charlton Heston. Watched by a pipe-smoking white adventurer, who explains to female interest that the hymn they are hearing was once sung before virgins were taken by the Sun God, Sumac grasps her moment.

Yma Sumac's Inca theme imagery connected with other branches of the populist exotic zeitgeist. Her 'Kon Tiki' hymned an Incan sun-god, though most listeners would associate the name with the documented exploits of Thor Heyerdahl. In 1947, this Norwegian explorer sailed across the Pacific Ocean on a Peruvian balsawood raft that he named after the sun-god. The voyage, and subsequent book, was intended to give substance to Heyerdahl's theory that the first settlers in Polynesia could have been Incan sailors, migrating from Peru.

Sumac undertook a minor migration sideways with her *Legend of the Jívaro* album. Whatever legends the Ecuadorian Amazon Jívaro may or may not have had buried in their history, the image of this supposedly bloodthirsty 'tribe' of headshrinkers made them archetypes of primitive life. As Michael J. Harner wrote in *The Jívaro: People of the Sacred Waterfalls* (1972), 'There was certainly no other tribe in South America about which less was known in proportion to what had been published.' According to Harner, 'their warlike reputation spread in the late nineteenth and early twentieth centuries when Jívaro "shrunken head" trophies, *tsantsa*, found their way to the markets of exotica in the Western world.'

By the fifties, enthusiasm for this ghoulish trade had leached into popular culture, feeding a hunger for uncensored sex and violence that could only be satisfied by pseudo-documentary material. In his essay on the Mondo series of shock anthology films, published in *Incredibly Strange Films*, Boyd Rice writes, 'One of the first movies ever made, *In the Land of the Headhunters*, is an obviously fake documentary with a contrived plot.' Rice finds similar examples of ethnographic exploitation cinema from the forties: *Dangerous Journey*, *Ingagi* and *Karimoja*. In the trade, these 'Jungle' films were known as goona-goonas, a sobriquet inspired by *Goona Goona*, an aphrodisiac plant adventure shot in Bali in the early thirties by André Roosevelt and the soon-to-be popular wildlife documentary broadcaster, Armand Denis.

The posters promised more than the films delivered: Armand and Michaela Denis's *Among the Head Hunters* showed the alleged headhunter casting a covetous sideways glance at the glamorous European couple; *Macumba Love*, in Flaming Eastman Color with music by Simonetti, promised 'weird shocking savagery in native jungle haunts, hypnotic frenzy, voodoo vengeance, bongos of Caibe'; *The Living Idol* was an 'amazing adventure beneath the curse of the jaguar god'; *Trader Horn* was the story of the 'white goddess of the pagan tribes. The cruelest [*sic*] woman in all Africa!' Even Carol Reed's attempt at Conrad, *Outcast of the Islands*, was advertised as 'Introducing Kerima, an excitingly exotic new screen discovery!'

There was nothing particularly new about such vicarious thrills and nonsensical exploitation. Writing about H.M. Stanley's African search for Livingstone in 1871–2, Victor Kiernan reported, 'It has been said that his newspaper sponsors really wanted him to find not Livingstone but sensational stuff for them to print, and that he manufactured excitement by moving with a huge retinue that could only feed itself by plundering. North America and Europe were indeed avid for blood-and-thunder yarns about Africa, as an outlet maybe for repressed blood-and-thunder impulses of their own.'

Eighty years later, sensationalist newspaper stories about rainforest initiation rites were still double-spread fodder for Sunday scandal sheets, fed by explorers. Travel books that exploited Jívaro *tsantsa* as their selling point were being published in the early 1950s, among them Bertrand Flornoy's *Jívaro: Among the Head-Shrinkers of the Amazon*, and Lewis Cotlow's *Amazon Head-Hunters*. Both of these examples salivated over the process of human head shrinkage, though Cotlow shows no compunction in distancing himself from all he observes. 'Why does a man cut off another man's head,' he enquires in the opening sentence of his book, 'shrink it to the size of his fist and then dance around it?' Though he dismisses much of what he sees as 'silly mumbo-jumbo', his many and various prejudices have begun to erode by the end of the journey. 'A steady rhythm can do strange things to people,' he confesses, 'and for a few minutes it almost made a Jívaro out of me.' Such writing inspired intrepid entrepreneurs into attempting to make a Jívaro out of every child in the western world. Growing up in the fifties I owned a replica of a Jívaro *tsantsa*, a grotesquely convincing, shrivelled, charred looking rubber toy, advertised in the small-ads in boys' comics and hugely popular at the time.

For the cover art of *Legend of the Jívaro*, Yma Sumac was photographed crouching behind a cooking pot. Dry ice froths out of the pot and Sumac, in an unaccustomed state of undress, flashes the spectacular whites of her eyes at a shrunken head that hangs in front of her. Behind her, naked Indians are throwing up their hands, either in ritual dance moves or dismay.

● naked as nature intended

In the period of great licence that followed the hostilities, jazz was a sign of allegiance, an orgiastic tribute to the colours of the moment. It functioned magically, and its means of influence can be compared to a kind of possession . . . In jazz, too, came the first public appearance of *Negroes*, the manifestation and the myth of black Edens which were to lead me to Africa and, beyond Africa, to ethnography.

Michel Leiris, *Manhood*, 1968

The ultimate goal of the true exotic is to erase history, stop time, manufacture memories; by force of will to fabricate an identity based on ethnic and cultural characteristics that have never before existed; to become a fabulous island, rising out of the sea, then sinking once more into the abyss.

Exotica and erotica are close, not just semantically, but in their promise of a life less ordinary, detached from the libido suppression of reality, responsibility, rationality and 'civilisation', hitched instead to a hopeless belief in the free physicality of primitivism. 'Thus, when confronting those possessors of sheer animal flesh unspoiled by intellect,' Yukio Mishima speculated in his *Confessions of a Mask*, 'young toughs, sailors, soldiers, fishermen – there was nothing for me to do but be forever watching them from afar with impassioned indifference, being careful never to exchange words with them. Probably the only place in which I could have lived at ease would have been some uncivilised tropical land where I could not speak the language. Now that I think of it, I realize that from earliest childhood I felt a yearning toward those intense summers of the kind that are seething forever in savage lands.'

Like naturism, exoticism was also a cheat, a way for pornographers to evade the censors, as with Barry Mahon's 1960 South Seas nudie film, *Pagan Island*, billed as 'one man alone with thirty beautiful girls'. No matter how stupid and generally exploitative such films might have been; they registered the need for a more open attitude to sex. Despite resistance from conservatives and harassment by police, Dr Alfred Kinsey's 1948 publication of his *Sexual Behavior in the Human Male*, followed by *Sexual Behavior in the Human Female* in 1953, revealed a breadth of private sexual practice among American whites that contradicted public images of straight, and straightforward, sex.

'Another favourite approach was to present a fake documentary film,' wrote Jim Morton in *Incredibly Strange Films*, 'in which it was acceptable to show bare breasts – as long as they weren't white. Consequently several movies were made purporting to depict native life in darkest Africa. Usually they were shot somewhere just north of San Diego, with the African "natives" appearing in a remarkable variety of shades. Often a man in a gorilla suit makes an appearance, stealing the tribe's comeliest maiden. Among them: *Bowanga! Bowanga!* (1938), *Ingagi* (1930) and *Love Life of a Gorilla* (1937).'

In his study of *fin de siècle* Paris, Raymond Rudorff concludes that 'In Paris and elsewhere, 1890-vintage eroticism was to a large extent a matter of stage settings and trappings ... A striking illustration of the mania for exotic decoration as a setting for sin is provided by the famous photographs of Sarah Bernhardt reclining in the midst of semi-Oriental luxury, against a stagy background of tiger skins, velvets and silk hangings, like a panther lying in wait for its prey in a claustrophobic, incense-heavy atmosphere.'

Exotic sensuality and sexual potentialities were externalised in the decadent period through theatricality. This was evident in the Orientalist, see-through costumes of dancer Maud Allan, who danced Oscar Wilde's *Salomé*. According to decadence authority Philip Hoare, she was accused by independent MP Noel Pemberton Billing of dancing for 'the cult of the clitoris'. As for illustrators, Aubrey Beardsley's *Japonisme*-style drawings are saturated with Orientalism, as is the elaborate theatrical erotica of the Austrian-born Marquis Franz von Bayros. As a boy, the Marquis had seen half-naked Gypsy women in Turkish Bosnia; the impression was lasting. Technically exquisite, his turn-of-the-century drawings depicted exploratory sex, often sadomasochistic, played out against an exotic *mise-en-scène* that might include Japanese *shamisen* players, dragons and naked geishas, shipwrecks, pornographic statuary and the kind of gardens described by Robert Harbison in *Eccentric Spaces* as 'a determined effort to make a mood eternal, to memorialize an intense disgust'.

The imagination of von Bayros was morbid, clearly tormented, yet lightened by playful self-mockery. In his work, only rarely did men penetrate women. Mostly, they chose (or are forced) to watch, to masturbate or sniff shoes. Men's genitals were severed and discarded, tweaked, tickled, tied up with ribbon, used for hoop practice, cut off and used as earrings, ridden like giant snails, played with a violin bow, used as a plectrum for plucking the *shamisen*, or, dark and bloated, they lurked in shade like grotesque giant slugs. With a few exceptions, the women in these scenes relegated the penis to a plaything, turning instead to an improbable wealth of alternatives for clitoral stimulation: a samurai sword, a cat's tail, an umbrella, the tongues of severed heads, a tiger's penis, an aeolian harp, statues, pillars, a sundial, a glass tube, a deer, a cow's ear, a tree branch, a rhinoceros horn (rhinoceros still attached), a candle, an axe blade.

The pencil, the pen and interior decor were ideal media for realising the exotic, theatrical, supposedly perverted fictions of erotic desire in this period, though fake harem photographs of turbaned European women fellating turbaned European men were not uncommon either. Raymond Rudorff quotes the *agent provocateur* Leo Taxil, whose exposé of Parisian sexuality disclosed the secrets of Europe's most famous brothel, 'rooms furnished in the taste of various countries of the world with a

Scotch room, a Chinese room, an Indian room, a Persian room, a Negro room etc.' Others offered Japanese, Spanish or 'Moorish' rooms; even a funerary chamber for those whose exotic fetish explored the furthest reaches of otherness.

● slaves to the rhythm

Alan Freed also brought Screamin' Jay Hawkins to movie fame: 'I did *Don't Knock the Rock*, but they cut it out – they even paid me for it, but they cut it out because I walked on naked with a loin cloth across here, white shoe polish marks on my face, my hair combed straight up, a spear in one hand and a shield in the other, like one of those wild Mau Maus and I was singing a song called "Frenzy". The movie people claimed it would be an insult to the black people of the United States. I bet it would go over today. Again, I was trying to explain to them that I was different, I do everything different. Do you realise they banned "I Put a Spell On You" because it had cannibalistic sounds? When they banned it, it had already sold a million. When they banned it, it sold another quarter of a million. I wish they'd ban every record I made.'

Screamin' Jay Hawkins, interviewed by Norbert Hess in *Blues Unlimited*, 1976

Paris in a later age became the spiritual, and actual, home of Josephine Baker, one of the most celebrated exotics of the twentieth century. Born in St Louis in 1906, Baker travelled to France as a dancer in *La Revue Nègre*. According to biographer Lynn Haney, the show's producer had been advised by the Cubist artist, Fernand Léger, to bring an all-black show to Paris. 'Give them the Negroes,' Léger told André Daven, after he had seen an exhibition of African sculpture at the Exposition des Arts Décoratifs. 'Only the Negroes can excite Paris.'

So Baker arrived in Paris in 1925, where she performed alongside Sidney Bechet at the Théâtre des Champs-Elysées. Picked out from the troupe as a relatively uninhibited body beautiful, she was persuaded to expose her breasts when she danced. The show-stopping climax was Baker's dance with Joe Alex: 'The drummer beat out a steady jungle rhythm, a tom-tom call. Josephine returned with Joe Alex to do their savage dance. She rode onstage upside-down, carried on Alex's broad shoulders. All she wore was a bright pink feather tucked between her thighs and a ring of feathers circling her ankles and neck. Alex swung her around in a slow cartwheel . . . Josephine and Joe then engaged in a primitive mating dance, filled with ardent passion.' A photograph of 'The Dance of the Savages' shows that Joe Alex was also near-naked, decorated with beads and feathers. The effect recalls R&B singer Screamin' Jay Hawkins, dressed in his parodic native garb in the 1950s. Three decades later, Grace Jones was art-directed as statuesque savage and caged animal, a 'slave to the rhythm', by Jean Paul Goude. A critic for *The New Yorker*, Janet Flanner, filed a review of *La Revue Nègre* which assumed an optimistic interpretation of Baker's appeal. 'Her magnificent dark body, a new model to the French,' she wrote, 'proved for the first time that black was beautiful.'

● the shadow of whom

Ellington speaks: 'Now this is really the "Chinoiserie". Last year, about this time, we premiered a new suite titled "Afro-Eurasian Eclipse", and of course the title was inspired by a statement made by Mister Marshall McLuhan of the University of Toronto. Mister McLuhan says that the whole world is going oriental and that no-one will be able to retain his or her identity. Not even the orientals. And of course we travel round the world a lot and in the last five or six years we too have noticed this thing to be true. So, as a result, we have done a sort of a thing, a parallel, or something and we'd like to play a little piece of it for you. In this particular segment, ladies and gentlemen, we have adjusted our perspective to that of the kangaroo and the didgeridoo. This automatically throws us either down under, and/or out back. And from that point of view, it's most improbable that anyone will even know exactly who is enjoying the shadow of whom.'

Duke Ellington, spoken introduction to *The Afro-Eurasian Eclipse*, 1971

Though she was notorious as the Ebony Venus, the black body, *la Sirène des Tropiques*, Princess Tam-Tam, Baker had always

wanted to sing. As with Yma Sumac, her fiction, her self-engen-
dered and imposed displacement, bled freely into other, distant
exoticas; her French recording, 'Ma Tonkinoise', for example, was
a strange little hybrid of chanson and Chinoiserie. The peculiarities
of these hybrids captivated others who suffered crises of identity.
Toru Takemitsu's adolescence coincided with Japan's extreme
nationalism during World War II, a period when Western music
was banned. For Takemitsu, Japanese traditional music evoked
the horrors of the war years. Drafted into military service in the
last two years of the war, he heard one of Josephine Baker's
Parisian records and was overwhelmed. When the war ended, he
decided to become a composer. The exotic focus of his pivotal
inspiration lived on in his film music, where influences from lounge
jazz, tape electronics, rock'n'roll, European Medieval music and
Japanese *gagaku* melted together in vivid heterogeneity.

Josephine Baker's role as an exotic was complex. Posed in
photographs with tiger-skin rugs, she was described as the 'Nefertiti of now' by Picasso. She danced encircled by rhinestone-studded
bananas that rose up around her waist like a girdle of sparkling
erections. As biographer Phyllis Rose observes in *Jazz Cleopatra*,
the bananas, set in 'jiggling motion, like perky, good-natured phal-
luses' evolved into stiff tusks. Photographed in *The Ziegfeld
Follies* in 1935, Baker wore a bikini that mutated her erogenous
zones into spiked weaponry, impeding any action other than
display, anticipating Madonna's spiked bra by more than half a
century. Walking her pet leopard along the Champs-Elysées, glorious in her role as stranger in a strange land, she colluded with
the crude fantasies of Africa that so enraptured the French (which
were, after all, a relief from the unequivocality of American racial
segregation or the racial abuse she suffered from Austrian Nazis),
yet she scrubbed her skin with lemon juice at night in the hope of
lightening her dark skin.

Duke Ellington raised contradictions also. His exoticisms were
the product of an enquiring mind, a life of travel and a need to
explore the sensuality of tone coloration in a bankable context.
Both Ellington, with his Cotton Club 'jungle' band, and Josephine
Baker, working at the Plantation Club, served apprenticeships in
Prohibition era, pre-Depression Harlem, performing to slumming

white New Yorkers (and foreign visitors such as Maurice Ravel) who came to indulge in the exotic atmosphere of a zone that seemed, from their brief forays, to conform to its description, by music critic and author Carl Van Vechten, as 'nigger heaven'.

'The creation of Harlem as a place of exotic culture was as much a service to white need as it was to black,' wrote Nathan Huggins in *Harlem Renaissance*. 'So essential has been the Negro personality to the white American psyche that black theatrical masks had become, by the twentieth century, a standard way for whites to explore dimensions of themselves that seemed impossible through their own *personae* . . . Thus the strands of identity for Afro-Americans in the 1920s were confounded in a tradition of white/black self-concept that could not be unravelled by simple proclamations of the birth of the New Negro.'

At the Cotton Club, drummer Sonny Greer played an incredible array of percussive instruments: tubular bells, suspended gongs, Chinese tuned woodblocks, timpani and Chinese drums. 'With such equipment, Greer could make every possible drum sound,' wrote Jim Haskins in *The Cotton Club*, 'and at the Cotton Club he awed the customers, conjuring up tribal warriors and man-eating tigers and war dancers . . . The featured Cotton Club singers and dancers completed the exotic image. Earl 'Snakehips' Tucker could twist his haunches and thigh joints into unbelievable contortions. He was called a human boa constrictor and became an immediate sensation.'

Complexities abound. Ellington, for example, was interested in Africanisms as a source of historical and cultural identity, yet at the Cotton Club his audience's voguish identification with percussion as tribal (still alive in the nineties as a stereotype in the beliefs underpinning 'tribal' techno and many Fourth World/New Age fusions) was not so far removed from the racist views of a bigot such as the Buzz character in *The Blue Dahlia*. For Buzz, the drumming is sheer barbarism. He staggers out of nightclubs, clutching his war-wounded head, complaining that the jungle music is driving him crazy.

● progressive

> Was McKay losing his marbles? The band should have come out
> roaring, as Dorsey had done. Instead, Marty Wynner stepped up to
> the mike and sang 'I Didn't Know What Time It Was.' The arrange-
> ment, an intricate one, demanded attention from the listeners, and
> Marty sang against the complex Eddie Sauter backgrounds with taste
> and understanding. When the song ended, there were no whistles,
> no shouts; just good, strong, long-lasting applause.
>
> Mel Tormé, *Wynner*, 1978

The lure of impressionism, heard in Ellington material such as 'Moon Mist', 'Dusk', 'Chelsea Bridge' and the exotic, otherworldly 'Bakiff', was tempered by his robust belief in swing and 'gut-bucket', the force of feeling and rawness that gives earth to aethereal, liquid experiment.

Postwar, this world of 'jungle' percussion and exotic arrangements, the primitive/modern concept, had found its way into the (mostly white, mostly West Coast) progressive jazz of the Sauter-Finegan Orchestra, Clare Fischer, Stan Kenton, Gil Melle and Don Ellis, whose sitar- and bongo-laden *Electric Bath* album was adorned with a classic Orientalist image – a reproduction of *The Turkish Bath* by Ingres.

'Sometimes the band sounded like a Balinese orchestra,' said Bill Finegan, reminiscing about his New York big band of the fifties, led with arranger Ed Sauter. In a long-winded sleeve note to his disappointingly tame *Primitive Modern* album, Gil Melle argued that 'Primitive fire reminiscent of African native drumming is essential . . . Modern polyrhythmic conception beyond the time-worn dactylic approach is a necessity. To the drummer belongs the world of Edgard Varèse and his realm of raw sounds.'

● the age of islands

> . . . rapidly gathering dusk with noisy cicadas – but the doves and
> chickens have now fallen silent . . . humid and smells of jasmine +
> sewage mingle sweetly . . .
>
> Postcard from Ubud, Bali, 1998

The vision of unconventional percussion combined with advanced harmonies had drawn many other exotics earlier in the century, such as composers Henry Cowell and Colin McPhee. Born in Canada in 1900, Colin McPhee moved to New York City in 1926, where he became fascinated with African-American culture. In 1928, for example, he accompanied a public recital by the black soprano Abbie Mitchell, who had been married to Will Marion Cook, composer of pieces such as *In Dahomey* and *In Abyssinia*. McPhee also wrote pieces inspired by the rhythms of machines in the hope of finding an accessible style that reached out to a less élite audience, one that connected to daily life. Then a small event changed the course of his life. In the late twenties, McPhee heard recordings of Balinese gamelan music, records made by German companies with the assistance of Walter Spies, a German painter and musician who lived on Bali, and then brought back to New York by friends of McPhee after an Indonesian sojourn.

Though McPhee claimed that this first encounter with the great passion of his life was accidental, biographer Carol J. Oja sees it as inevitable. 'New York in the late 1920s was a place of prosperity and experimentation,' she writes in *Colin McPhee: Composer in Two Worlds*, 'where "the *new* – the thing of the latest moment – became almost violently desirable and important," as one chronicler of the period has put it. Among these "new" ideas was an interest in the exotic, whether found in nearby Harlem nightclubs or far-off South Sea islands. Through a widening circle of friends, McPhee came in touch with several key figures, including especially the anthropologist Jane Belo, the writer Carl Van Vechten, and the artist Miguel Covarrubias, all of whom were involved in exotic explorations. By 1931 he found himself at the edge of an exciting musical frontier.'

These friendships introduced McPhee to an expansive milieu of cultural curiosity: Van Vechten was equally confident writing about Erik Satie or the blues; the Mexican artist, Covarrubias, had designed the sets for *La Revue Nègre*, Josephine Baker's debut in Paris. Others in the circle included Langston Hughes, Zora Neale Thurston, Paul Robeson, Somerset Maugham and Bessie Smith.

Belo and McPhee married in 1930; Belo was aware that her

new husband was homosexual yet she approached the relationship in a spirit of psychological experiment. Following Covarrubias, they decided to travel to Bali. For McPhee, the journey was escapist, a nostalgic flight from modernism and the brute thrust of capitalist values. Oja quotes another author of the period, Malcolm Cowley, who named the 1920s 'The Age of Islands'. In this age of islands, 'Americans by thousands and tens of thousands were scheming to take the next boat for the South Seas or the West Indies . . . Or without leaving home they could build themselves private islands of art or philosophy . . . they could create social islands in the shadows of the skyscrapers, groups of close friends among whom they could live as unconstrainedly as in a Polynesian valley, live without moral scruples or modern conveniences, live in the pure moment, live gaily on gin and love and two lamb chops broiled over a coal fire in the grate.'

McPhee may have been ready for a life of living gaily on gin and love, 'away from all the modern virtues', but he was also ready for gamelan. 'I had in mind some idea of crystal sound,' he wrote, 'something aerial and purely sensuous. It is strange that another ten years should find me in Java and Bali where music sounded exactly like that.' After his first trip to Bali with Jane Belo, McPhee found he was unsatisfied by concerts of contemporary music in New York. In 1932, they returned to look for property. Finding a site in Sayan, a small village near Ubud, they built a house of four buildings with two kitchens. Collecting information, absorbing music and the island, McPhee lost the motivation to compose. 'Composing had become an "oppressive responsibility," ' writes Oja. 'As the drive to write music left, he felt "free and happy, liberated from [something] in which I no longer believed." '

Colin McPhee portrayed his private paradise in his book, *A House in Bali*, first published in 1946. The book is magical, like the document of a dream so rich and detailed as to be a seductive substitute for waking life. Strange to discover, then, in retrospect, the circumstances under which it was written. McPhee's wife, Jane Belo, is invisible in the story. During their times in Bali, the marriage proved to be unworkable. 'Even though Jane had known from the beginning that Colin had male lovers,' writes Oja, 'she eventually found this intolerable. In his Bali field notes Colin occasionally alluded to affairs with Balinese men, but he was mostly discreet and extremely private. Several of his friends have suggested that one of the appeals of Bali was its openness to homosexuality.'

Anthropologists are reluctant to reveal sexual liaisons that happen 'in the field'. James Clifford questions the taboo. 'At its inception, though,' he writes in *Routes: Travel and Translation in the Late Twentieth Century*, 'the taboo on sex may have been less against "going native" or losing critical distance than against "going travelling," violating a professional habitus. In travel practices and texts, having sex, heterosexual and homosexual, with local people, was common. Indeed in certain travel circuits, such as the nineteenth-century *voyage en Orient*, it was quasi-obligatory. A popular writer such as Pierre Loti consecrated his authority, his access to the mysterious and feminised Other, through stories of sexual encounter. In fieldwork accounts, however, such stories have been virtually nonexistent.' Clifford adds a note: 'One might also mention Bali as a site for gay sex tourism before 1940.'

Eventually, the homosexual activities of various Westerners on Bali led to crackdowns by the Dutch authorities who were preparing for Indonesian independence. Walter Spies was arrested and jailed on charges of hosting 'a rendezvous for homosexuals' and having sex with minors. 'Nowhere does McPhee record that he might have been the object of such suspicion,' notes Oja, 'yet the timing of his departure suggests he was affected.' Despite the collaboration and friendship of McPhee and Spies with academics such as Margaret Mead, Gregory Bateson and Jane Belo, or their own ventures into serious studies of Balinese arts, they were essentially bohemian exotics, little different in some respects to Paul Gauguin in Tahiti or to the sexual and literary adventurers – Paul Bowles, William Burroughs, Brion Gysin, Allen Ginsberg – who travelled to Tangier to explore freedom of behaviour, displacements of consciousness and language.

● the sunless zone

'I write to you from a far off country,' Chris Marker says in his *Letter
from Siberia*. The line could stand at the beginning of many of his
films, for Marker belongs to a grand French tradition of artists as
travellers and adventurers, a tradition that includes Gauguin, Saint-
Exupéry, Malraux, and, perhaps most relevantly, the corps of glob-
etrotting cameramen assembled by the Lumière brothers . . . [A]ll of
Marker's major films . . . are really variations on the same great
theme, the intellectual and spiritual homelessness brought about by
the inhuman pace of recent historical change. In *Sans Soleil*, as
elsewhere, Marker uses the alienation experienced in travel as the
opening trope for meditations on other types of modern distances:
the distance between East and West, between past and present,
between personal and historical time, and finally, between the filmed
and the filmmaker, the perceived and the perceiver . . . He further
deconstructs and transforms documentary images by running them
through a video synthesiser to create what he calls 'the zone,' an
imaginary counterworld in which past, present and future merge.

Steven Simmons, 'Man Without a Country', 1983

● the interzone

Tangier was 'Interzone' for Burroughs, described by biographer
Ted Morgan as being 'as much an imaginative construct as a
geographical location, a metaphor for limbo, for a dead-end place,
a place where everyone could act out his most extreme fantasies'.
After Edward Said's *Orientalism* and with the growth of colonial
studies, artist-exoticists such as Michel Leiris have come under
increasing attack. In *Gone Primitive: Savage Intellects, Modern
Lives*, Marianna Torgovnick characterises Leiris – surrealist, ethnographer, art historian and writer – as a sexual obsessive who
exploited primitivism in a personal drama more representative of
his own inner fixations than the outer world he observed. Her
critique acknowledges that the unusual frankness in Leiris's writings – a disarmingly exposed intimacy more than a memoir –
may willingly reveal disturbing desires ('desires implicit in Leiris's
metaphor of the museum as whorehouse') that are common in
others yet carefully hidden. In his 'portrayal of the self as kaleido-

scopic and changeable', Leiris was an example, she claims, of 'transcendental homelessness', the phrase used by Georg Lukács to describe the condition of the modern Western mind.

In *The Predicament of Culture*, anthropologist James Clifford offers an alternative view of Leiris (particularly *L'Afrique fantôme*, his journal of the Dakar-Djibouti mission of 1931–3) as a pioneer in the development of surrealist ethnography. Clifford defines surrealism as 'an aesthetic that values fragments, curious collections, unexpected juxtapositions – that works to provoke the manifestation of extraordinary realities drawn from the domains of the erotic, the exotic, and the unconscious . . . Surrealism is ethnography's secret sharer – for better or worse – in the description, analysis, and extension of the grounds of twentieth-century expression and meaning.'

Colin McPhee was not a surrealist, but his self-willed displacement in Bali projected him into the Interzone, the imaginative construct, a place that encouraged 'extraordinary realities drawn from the domains of the exotic, the erotic, and the unconscious'. Though McPhee was too discrete to make a connection public, the 'sensuous charm' that he heard in Balinese music seems connected to his enjoyment of other sensual pleasures: cooking, drinking, sexual freedom. In his essay, 'Eros and Orientalism in Britten's Operas', musicologist Philip Brett quotes a letter from McPhee in which he wrote: 'Many times there was a decision to be made between some important opportunity and a sexual (homosexual) relationship that was purely sensual. I never hesitated to choose the latter. This I did deliberately and would do again and again, for it seemed the only thing that was real. The Balinese period was simply a long extension of this.'

Brett argues that gamelan is a 'gay marker in American music', referring to John Cage, Lou Harrison, Colin McPhee and Henry Cowell as important twentieth-century composers who had taken inspiration from Indonesian gamelan. Colin McPhee introduced Benjamin Britten to Balinese music after they met in Long Island, at the home of the Mayer family, 'where they were welcomed like many other gay men in music and literature'. In 1941 the two of them recorded McPhee's gamelan transcription for two pianos, four hands, *Balinese Ceremonial Music*. Brett finds echoes of gamelan in many of Britten's works, including *Paul Bunyan, Peter Grimes, The Turn of the Screw, The Prince of the Pagodas* and *Death In Venice.* 'In 1955–1956,' he writes, 'Britten, Pears, and their friends the Hesses went on a world tour during which the composer heard not only Balinese gamelan music, whose technique – which he found "about as complicated as Schönberg" – he now became involved with, but also Japanese music drama.'

Britten composed during a time when homosexuality was demonised and hunted out. Brett speculates that orientalism spoke for a deeper text in his music, the sexual leanings that he was unable to express freely, both through his own conservatism and the repressive attitudes of his time. He suggests that Britten 'indicates a rich if dangerous enchantment of life and art beyond the world that imprisons him . . . [O]rientalism is one of the means by which desire unacceptable to or feared by the (Western) subject can be projected on to the Other.'

The sadness for McPhee was that he was overwhelmed by Bali. Outside events turned paradise to ashes. First, the sexual persecution, then the growing popularity of Bali as a tourist resort (resented by McPhee, even though he was one of the forerunners), finally the imminence of World War II and the first suspicious Japanese interest in the island. Walter Spies was finally released from jail, then arrested again as a German after Hitler's invasion of Holland, finally killed during a Japanese aircraft attack on a boat transporting prisoners from Sumatra to Ceylon. Paradise lost.

Back in New York, McPhee struggled with composing and the writing of a lengthy musicological study, *Music in Bali.* Frequently discouraged by the sporadic attention given to his music, he drank too much alcohol, suffered poverty, depression and poor health, supplementing his meagre income either with journalism or by selling his collection of Balinese artefacts and music transcriptions. *Tabuh-Tabuhan,* his Balinese influenced 'Toccata for Orchestra and 2 Pianos', was released on record in 1959, twenty-three years after he completed its composition; *Music in Bali* was published in 1966, thirty years after he began writing it and two years after his death.

● swimming in text

He [Lafcadio Hearn] records in *Glimpses* how, on his first day, he was fascinated by the sight of Japanese writing. He went to sleep dreaming of an active Japanese script moving around him, as though he had somehow already entered the inner mental world of Japan.

George Hughes, 'Entering Island Cultures', 1997

● phantoms keeping watch

In Joseph Conrad's short story, *Youth*, the narrator Marlow lives to be in the East. Nothing else will do, even though (or maybe because) this is a generalised East, full of Eastern promise. 'This was the East of the ancient navigators, so old, so mysterious, resplendent and sombre, living and unchanged, full of danger and promise.'

Compare his youthful, romantic enthusiasm for Siam and (for him) its new horizons with the ageing, near-blind sea captain who is the fulcrum of another short story, *The End of the Tether*. Forced into captaincy of a trading steamship, *he* sees only decline, the collapse of beauty into functionalism and hard commerce, the end of sail, the adventure of old Asia revealed as naked Empire. 'In this evocation, swift and full of detail like a flash of magnesium light into the niches of a dark memorial hall, Captain Whalley contemplated things once important, the efforts of small men, the growth of a great place, but now robbed of all consequence by the greatness of accomplished facts, by hopes greater still.'

Reading Conrad gives the sense of a turbulent, emergent world of contradictory impulses. A glut of new stimuli was flooding in from the technological future, the geographically remote, the culturally alien. Steamers brought change and destruction. In his story, 'Freya of the Seven Isles', the Dutch gunboat *Neptun* drags the elegant trading brig *Bonito* onto Tamissa reef, off Makassar, Celebes. 'The deep-toned blast of the gunboat's steam-whistle made him shudder by its unexpectedness ... In an instant the subtle melancholy of things touched by decay had fallen on her in the sunshine; she was but a speck in the brilliant emptiness of space, already lonely, already desolate.'

For the exoticist, technology embodies the contradictions embedded in the desire to be an island in a changing world. Technology carries them to paradise, or records it, yet erases the fantasy of utopia on impact. 'Every one wants to be Robinson Crusoe,' grumbled Colin McPhee, 'and takes other footprints in the sand as personal insults.' Both Paul Gauguin and Robert Louis Stevenson were fascinated by the new medium of photography, for example, yet, as Stevenson wrote at the end of his life, 'our civilisation is a hollow fraud'. Sophistication, then as now, was condemned as a pernicious alienation from nature and the primal self.

Comparing the work of Pierre Loti with two of his admirers, the Irish writer J.M. Synge and Lafcadio Hearn, half-Irish, born in Greece but forever associated with Japan, George Hughes writes: 'They all feel that modernization or social evolution is inevitable, but that islands represent a possible safe place, a kind of purity through otherness, and of course a place where one may find oneself.'

The interpenetration of the West with regions perceived as other, as exotic, was symbolised by a dual language. One device for evoking the twenty-first century in Ridley Scott's *Blade Runner* was Cityspeak: 'some sort of weird, futuristic gutter language', scriptwriter David Peoples told *Blade Runner* archaeologist Paul M. Sammon. 'That clicked with me, because at one time I had lived in the Philippines Islands, and I could still remember sitting in these public taxicabs called Jeepneys there and listening to the Filipinos speaking in Tagalog, their native language, with all these other English words stuck in.' Similarly, Loti, Synge and Hearn spiced their texts with exotic words. '[A]ll three writers share an attempt to create a sense of the interlinguistic,' writes George Hughes, 'a sliding between languages or a mixture of languages, that can represent the feel of another culture to the reader.'

Lafcadio Hearn had attempted to slide between cultures by living in Japan, adopting Japanese behaviour and rewriting Japanese tales. Best known, perhaps, are his ghost stories, published as *Kwaidan* in 1904 and filmed so vividly by Masaki Kobayashi in 1964.

A creature of decadent, *fin de siècle* sensibilities, Hearn

claimed to be attracted to 'the Revoltingly Horrible or the Excruti-
atingly Beautiful'. Born on the island of Leucadia (now Levkas)
in 1850, Hearn was abandoned by his Irish father and Greek
mother. After a difficult childhood in Dublin, he travelled to
London, then America. He worked as a journalist in Cincinnati,
moved to New Orleans, then to the French West Indies. Like Colin
McPhee, he had been attracted to black culture, or even blackness
itself, before moving East (anticipating Norman Mailer's White
Negro, McPhee had expressed privately a desire to be black; as
for Hearn, he married a former slave in 1875, despite the law
against miscegenation). Finally settling in Japan, Hearn became a
naturalised Japanese, taking the name Koizumi Yakumo, and lived
there until his death in 1904.

As an example of the sensory appeal of the macabre, George
Hughes quotes an example of Hearn's journalism, a description
of a tan-yard murder in Cincinnati: 'The skull had burst like a
shell in the fierce furnace heat, and the whole upper portion
seemed as though it had been blown out by the steam from the
boiling and bubbling brains ... The brain had all boiled away,
save a small waste lump at the base of the skull about the size of
a lemon. It was crisped and still warm to the touch. On pushing a
finger through the crisp, the interior felt about the consistency of
banana fruit.'

Though Hearn was obsessed by the supernatural, by ghosts
and morbid subjects, Hughes separates him from the limpid, suic-
idal face of *fin de siècle* romanticism. 'His version of the artist,'
Hughes writes, 'is a figure who despises what he calls the "ridiculous and *moral*" in modern society, and is committed to an
experimental attitude towards life.' To move to a country as different as Japan, taking a Japanese name, identity, customs and
family responsibilities, is an extreme expression of that attitude.

'[S]uch a move into the exotic is quite simply one of the basic
fin de siècle narratives ("Lève l'ancre," as Mallarmé writes, "pour
une exotique nature! ..."),' Hughes continues. 'Behind such a
move is the implication that there are two distinct and very different worlds: an occidental world and an oriental world; a
mundane world and an exotic world; a materialist world and

a world of fantasy. The artist is the person who can go between them.'

● bugs in the box

In his study of the musical insects of Japan, caged insects that would sing at night (living interior decor, a precursor of the electronic chirping bug-boxes now sold in Chinatowns and New Age shops), Lafcadio Hearn asked, 'Does not the shrilling booth of the insect-seller at a night-festival proclaim even a popular and universal comprehension of things divined in the West only by our rarest poets: the pleasure pain of autumn's beauty, the weird sweetness of the voices of the night, the magical quickening of remembrance by echoes of forest and field?'

. . . the essence of the spell . . .

10

how to stuff a wild bikini

◆◆◆◆◆◆◆◆◆◆◆◆◆◆◆◆◆

And the silken sad uncertain rustling of each purple curtain
Thrilled me – filled me with fantastic terrors never felt before

Edgar Allan Poe, *The Raven*

. . . Charlton Heston stretches his arms wide, Moses parting the Red Sea in Cecil B. DeMille's *The Ten Commandments*. Behind him, the sky is black and blue, bruised by God's wrath. In J.R. Eyerman's 1956 *Life* magazine photograph of a drive-in movie, these arms are opened to enfold a congregation of cars, blue-hooded, soft and silent. The cars are immobile, film-fixated, but the way they are ranked, pointing in a V towards the huge screen, gives the impression that they are racing forward, like penitents running into the healing arms of an evangelist. Behind the huge screen, a sparkle of city lights, like fireflies over a field, and then beyond that, another sky, sulphurous and poisoned. If J.M.W. Turner had lived in the twentieth century, painting traffic tailbacks and exhaust emissions, this would be his sky . . .

Up-against-the-wall cheap quickies, American exploitation films of the fifties and early sixties, traded in suspensions of disbelief. The distance between the screen world of exotic extremes and the mundane world off-screen was stretched to absurdity and beyond. Fears, paranoias and social panics were parcelled for easy comprehension, then sucked dry in an ecstatic rush.

For a sixteen-year stretch between *Hot Blood* and *Baron*

Blood, Les Baxter was the banana republic emperor of exploitation music. Having composed music for *The Yellow Tomahawk* in 1954, he went on to underscore every permutated subgenre in the cheap knock-off canon: Western, gangster, gang, sci-fi, sword 'n' sandal, nuclear attack, horror, Mondo, monster, occult, teen-comedy, mummy, voodoo, delinquent, beatnik, biker, dragster, surf-and-beach-blanket films as they zipped in and out of fashion's window of opportunity.

Often working for American International Pictures under the aegis of producer Roger Corman, Baxter wrote soundtracks for more than seventy films. Floyd Crosby was in charge of cinematography on many of them, including the Edgar Allan Poe adaptations and *X – The Man with X-Ray Eyes*.

The Baxter filmography includes *The Raven*, *Pit and the Pendulum*, *Pharoah's Curse*, *House of Usher*, *X – The Man with X-Ray Eyes*, *Tales of Terror*, *Bop Girl*, *Voodoo Island*, *Panic in Year Zero*, *The Young Racers*, *Beach Blanket Bingo*, *How to Stuff a Wild Bikini*, *Black Sabbath*, *Dr. Goldfoot and the Bikini Machine*, *Savage Sisters*, *Terror in the Jungle*, *Wild in the Streets*, *Hell's Belles*, *Cry of the Banshee*, *The Dunwich Horror* and other psychotronic 'classics'. Most of these films were B-pictures; many dipped below the alphabet into letters from unknown tongues. One of them, *The Bride and the Beast* (also known as *Queen of the Gorillas*), was directed by Ed Wood Jr., the so-called worst filmmaker of all time, so awarding Baxter a heavenly chair among the immortals of Hollywood kitsch.

'I was astounded by what I saw,' wrote Ed Naha, author of *The Films of Roger Corman*. 'I mean, some of these movies were *bad*. They weren't just run-of-the-mill bad, either. They were *vigorously* bad. Creatively *awful*. Argh . . . It was pretty traumatic for a ten year old. It must have been worse for an adult.' Baxter also wrote new scores for Italian horror and mythology films, their original music so execrable in both artistic quality and fidelity that even the American exploitation market imposed higher standards. 'I don't know how much improvement I made because I had such small orchestras,' Baxter told David Kraft and Ronald Bohn of *Soundtrack!*, 'but at least we improved the fidelity.' For a composer who modelled himself on Stravinsky and Ravel, this descent into the maelstrom must have tested Baxter's faith in his true worth.

'If you're thirty, you're through!' screamed the poster for *Wild in the Streets*. Les Baxter was forty-six when he worked on this film. 'I never turn anything down,' he admitted, heroically. Despite his elevated ambitions he survived at this lowly level, also working extensively in television. If *Baywatch* had been primetime thirty-five years ago, Les would have taken the call.

In the true spirit of exploitation, a film score would take two weeks at the most. 'Roger Corman never took any interest in the music,' Baxter told *Soundtrack!*, 'never attended a recording session. He would make a picture at breakneck speed, I would score it quickly while he went on to the next one.' Eventually, Baxter began to lose track of his own music in this frenzy of fragments: 'Offhand I don't recall working on *Warriors Five* or *Premature Burial* although the studio sometimes used my left-over cues or took my cues illicitly from other pictures. I don't think I worked on *Samson and the Slave Queen*, but if you watch the film you can hear practically half the music from *Goliath and the Barbarians*. Actually, some of the titles in my filmography are things I could never dream of scoring . . . *Dagmar's Hot Pants, Inc.* . . . what on earth's that?'

The date of Baxter's entry into film composing is significant. *Tanga Tika*, the sailboat travelogue, appeared in 1953; Leslie Selander's *The Yellow Tomahawk* followed a year later; then came the full flood, anything up to seven pictures a year, beginning in 1956 with Reginald Le Borg's somnambulist drug thriller, *The Black Sleep*, Nicholas Ray's *Hot Blood*, Paul Henreid's *A Woman's Devotion*, another Selander Western, *Quincannon, Frontier Scout*, and a richly suggestive trio of obscurities: *Wetback*, *Hot Cars* and *Rebel in Town*.

In *The Sound of the City*, Charlie Gillett identified five distinct forms of popular music that surfaced between the years 1954 and 1956. Despite their differences, they became known as rock'n'roll. 'The styles gave expression to moods of their audience that had not been represented in popular music,' he wrote. 'Each style was developed in particular regions or locales and expressed personal responses to certain experiences in a way that would make sense to people with comparable experiences. This grass-roots character gave the styles of rock'n'roll their collective identity, putting it in sharp contrast with established modes of popular music, which were conceived in terms of general ideas formulated in ways that made the finished product available for millions of people to accept.'

Between 1951 and 1956, Baxter had been hitting the pop charts with schmaltzy arrangements of standards such as 'The Poor People of Paris' and 'Unchained Melody'. Easy listening at its impermeable *Stepford Wives* apex, they claimed a homogeneity at the centre of flattened culture, sweeping rougher, more disorderly expressions to the outer limits. This artificially cheerful situation was about to change. 'Well, here's what happened,' Baxter explained to *Soundtrack!*. 'I was going great guns until rock'n'roll came along. Then, they discovered they could sell a lot of records with just four or five guys in a rock group, they became disinterested in strings.' These Baxter hits, apparently recorded only for the money, were the apotheosis of 'general ideas'. Their representation of a middle-aged, middle-class, white, suburban, de-regionalised, politically conservative and emotionally imperturbable America made them extremely vulnerable to the explosive encroachment of rock'n'roll. Baxter continued to make these easy listening records, but they were overshadowed artistically by the more personalised expression of his exotica obsessions.

Although the first Baxter exotica album – *Ritual of the Savage* – had been made in 1951, the majority of his recordings in this genre were made during the peak years of rock'n'roll. 'Even in an age of electronic media, some historic moments go unrecorded,' wrote R.J. Smith in the sleeve notes to *The Exotic Moods of Les Baxter*. 'Such a turning point occurred in early 1956, when Les Baxter shared a TV variety show billing with a young Elvis Presley. Here was the immovable object meeting the irresistible force.' One moment, Baxter had been at the centre; the Perry Como Show was his. Then, with an insolent flick of the hips, rock'n'roll spun him into outer nothingness to land in a trashcan of bugmen, saucers, somnambulists, necrophiles, speed fiends, beach bums, biceps and bikinis.

● the wildest bikini

the Peace Museum, Hiroshima ... melted bottles ... a school uniform in tatters ... shadows etched onto a piano ... the absence of light, captured by a flash ...

Extracts from the Les Baxter filmography:

1962, *Panic in the Year Zero!* A family take a fishing trip. While they are relaxing in the mountains, Los Angeles is destroyed in a nuclear attack. Society in chaos ... Features Frankie Avalon.

1963, *Operation Bikini* American submarine captured by Japanese in World War II. Features Frankie Avalon.

1964, *Bikini Beach* Beach fun with drag strip racing. Stars Frankie Avalon and ex-Mousketeer Annette Funicello. Cinematography by Floyd Crosby.

1965, *Dr. Goldfoot and the Bikini Machine* Young female robots constructed by mad scientist Dr. Goldfoot are programmed to seduce wealthy men. Features Frankie Avalon and Annette Funicello.

How To Stuff a Wild Bikini. 'For beginners and experts ... an interesting course in the birds ... the bees and bikinis ... you gotta practice on a tame one first!' Features 'wildest motorcycle race ever run!' Also features Frankie Avalon and Annette Funicello. Cinematography by Floyd Crosby.

1966, *The Ghost in the Invisible Bikini*, ghosts meet women in bikinis.

Imagine the bikini as a central icon of the postwar period: frivolous, modern, daringly sexual, exotic, imperialist, paranoid, a homage to fast global communications, an item (or two items) of clothing that marked the nuclear age by trivialising it. Bomb culture.

Launched at the Paris fashion shows of July 1946, the bikini was devised by an engineer named Louis Reard. Working for his mother's lingerie company, Reard's 'invention' of the garment coincided with a parallel invention by another designer who, referring to its diminutive size yet helplessly drawn to the Bomb, called his micro-swimsuit the *atome*. Anxious to make a splash, Reard took inspiration from the US government's atomic test on the island of Bikini, four days before the bikini's catwalk debut.

Bikini Atoll is grouped among the many Pacific islands that constitute the Marshall Islands, Micronesia. Captured from the Japanese during World War II, Bikini was chosen by the US government as an ideally remote site for testing atomic bombs. The inhabitants were persuaded to leave their home for a smaller island, where they found that a very limited stock of food had been provided for them by the Americans. The natural resources of the island itself compared badly with Bikini Atoll. In a short time, all of them began to suffer from malnutrition. Meanwhile, two atomic bombs were exploded on the atoll, both of them a similar size to the bomb dropped on Nagasaki at the end of the war. A later blast, far larger than the Nagasaki and Hiroshima bombs, showered a deadly radioactive dust on nearby fishermen and the islanders. Coconuts were blown off trees by the atomic wind, exacerbating the food crisis.

After paradise had been irradiated and blasted, American teen-culture created its own temporary idyll in California. Youth culture, a growing economic force, required chronicles, demanded product. With Brian Hyland's 1960 pop number 1, 'Itsy Bitsy Teeny Weeny Yellow Polka Dot Bikini' setting the tone, bikinis, beach living and Hawaiian surfing converged in a film series that began with *Bikini Beach* and ended in 1966 or thereabouts (shortly before Jimi Hendrix mumbled 'may we never hear surf music again') with Don Weis's ignominious *The Ghost in the Invisible Bikini*.

The world shivered in the chill threats of the Cold War. With the Cuban missile crisis of 1962 still fresh in everybody's mind, nightmares were invaded by post-Freudian content: nuclear flash, radiation burns, melting flesh, gangs on the rampage, the hungry dead. Annette Funicello revealed her personal suffering during the shooting of the beach 'n' bikini movies to Rob Burt (*Surf City, Drag City*): 'I was tired of wearing the heavy pancake makeup, so I decided to buy a sunlamp to get a face tan. Well, I fell asleep

underneath it. The next day my eyes were glued shut, and I had
these horrible blisters all over my face, but I still went to work.'

Aside from its celebration of endless summers in the neo-
Polynesian paradise of Southern California, the beach 'n' bikini
genre was spotted with cameo performances in surf clubs by pop
acts. While Les Baxter and other Hollywood pros scored incidental
cues, Little Stevie Wonder (an unlikely surfer), Brian Wilson, the
Pyramids, the Hondells, the Kingsmen and Dick Dale and the
Deltones gave added teen value.

Now into his second career thanks to the adrenaline shot of
'Misirlou' that opens Quentin Tarantino's *Pulp Fiction*, Dick Dale
invented surf guitar. A surfer, guitarist and electronics enthusiast
who lived on the beach in Southern California, he wanted to
make music that captured the essence of surfing. 'There was a
tremendous amount of power that I felt while surfing,' he told
John Blair in *Who Put the Bomp!* magazine, 'and that feeling of
power was simply transferred from myself into my guitar when I
was playing surf music. I couldn't get that feeling by singing, so
the music took on an instrumental form . . . One day I just started
picking faster and faster like a locomotive. I wanted to make it
sound hard and powerful.'

Dale had learned to play country music on the ukulele, an
improbable apprenticeship; now he played the Fender Stratocaster
with speed, hacking a relentlessly fast, loud tremolando on heavily
reverbed bass strings. There was nothing subtle about it. 'Night
Rider', 'Misirlou' and 'Ghost Rider in the Sky' were like nocturnal
field recordings of the Four Horsemen of the Apocalypse. When
Dale stopped to make space for a saxophone solo, it was as if
three of the horses had collapsed and died. Tom Wolfe caught a
celebrity appearance by Dale at a Burbank teen fair. This was the
custom car and hot-rod fair that Wolfe documented famously in
his *Esquire* article, 'There Goes [Varoom! Varoom!] That Kandy-
Kolored Tangerine-Flake Streamline Baby'. Dick Dale was wearing
a 'Byronic shirt and blue cashmere V-neck sweater and wrapar-
ound sunglasses', according to Wolfe. 'The surfers also get a hell
of a bang out of slot racing, for some reason,' he wrote, 'so with
Dick Dale slot racing at the Teen Fair, you have about three areas
of the arcane teen world all rolled into one.'

This was true of the films Les Baxter was scoring. They draped themselves loosely around invasions from without – space monsters, voodoo zombies, revivified mummies, commie rockets – or they sparked paranoid alarms of panic within – biker gangs, body snatchers, vertical corpses, vampires roaming the suburbs – ensuring teen appeal by a judicious combination of fixations. They were dedicated to the alienated outsider: the alien, the creature, the thing, the biker, the drunk, the lonely surfer, the man who shrinks to nothing, the woman who grows into a fifty-foot monster, the man with X-ray eyes whose nightmare of perception was to see through the surface of society, so incurring his own destruction. As a happy coincidence, the solid-body electric guitar with chromium tremolo arm, multiple pickups, extravagant switches and amplifier vibrato, the kandy-kolored tangerine-flake streamline baby, had evolved in parallel with the fashions for speed, for noise, for kustom-kar kommandos who lived fast, died young.

Popular with teenagers from 1958, when twang-king Duane Eddy hit number 6 in the US charts with 'Rebel Rouser', guitar instrumentals chain-whipped generic mood music until it pledged allegiance to a more localised, aggressive and *ad hoc* garage band aesthetic. Instrumental pop had been dominated by the Teflon-smooth, grease-free easy listening of Lawrence Welk, Percy Faith and Ray Conniff. 'Of all the easy-listening maestros in the Cold War landscape,' wrote Joseph Lanza in *Elevator Music*, 'Ray Conniff comes closest to furnishing music that is "to the super-market born." Conniff's music connotes the mystically metallic clanking of shopping carts trailing down aisles, the rustle of cash registers, the tinkle of loose change, and the grunt of chromium doors automatically opening for the next phalanx of shoppers.'

As Lanza persuasively argues in his pro-Muzak polemic, mood music is a variety of extreme modernism, a music tailored to the era of pop psychology, drive-in movies, automatic industrial production lines, TV dinners, electric kitchens, elevators, parking lots, fast food, Tupperware parties, themed malls, superhighways, synthetic environments and other (mostly) American innovations in urban, robotopian lifestyle and work. 'Muzak and mood music are, in many respects, aesthetically superior to all other musical forms,' he jibes. 'They emit music the way the twentieth century is equipped to receive it.'

dine-a-mike

A new language was evolving in order to describe the shape of this strange world, a corruption of English some might say, but brash, vital, quickened, explosive and highly evocative of its subject. The language of an island, emerging from the deeps. In his study of American chain-restaurant architecture, *Orange Roofs, Golden Arches*, Philip Langdon documented inventions that swept through the business of serving food. The electronic ordering system was one gadget that took off during the fifties. 'From 1951 to 1959, a succession of electronic call-in systems appeared,' he wrote. 'Aut-O-Hop, Auto-Dine, Dine-A-Mike, Dine-A-Com, Electro-Hop, Ordaphone, Fone-A-Chef, Servus-Fone, Teletray, TelAutograph, and the Lindley Wireless Expeditor.'

The open road, the lost highway, the vanishing point, darkness eaten by headlights and the flashing neon of roadside signs; a strip of culture rolled out into the desert or terminating at the ocean's edge; new materials ripping into the essence of sand, wind, seawater. For the sexual/oceanic take on this theme, listen to surf instrumental classic 'Penetration' by the shaven-headed 'crazies of the surf scene', the Pyramids.

the legend

There is an obscure legend that may or may not be true. This convoluted story describes the arrival of the first electric guitar in the United States. The object, flat and shaped like a frying pan, was carried from Hawaii over towering Pacific rollers, born aloft by four big-wave surfers who braved shark attack and storms. Cast from aluminium, the guitar blazed so fiercely in the sun that the surfers wore whalebone sunglasses, acquired through trade with northern hemisphere Inuit, to protect themselves from blindness.

They landed near Ventura, California, and walked south to Los Angeles. Broke and exhausted, the surf kings picked up loose change in a Tiki shack on the edge of Watts by demonstrating the electrical invention, played in their so-called Kekuku style. This was something rarely seen before in America: sliding a broad two-edged, gut-sticker knife along amplified strings to conjure mind movies of rupturing hi-tension wires, bears on fire, smokestack lightning, thunder over Pyramid Lake, a landslide in Death Valley, a Japanese typhoon.

Copies were manufactured, coated in new plastics and mirror chrome, finished in colours of shocking pink, baby blue, the new rays of the rising sun, their shapes pulled in all directions as if melted in the heat. The invention inspired a whole new way of living. Somehow, the future seemed to be wrapped up in the aluminium frying pan and busting to break out.

A coven of occult bikers from Bakersfield tuned into the story and turned their hogs south. Lured into a peyote ceremony, the Hawaiians wandered in the underworld; the bikers stole the guitar and headed home but the legend says that their leader was blinded by the lights of a UFO hovering in the Mojave desert. Shaken to the soles of his motorcycle boots, he pushed the guitar onto a bewildered cowboy in a bar on the outskirts of Tehachapi. Crazed by corn liquor and snakes, the cowboy worked up a high octane routine that seemed to the desert pilgrims of southern California to speak in devil tongues.

In time, the cowboy – Hasil was his name – truly believed he had plucked something original out of thin air. But news of the invention had already spread from the Tiki shack like shock waves from a depth-charge explosion. There were rumours of a violinist on Chicago's Southside who constructed his own guitars in rec-tangular shapes, upholstered with pink nylon fur. Some whispered *vodun* tales: these guitars mumbled and shouted, used as a mouth-piece by Papa Legba, guardian of the sacred crossroads.

When the Russians launched Sputnik 1 a fire was lit under the backside of every electric guitar strangler in the world. There were guitarists who had tuned their instruments to the pitch of ocean surf or hot-rod engines; some knocked amplifier valves halfway out of their sockets, twisting and spiking the sound of gleaming steel strings into barbed wire. After a car accident, one fanatic had his broken arm reset at an angle in order to keep on playing.

But the dark void of space and distant planets . . . outer space was the most enthralling frontier of them all. The electrical frying pan and its offspring had permeated every zone of the globe – from Thailand to Congo, from England to Kalimantan. Tracking the glow of the Sputnik as it fell below the edge of the world, guitarists dressed in space suits would stand in front of their space-age amplifiers, bleeping and howling in awe-struck homage. So began the modern era.

● space guitar

As 'I Will Follow Him' fades into the joker's laugh of the Surfaris 'Wipe Out', the famous *Life* cover of 'America's Youth Today' appears: a skeleton head marked YOUTH in a woman's wig, smoking a cigarette. Superimposed over the black eye sockets is a bathetic picture of Jesus with his hand on a young boy's shoulder, pointing him towards the right-hand path.

Scorpio Rising closes with rapid-fire cuts rhythmically set to the manic surf guitar of 'Wipe Out'. Scorpio ranting. Nazi flags. A checker-board with swastika checkers. Assorted shots of bikers in Coney Island. The Back posing. A guy spilling out in the motorcycle race. A skull. Three guys yelling 'Hooray!' Ambulance arriving. A dead hel-meted face seen under a red strobe.

Bill Landis, *Anger*, 1995

Youth crazes for hot rods, custom cars, surfboards and motor-cycles regurgitated fascinations with speed, mobility, economic independence and customised technology, a multiple collision of avant-garde city life with nature. 'The concept of the "motorcycle outlaw" was as uniquely American as jazz,' wrote Hunter S. Thompson in *Hell's Angels*. 'Nothing like them had ever existed. In some ways they appeared to be a kind of half-breed anach-ronism, a human hangover from the era of the Wild West. Yet in other ways they were as new as television.'

Guitar instrumentals – hybrids of rough R&B, gimmick instrumentals by Johnny and the Hurricanes, exotic easy listening and cinema soundtracks – evoked the mood of this contradictory lifestyle. Sputniks, Telstar and the space race, the atomic bomb, science fiction, westerns and horror films all inspired imagery that dovetailed with the futurist abstractions of motion, violence, nomadic modernity, the opposition of open landscapes and claustrophobic oppression. This outsider art demanded exotic, otherworldly sound design, its populism introducing an expanded sonic vocabulary to the teen audience. Les Baxter's more outlandish arranging added aural chills to the image bank. Occupying similar territory was Louis and Bebe Barron's late forties electronic score for *Forbidden Planet*, along with the theremin soundtracks played by Dr Samuel J. Hoffman (*The Day the Earth Stood Still*, *Spellbound*, *Lost Weekend*) and the eerie music vibrating around the edges of fantasy television shows such as *Outer Limits*, *Twilight Zone* and Rod Serling's *One Step Beyond*, scored by composers like Dominic Frontiere and Harry Lubin.

Musically, an obsession with weirdness, threat and rebellion merged with instrumentals that represented marginalised American communities. The first serious opposition to the easy-listening school of instrumental pop came from rhythm and blues artists like Bill Doggett, Bo Diddley and Johnny 'Guitar' Watson or from jazz-influenced country players like Les Paul, Hank Garland, Speedy West and Jimmy Bryant. Their music was an alternative view of futurism, either a regionalised expansion of sound technology and recording techniques, or, at its most extreme, a dystopian leer facing off against the utopian charm school smile of Welk and Conniff.

No guitarists were more daring. Johnny 'Guitar' Watson's 'Space Guitar', recorded in Los Angeles in 1954, takes off from conventional LA 'jump' blues and plunges into a dark abyss of echo. In between convoluted, metallic blues runs and cliffhanging silences, Watson slides, slurs and chops his way over the fret board of his Fender guitar. Similarly, Speedy West's 'Space Man in Orbit', recorded for Capitol Records in Hollywood in 1962, pushes pedal steel guitar technique to the brink of impossibility. Descended from the jazz and country hybrid of Western Swing, Speedy's extraterrestrial adventure burns on electricity, crackling and sparking, chattering and barking at dizzying speed. Although the future of these records was doomed by the ascendance of garage rock, their exploration of electric tone colours within concise, entertaining musical structures was revelatory.

'I play guitar like a drum,' said Bo Diddley. After decades of fighting against the volume of big bands, drummers and saxophone soloists, the electric guitar had mutated into the loudest drum on the bandstand. An earthy eccentric who reconciled image gimmickry with sonic invention, Bo Diddley recorded two guitar instrumentals remarkable for their tightly concentrated exoticas. 'Mumblin' Guitar' and 'Bo's Guitar' exploit the electric guitar's percussive potential: a bass string played tremelando, through amplifier reverb, sounded more like a ceremonial drum hollowed from a tree than an instrument related to the Spanish guitar. Both tracks, particularly 'Mumblin' Guitar', overtly explore the symbiosis of speech and instrumental voicing that is central to so much blues and jazz; both stretch the formula of twelve-bar blues, edging it towards a kind of drone, punctuated by yelps and explosions as Diddley slides rapidly up and down the neck, or hits a string with force.

Looking at photographs on the covers of Bo Diddley albums and 7-inch EPs, we see the bizarre shapes he created for his guitars: elongated tail-fins, like spacecraft; a red rectangle; a covering of pink fur, like a benign synthetic bathroom-rug-creature knocked up for a Roger Corman B-quickie. 'Bo's Guitar' is his self-styled 'jungle music' of those shapes: a fast, sparse Latin rhythm, crossed with Diddley's shave-and-a-haircut beat, hammered out on tom-toms and hissing, imprecise maracas, a mercilessly clipped guitar sound that is bongos, barbed wire, a running gang-fight in echoing streets, zip guns and razors. In the background, a piano tinkles its counterpoint, a muttering from the old world.

At Chess Records, there was a misguided attempt to finesse Bo into the world of surf sonics. A whole album of 'Bo's Guitar' would stand as one of the greatest instrumental albums ever made; regrettably, *Surfin' with Bo Diddley* is far from being that. Only on 'Surf, Sink or Swim' and 'Low Tide' does Diddley's off-centre Chicago brutalism mesh with naïve garage band energy and, even then, the results are arthritic rather than stomping.

In the unlikely event of Bo Diddley wanting to research his surf album, he would have been carried off the beach on a stretcher. Despite its musical roots in black R&B, its Chicano musicians, its gymnastic roots in Hawaii, the image of Californian surfing was Aryan, a pursuit of leisured blonds who wanted to darken their skin temporarily and walk on water. In *Waiting for the Sun*, Barney Hoskyns quotes a black writer, Lenwood O. Sloan, who was equipped with the perspective to X-ray contradictions: 'The culture of the beach and the barbecue and the surfboard is Polynesian, but if you stopped a blond-haired, blue-eyed surfer on the beach and told him he was a Hawaiian Polynesian, he'd bust your teeth out.'

● guitar noir

But the moments of convergence could be incendiary, the moments when music from guarded enclaves of race and class took on an unknown identity and rose up, like The Thing, to terrorise the faint-hearted. Link Wray's 'Rumble' is one of the finest examples, a record so notorious that it threatens its own reputation with critically generated disappointment. Yet despite countless words written about 'Rumble', this million-selling single still moves with a trembling, psychotic, primate lurch. If the Walkman had existed in 1958, humanoids would have listened to 'Rumble' on their headphones as they stalked the naked city.

Born in North Carolina, Wray was a one-lunged TB survivor who, in his early years, bore a passing resemblance to Kenneth Anger. Like John Lee Hooker and Bo Diddley, his approach to the electric guitar seemed unfettered by precedent. The nature of the beast was grasped. The second solo Wray takes on a clanging, punk-prototype version of Willie Dixon's 'Hidden Charms' moves beyond the discrete pitches of the guitar fret board into a zone of tortured, arcing electricity. Other records he made with bassist Shorty Horton and drummer Doug Wray – 'Jack the Ripper', 'The Black Widow', 'I'm Branded' and 'Ace of Spades' – promised electric savagery with their bloodshot, homoerotic titles but fell short of the primitivist psychobilly spirit of 'Rumble'.

Link Wray portrayed the leather-armoured urban warrior;

Dick Dale conjured up the wave-whipped bare flesh of the surf
rider. To the casual listener, the conflict of culture versus nature
generated fairly similar end products: basic electric music played
with aggression. Through their exploration of mood through
sound, guitar instrumentals planted the seeds of punk and psychedelia. Merrell Fankhauser, for example, claimed he composed
the Surfaris' 'Wipeout', the manic garage-blues that took surf into
international pop charts in 1963. By 1966, Fankhauser had formed
a psychedelic folk-rock band, Fapardokly; next, he formed Mu
with slide guitarist Jeff Cotton, known as Antennae Jimmy Semens
during his tenure on Captain Beefheart's *Trout Mask Replica*; by
1973, Mu had left Los Angeles for the Hawaiian island of Maui
where they grew bananas and papaya, watched UFOs hovering
around the crater of Haleakala volcano and received messages
from 'the space brothers' through a switched-off television set. By
the nineties, Fankhauser was presenting a five-nights-a-week surf
music television show in California. Sadly, little of this exotic
trajectory survived to enliven Mu's sentimental, staid mysticism,
though the sitar dream-state melancholia of Fankhauser's 'A Visit
with Ayisha', recorded with HMS Bounty in 1968, is classic psychedelic exotica.

Appropriately for oceanic music created by suburban teens,
there were two sides to guitar-driven surf music: either mystical,
atmospheric, dreamy or pounding, physical, aggressive. Though
neither act is now associated with the surf subcult, Santo and
Johnny and Sandy Nelson represented the binary opposition.
Santo and Johnny's million-selling steel guitar hit of 1959, 'Sleep-
walk', is an exotic reverie, aspired to by the Survivors' 'After
the Game' (the Beach Boys releasing a single under an alias), the
Chantays' 'Pipeline', the Shadows' 'Midnight' and the Ventures'
'Beyond the Reef' yet never quite matched.

As for the one-footed Hollywood session drummer Sandy
Nelson, his drum instrumentals seemed direct descendants of Les
Baxter Latin bongo-party albums such as *Skins!* After the massive
success of Nelson's 'Teen Beat' in 1959, Baxter replied with his
Teen Drums album. The contrast is instructive: Nelson thrashing
out a barely coherent, cymbal-splashing beat against absolute
beginner guitar and bass riffs; Baxter spicing soft conga and tom-

tom patterns with fluttering alto flute, sliding into Cuban clave and a riff that anticipates Lalo Schifrin's *Mission Impossible* theme by five years, finally flicking out piano fills that sound as if (and I doubt this) they are influenced by the 'new thing' jazz of Cecil Taylor.

If Baxter hoped to cash in on teenage drum mania, his efforts were sabotaged by their cool sophistication. Exotic cash-ins abounded, more finely attuned to the zeitgeist than Baxter's disarmingly sincere polymeric jet-setting. The Champs' quasi-Mexican grindhouse instrumental, 'Tequila', was the perfectly proportioned template. A river of sludge surrounded it, typified by obscure tracks collected on the Strip label's two-volume CDs, *Jungle Exotica* – The Zirkons' 'Congawa!', the Highlights' 'Ah So!', the Revels' 'Conga Twist', the Nite Cats' 'Jungle' – crude party instrumentals with 'native' chants, animal sounds, Chop Suey vocals, jungle drumming and a leering Ku Klux Klan insensibility that sours the appeal of their lunatic energy.

● one step beyond

> Bo Windberg did not use leads from his guitar to the amplifier at that time [1963]; the connection was made by radio waves transmitted from the electronic box of tricks built into the back of the guitar. However, the extra mobility this gave was neutralised by the enormous space suits in which the group played live in those early times.
>
> Willi Dowidat, 'The Spotniks', 1977

The most enduring instrumental groups combined all of the late fifties/early sixties tropes of paranoia and exploration into a single mood programme. With 'Perfidia', 'The Ninth Wave', 'Sukiyaki', 'Apache', 'The Savage', 'Night Drive', 'The Lonely Bull', 'Watusi', 'One Step Beyond', 'Twilight Zone', 'Love Goddess of Venus' and 'The Bat', the Ventures stick-shifted their way through Latin, surf, orientalism, jungle, Western, Mexican, space, sci-fi, fantasy, erotica, horror and every other area of the 'arcane teen world all rolled into one'. In Britain, the Shadows followed a similarly inclusive, though more prissy approach to the electrification of imagistic music with 'Apache', 'Man of Mystery', 'The Frightened City', 'Midnight', 'Kon-Tiki', 'The Savage' and 'Peace Pipe'.

Usurped by the Beatles and the Rolling Stones, guitar instrumental bands either vanished or veered off into easy listening, psychedelia or trend-chasing opportunism. The Shadows and Sandy Nelson followed the easy path, while psychedelic recordings as diverse as Pink Floyd's 'Interstellar Overdrive', Quicksilver Messenger Service's 'The Fool', the Byrds' 'Moog Raga', Captain Beefheart's 'Dali's Car', Jimi Hendrix's '3rd Stone from the Sun' and the Electric Flag's soundtrack for Roger Corman's acid movie, *The Trip*, all owed varying sizes of debt to surf, biker, exotica and drag strip instrumentals.

● cycle-delic

There was another option. This was the difficult career path of disappearing for thirty years and then springing back into view at a sympathetic moment of retrospective curiosity: a Tarantino moment, a Jim Jarmusch moment. Having launched the surf instrumental craze in the early sixties, Dick Dale vanished from sight, emerging again after *Pulp Fiction* as a hard-ass, ponytail desert mystic who incorporated didgeridoo and Native American chants into a thunderous tremolando twang otherwise unchanged since his first recordings. 'Jimi, I'm still here, wish you were,' growled Dale in a 1996 cover version of '3rd Stone from the Sun'. Though Hendrix believed he had spoken the last word on surf music, Dick Dale ended up the survivor.

Also unchanged, except for the loss of an impressively surly facial expression and a personnel change in his Arrows, was Davie Allan. Walled up in cover band purgatory during the seventies, Allan suddenly discovered dedicated fans who cherished his bruising, distorted biker instrumentals. Film director Jim Jarmusch was among them. His use of 'Cycle-Delic' in *Night on Earth* gave Allan extra impetus to break into his self-imposed exile from distortion with ferocious nineties albums like *Fuzz Fest* and *Loud, Loose and Savage*. The titles alone – 'Polycarbonate', 'Polyurethane', 'Malfunction in Sector 9', 'Metal Fatigue' – evoked a Mad Max world high on fuel and impact. Regrettably, the bikers who inspired the music had aged less well. When Davie Allan played at the Love Ride, a Californian charity event, the bikers complained that he was too loud. 'They wanted to hear country-western music,' Allan told Greg Douglass at *Outré* magazine. 'At that same gig, the soundman, who didn't have a clue as to what we do, comes up to me after the soundcheck and says, "Can you get rid of that buzzsaw effect".'

Beginning with a 1966 short film on skateboarding, *Skaterdater*, Davie Allan and the Arrows had recorded instrumental cues for a series of teen films, including Roger Corman's *Wild Angels* in 1966, Dan Haller's *Devil's Angels*, Tom Laughlin's *Born Losers* and such youth film 'landmarks' as *Riot on Sunset Strip* and *Dr. Goldfoot and the Girl Bombs* (a cheap 1965 Italian production scored by Les Baxter).

'Their credo is violence . . . Their God is hate' trumpeted the poster of *The Wild Angels*. Like Baxter, Allan was running to keep pace with the American International Pictures treadmill. Les Baxter had scored a number of biker films, but disliked certain aspects of the job. 'Dubbing can ruin a score,' he told *Soundtrack!* 'When I did the gang picture series like *Hell's Belles* I would usually say if a cue included motor cycles revving away . . . forget it. I don't see any reason for composing music to get buried by things like that.'

With his decomposing fuzz tone, screeching wah-wah and exhaust pipe one-note sustains, Davie Allan's guitar playing sounded as if it was already buried under extraneous machine noise, dirt, grease, throttle roar, rust and fungus. Working under the auspices of a school friend, the notorious Mike Curb, Allan recorded a stream of delirious instrumentals, not always thoroughly familiar with their ultimate cinematic destination. Barney Hoskyns describes Curb as 'a millionaire brat from the Valley' in *Waiting for the Sun*. 'Curb was a typical Hollywood operator,' Hoskyns writes, 'and ideologically unsound to boot. Despite cashing in with soundtracks for such AIP exploitation classics as *Riot on Sunset Strip* and *Wild in the Streets*, he was a staunch Nixon supporter who in 1970 – as the twenty-six-year-old president of MGM Records – purged that label of all known drug users.'

Curb crossed paths with Brian Wilson. His co-production, with Nik Venet, of 'Little Honda' by the Hondells featured a Brian Wilson lead vocal on a Brian Wilson song. Curb's hypocrisy knew no bounds. Despite being credited with music on many of these films, he simply administered the sessions, hiring Davie Allan to record B-movie tripfests such as 'Cycle-delic' and 'Mind Trans-ferral'. Allan described the process to Douglass in *Outré*: 'Mike Curb was basically in charge of most of these movies, although he wasn't there a lot of the time. It'd be, like I said, just the three of us, going in and recording tracks. We didn't actually go in and have so much time where we were supposed to do this cue or that cue. A lot of times they would just take pre-recorded stuff and kind of cut it up.' Inspired by the melodic genius and craftsmanship of Henry Mancini, Davie Allan found himself in the unknown, a cut-up zone of fast-art Otherness.

Les Baxter, carrying that burning symphonic desire in his back pocket, was struggling with the set-up. Another film shared by Allan and Baxter was *Wild in the Streets*, an AIP satire from 1968, directed by Barry Shear. Set in the near future, the film pandered to a growing teenage demand for independence from parental controls with a plot about a pop singer elected as US President. Baxter was clearly unhappy about the practice of mixing pop music into the underscore. 'I did a lot of successful rock movies and the "beach" series made a lot of money,' he told *Soundtrack!*, 'but I always felt capable of writing a rock song myself if I was asked. I'm only sorry more of my music didn't get on the albums. In *Wild in the Streets* – a fine, futuristic movie – I wrote a, for then, "current" piece of music for the Sunset Strip sequence, which was a prediction of disco, progressive jazz and so on. But they left it off the LP, which is a pity ... Sometimes a producer of a non-musical picture would try to persuade me to use somebody else's theme song, but I generally fought against that.'

But while Baxter fought skirmishes against the zero ethics floating world of generation gap Xploitation cinema, the action moved further and further from his orbit.

11

beyond the reef

◆◆◆◆◆◆◆◆◆◆◆◆◆◆◆◆◆◆◆

What precious jewels these are, that change hue at the slightest whim, that drift lazily for a while, then transform themselves into a million dazzling sparkles. Les Baxter's orchestra plays their praise, in a composition as rich in beauty and varied movement as these magnificent jewels of the sea.

Les Baxter's Jewels of the Sea, sleeve notes

By circuitous route, using an ancient surrealist map of the world, the electric guitar, plasticised, chromed and wired, a surfboard with strings, can be traced back to that revered and reviled pre-modern adventurer, Captain Cook. 'When Captain James Cook discovered the Sandwich Islands in 1778,' wrote Andy Martin in *Walking on Water,* 'on the third and last of his voyages of discovery, he was mistaken for a god. As it happened, his arrival in Hawaii coincided with the culmination of the three-month festival of dancing and sports known as the *Makahiki.* It was January, the climax of the season of rough seas and high surf, when warfare was forbidden and men and women left their work in the fields to swim and play in the ocean ... The high priests, first on Kauai, then on the Big Island, assumed Cook was Lono. The god of surfing, aboard his big canoe, had returned.'

The first surfer to hang ten in California was a Celtic-Hawaiian named George Freeth, who performed on the ocean in front of Redondo Beach at the behest of the Pacific Electric Railroad. Freeth was followed by Duke Kahanamoku, who swam front crawl so powerfully that he broke the womens' fifty-yard world record without using his arms. '[Jack] London watched him racing in Honolulu Harbour,' writes Charles Sprawson in *Haunts of the Black Masseur*. 'It was in the Pacific Islands that London, like [Rupert] Brooke, enjoyed his most romantic bathing, often by moonlight, among the rollers, in pools below waterfalls or the rock basins of ravines, once in the mouth of a river while the sailors of his yacht stood on guard in the bush to protect them from possible headhunters.'

In *Surf City, Drag City*, Rob Burt compares Kahanamoku to Bruce Lee. Both the Hawaiian surfer and the Chinese martial artist were athletic exotics who spearheaded crazes in America and worked in feature films. In 1948, Duke appeared in *Wake of the Red Witch*, an East Indies adventure yarn starring John Wayne. Surfing up and down the Californian coast, he drew increasing numbers of converts to this strange sport of standing still on an unstable surface. America's annexation of Hawaii in 1898 sparked Island fever, an excitement that was amplified by the appearance of Hawaiian troubadours at international expositions. Irene West and her Royal Hawaiians, Toots Paka's Hawaiians, Sonny Cunha and others played at expos held in Chicago, Buffalo, Atlantic City, San Francisco, Seattle and Boston; in Japan, Helen Makela performed at the Yokohama World's Fair of 1923 while in London during the same year the *Bird of Paradise* troupe played at the Wembley Exhibition.

At the seven-month-long Panama-Pacific International Exposition of 1915, held in San Francisco, the Hawaiian Pavilion featured hula dances and music. According to George S. Kanahele's *Hawaiian Music and Musicians*, 'The music created a sensation. Thousands of people were hearing Hawaiian songs and instruments for the first time, and songs like "Waikiki Mermaid", "Song of the Islands", "One, Two, Three, Four" and "Tomi Tomi" became hits. The greatest hit of all was Henry Kailimai's "On the Beach at Waikiki", which was introduced at the exposition. People went away humming the melodies and making the Hawaii Pavilion one of the most popular at the exposition.'

America's professional songwriters responded with a glut of

faux Hawaiiana, released in huge quantities by companies such as Edison and Brunswick. In 1916, more Hawaiian records were sold on the mainland than any other type of popular music. These depictions of sensuality in a tropical paradise included 'Oh, How She Could Yacki Hacki Wicki Woo', 'They're Wearing 'Em Higher in Hawai'i' and 'Yacka Hula Hickey Dula', the latter recorded in military style by His Majesty's First Lifeguards in London in 1917.

Instrumentalists all over the world took up the two main instruments associated with Hawaiian music: slide guitar and ukulele. In Britain, Lancashire comedy vocalist George Formby was famous from the thirties through to the end of the fifties, satisfying an appetite for *double entendre* by singing about his 'little ukulele in his hand'. Other 'daft little songs' (as he would call them), all onanistically strummed at frantic pace on a hybrid banjolele, sketched caricatures of such exotic absurdities as the Hindoo-Howdoo-Hoodoo-Yoodoo-Man, Madame Moscovitch the Moscow witch and Mr Wu, a lovestruck Chinese launderer of Limehouse.

Whereas the ukulele can be traced to Portuguese origins, steel guitar technique was invented by a Hawaiian musician. A number of conflicting claims to this invention have surfaced, but the most convincingly documented evidence points to a young guitarist from Laie, on Oahu, named Joseph Kekuku. According to Kanahele, 'Kekuku himself is said to have told a guitar enthusiast in London in 1919 (while he was touring England with the *Bird of Paradise* company) that he produced his first steel guitar sound in 1885 at the age of eleven. He was walking along the railway strumming his guitar, according to his story, when he picked up a bolt, slid it across the guitar strings, and effected the characteristic slur of the steel . . . Kekuku progressed from bolt, pocket comb, knife, and tumbler to the steel bar which he designed and made himself in the school shop.'

Another claimant to the invention was Gabriel Davion, a musician who had been 'born in India, kidnapped by a sea-captain and finally brought to Honolulu'. This Pierre Lotiesque adventure yarn raises speculation that Davion may have learned the technique from Indian players of the *gottuvadyam*. A rarely used fretless four- or six-stringed instrument from Southern India, the *gottuvadyam* was similar to the drone-playing *tanpura* but stopped and struck with two light bamboo, horn or polished wood blades, one held in each hand.

The story brings to mind Tau Moe, transcribing Carmen Miranda songs in India. In *Routes*, James Clifford cites Bob Brosman's research on the Moe family and their life of constant touring. Although the Moes play an authentic version of Hawaiian slide music, their extended absence from home raises contradictions. 'They played music in Hawaiian "exoticist" shows all over the Far East, South Asia, the Middle East, North Africa, eastern and western Europe, and the United States,' writes Clifford, 'and they performed, too, the gamut of hotel-circuit pop music.'

Tau Moe's Tropical Stars even collaborated with ersatz Hawaiians, including the British-based impresario, Felix Mendelsson. Booked into a long run at the Taj Mahal in Bombay, the Moes recorded for HMV, and in Tokyo they recorded for Columbia. Clifford asks how the family retained its sense of identity during nearly six decades of presenting exotic music in (to them) exotic locations. 'How did they compartmentalize their Hawaiianness,' Clifford asks, 'in constant interaction with different cultures, musics, and dance traditions – influences they worked into their act, as needed? How, for fifty-six years in transient, hybrid environments, did they preserve and invent a sense of Hawaiian "home"? And how, currently, is their music being recycled in the continuing invention of Hawaiian authenticity?' Perhaps the question holds less mystery for the Moes themselves. For musicians who constantly tour the world, their music embodies a portable and fluid, though nonetheless sustained (and sustaining) sense of place. Music's capacity to carry memory and identity in this way may be the means of surviving such a "rootless" life of movement.

● frying pan on air

'I hired a talking drummer and a Hawaiian guitarist to give the music its proper African background,' says [Prince] Nico.

Chris Stapleton and Chris May, *African All-Stars*, 1987

The impact of the Hawaiian slide guitar was global: the Indian success of 'Everybody Does It in Hawaii' by country singer Jimmie Rodgers demonstrated an enthusiasm that survives in the extensive use of steel guitar in Bollywood film soundtracks and the slide guitar playing of Vishwa Mohan Bhatt; a surge of pre-World War II popularity for the steel guitar inspired Hawaiian bands in Java and Bali; recent recordings, made in Rangoon by Rick Heizman and Henry Kaiser, feature a Burmese lap-slide guitarist named U Ohn Lwin; in Kenya, Zaire and Nigeria, guitarists tuned their strings to open chords and experimented with knife blade slides; in Japan, a number of Hawaiian bands were formed, led by steel guitarists such as Kazunori Murakami, whose passion for Hawaiian music was ignited in a Tokyo cinema when he saw Cliff Edwards (known as Ukulele Ike) perform 'Singing in the Rain' in MGM's 1929 *Hollywood Revue*.

Most dramatically, Hawaiian music added a new sound to country music and the blues, as well as playing a pivotal role in the total electrification of the guitar. America's fanatical devotion to Hawaiian guitarists such as Sol Hoopii, Jim and Bob (the Genial Hawaiians) and the Portuguese cowboy, Frank Ferera, inspired blues and country players to experiment with the slide technique. Often playing Dobro or National guitars – acoustic instruments fitted with metal resonator dishes – players such as Frank Hutchison, the Johnson Brothers, Tom Darby and Jimmy Tarlton, Cliff Carlisle, Kokomo Arnold, Blind Willie Johnson and Robert Johnson all recorded slide guitar performances in the twenties and thirties. What is striking about these records is the speed with which slide technique was adapted to mirror the emotional tenor and harmonic character of these musical genres. The Hawaiian influence could still be acknowledged: country acts called themselves Hawaiians, and the great postwar blues singer, Elmore James, recorded 'Hawaiian Boogie' in the early fifties. Yet despite these postcards to Hawaii, slide guitar blended perfectly with either the string bass, fiddle and high mountain singing of country or the intense interplay of voice and guitar that typified rural blues. Later, with electrification and the mechanical wizardry of the pedal steel guitar, Joseph Kekuku's knife blade glissandi slid into new dimensions.

The National 'resophonic' guitar was invented by the Dopera
Brothers, who later approached an engineer named Adolph Rickenbacker for metal components. Rickenbacker met two other
engineers at National, George Beauchamp and Paul Barth. This
trio formed the Electro String Company, which produced their
first solid-body electric guitar in 1931. Known as the 'frying pan'
or 'pancake', this odd-looking instrument, cast from a single piece
of solid aluminium, proved to be difficult to sell. The breakthrough
came from a Hawaiian steel guitarist who agreed to play the
'frying pan' on air. As Adolph Rickenbacker has said, 'In a few
days, every Hawaiian and hillbilly in the city was on our trail.
They lined up in front of the shop every morning to pick up all
that we could produce the day before.'

Of course, other inventors were involved in parallel developments: Thomas Edison's solid-body violin inspired guitar
experimenter Les Paul to do the same with the guitar, while Leo
Fender, Paul Bigsby and Merle Travis all worked on design proto-
types of their own. Aside from opening up the possibility for new
guitar shapes, the combined effect was to revolutionise the sound
and the economic infrastructure of music. The leap was typified
by a blues player like Muddy Waters, who began his musical life by
playing acoustic country blues and ended it with an electric slide
guitar style that sounded like the attack of the killer bees.

Hawaiiana persisted, though transformed by electricity.
Speedy West was born in Missouri in 1924. He began playing a
$12 Hawaiian guitar, then progressed to a $125 National steel-
bodied resonater model. Encouraged to turn professional after
hearing the Hawaiian-style country playing of Little Roy Wiggins,
he took up a musical career, moving from Missouri to the Western
Swing scene then flourishing in Los Angeles, a city expanded out
of recognition during the war years. Once in the centre of the
action, West bought one of Leo Fender's new amplifiers and commissioned Paul Bigsby to build him a three-neck, four-pedal steel
guitar, so becoming the first country player to use one of these
extraordinary instruments. 'West's technical precision was beyond
question,' wrote Rich Kienzle in his notes for *Flamin' Guitars:
Speedy West, Jimmy Bryant*, 'but he didn't feel bound by the
normal physical or musical restraint . . . The crazy, swooping runs

and the richly articulated, expertly voiced chords were only part
of his style. When he ripped loose, he could create crashing,
metallic, futuristic chords that exploded like a volcanic bubble.'

Indelibly associated with a technique so fast, unfeasible and
outrageous that it terrified other guitarists, West also recorded a
number of slow, impressionistic mood pieces that exploited other
aspects of his electric steel. 'Reflections from the Moon', 'Sunset',
'Lazy Summer Evening', 'Afternoon of a Swan', 'Rippling Waters',
'Deep Water' and 'West of Samoa' were made for exotic dreaming,
music suspended in a glass bubble, swirling with artificial snow.

For 'West of Samoa', recorded in 1954, he played sound effects
that anticipated Jimi Hendrix's submarine sounds on '1983 . . . (a
merman I should turn to be)'. 'To create the sounds of birds,'
wrote Kienzle, 'he overdubbed the scrapes of his picks, an effect
he'd used elsewhere, up and down the strings, creating what for
all the world sounded like tropical bird effects. It was a measure
of Speedy's impromptu genius in the studio.' In 1957, after the
break-up of West's long-running partnership with guitarist Jimmy
Bryant, producer Ken Nelson persuaded West, under protest, to
record a Hawaiian album. 'Well shit, I don't play Hawaiian music,'
said West, 'but it come out pretty good.' Once again, the title was
a pun. Pictured on the front cover of *West of Hawaii* at the steel
– a Hawaiian *lei* hung around his neck, *hula* dancer and Hawaiian
backing band soft-focused into the background – West interspersed the up-tempo corn of standards like 'Yaaka Hula Dickey
Hickey Dula' with more of his serene tone poems, including a
shimmering version of 'The Moon of Manakoora'.

● firecrackers

If you wish to escape the pressures and tensions of sophisticated
commercialism, daily hypnosis of television, undercurrents of social
and political tidal waves, then follow the sun to islands in the
Pacific and find your peace in the trade winds of Polynesia and
relaxed friendliness in Hawaii. More and more the searching traveller
seems to find in the Hawaiian Islands an intangible but real elixir
which rejuvenates the mind, body and spirit. Until 1957 easy access
to these islands of escape was limited. Today, with the magnificent,

awesome experience of a jet flight you can follow the sun and be
there within hours – the Islands are waiting for you!

Tony Lease, radio voice of the Pacific, sleeve notes to Arthur Lyman's
Isle of Enchantment

Speedy West's version of 'The Moon of Manakoora' was recorded
by other exoticists. In sun-drenched Finland, steel guitarist Onni
Gideon's Aloha Hawaii group, featuring Annikki Tähti, enjoyed a
local hit with a vocal version, entitled 'Manakooran Kuu'. Much
closer to the source, vibraharpist Arthur Lyman recorded 'Moon
of Manakura' for volume two of his *Tabou* album. This moon
wanes even more ethereal than West's, the Lyman group taking
the tune at a tempo so slow that it threatens to stumble to its
knees. Strummed with great deliberation on ukulele, the chords
lead a ghostly procession through gathering mist – organ, vibraphone, double bass and a conga drum that booms like a bittern –
all seemingly huddled together, in fear of startling a moon wraith.

Lyman, born on Kauai Island, Hawaii, in 1936, originally
played vibraphone for the Martin Denny group. It was Denny, a
classically trained jazz pianist from New York, who had popularised the exotica boom with his 1957 hit version of Les Baxter's
'Quiet Village'. Having fallen into a career trough in the mid-
fifties, Denny was asked to take over from a pianist friend at Don
the Beachcomber's Waikiki tiki bar. The exact transition from
Denny's journeyman jazz and cabaret existence to the blossoming
of his identity as the popular figurehead of exotica is unclear.
Much of the appeal of this music in the nineties, aside from the
kitsch experimentalism, is its barely documented air of mystery
and strangeness.

This was a style reputed to have been cross-fertilised in outer
space, then injected, fully formed, into urban lounges and resort
bars across the world. Where did it come from? Part of the answer
lies with Les Baxter and his early-fifties synthesis of Machito
mambos, jazz (particularly the highly arranged big bands of Stan
Kenton and Claude Thornhill), Ernesto Lecuona, Stravinsky,
Ravel, string arranging and Hollywood orientalism.

Denny took a number of Baxter's melodies, along with his
pop exoticism, and used them in cocktail jazz (that is to say,

background jazz played for an audience pursuing notions other than music). This lounge or supper-club jazz had its roots in players such as Noro Morales, Milt Buckner and George Shearing. A Puerto-Rican pianist who arrived in New York City in the mid-thirties, Noro Morales became popular with Latin and non-Latin audiences. '[H]e excelled in a style that peaked during the 1940s,' wrote John Storm Roberts in *The Latin Tinge*, 'and has totally vanished since then, the quintet for piano and percussion.' Roberts's view of Morales is that he was torn between an exciting Latin style and the demands of his downtown audience. 'A reissue album of Morales' work on the small Tropical label shows him at his best and worst,' he wrote. 'Some tracks are essentially skilled cocktail piano. But many of the sextet numbers show highly effective contrasts between busy Afro-Cuban percussion and a sometimes florid but always interesting piano style that occupies a very personal piano space between "international" Latin and more traditional Cuban playing.'

Morales also dabbled in exotica, of a kind. 'A late recording for MGM on two sides of a 78rpm record, *Puerta de Tierra*,' writes Roberts, 'opened as an effectively brooding Latin jazz piece, but soon degenerated into wide-horizons mood music with Hollywood strings and brass.' Arthur Lyman covered a Morales number, 'Jungle Fantasy'. This Latin workout follows the Tin Pan Alley Hawaiiana of 'Moon of Manakura', three Lyman originals (Polynesian and oriental exotica and Latin-jazz) and a dreamy standard, 'Ebb Tide', a sequence that illustrates the true sources of cocktail lounge exotica.

Lyman's piano player, Alan Soares, often played in the locked-hands style of parallel chords pioneered by Milt Buckner and popularised in the fifties by English-born pianist George Shearing. Blind from birth, Shearing had worked in dance bands in England, then moved to America where he worked with Oscar Pettiford and Buddy DiFranco. He formed his own post-bop quintet in 1949, featuring Margie Hyams on vibes and guitarist Chuck Wayne. Shearing's sound turned out to be a huge success, a kind of pop-jazz whose secret lay in the tonal compatibility of vibraphone, piano, guitar and double bass. Clinking together in unisons or gentle counterpoint, these instruments functioned as a soothingly melodic percussion orchestra, their tranquil, mildly invigorating effect not totally removed from similar tonal blends in Balinese, Javanese, Thai and Burmese musics. Was this music that evolved camouflage to survive in a soundscape of chinking cocktail glasses, then found the disguise so effective that by degrees it vanished, like a chameleon in foliage, into the deadly embrace of piano bars, executive lounges, hotel lobbys, elevator hum?

In 1953, Shearing changed the personnel of his group, bringing in percussionists Willie Bobo, Mongo Santamaria and Armando Peraza and vibraphonist Cal Tjader. 'The quintet's music was an odd hybrid of cocktail piano, small group bop, and a full Cuban percussion section,' writes Roberts. 'Though it was enormously popular at the time, it has been critically somewhat underrated for several reasons. The tight-piano-vibraphone work had a dulcet quality that *sounded* a little trivial, and the band's repertoire included a lot of boleros and other slow numbers that fitted right into the background music image ... Shearing's large popular success was another example of the fact that jazz has frequently reached its widest audiences in Latin fusions. It also gave impetus to the whole jazz quintet movement, for it had the economic advantages of a small group at a time when most big bands were in financial trouble.'

Bassist Al McKibbon had taken Cal Tjader to New York's Palladium ballroom in 1953, to hear the mambo kings who played there; Tjader went on to form his own Latin jazz quintet in the middle of 1954, playing a more vigorous though still commercial-ised form of crossover at the Macumba in San Francisco. At his best, Tjader could be thrilling, as on 'Soul Sauce'. This echoing version of Chano Pozo and Dizzy Gillespie's 'Guacha Guaro' was produced by Creed Taylor, the architect of two wonderfully bizarre psychodramatic mood albums, *Shock* and *Panic*. Ironically, Tjader came to be influenced by the exoticists. In 1963, persuaded by Creed Taylor, he recorded two albums in an exotic vein: *Several Shades of Jade* and *Breeze From the East. Several Shades of Jade* is notable for the participation of arranger Lalo Schifrin, who had studied ethnomusicology in Paris. So 'Cherry Blossoms' begins with string drones and shrill piccolo, their gnawing tension heightened by sharply struck woodblocks, hit in an accelerating pattern that simultaneously suggests Japanese *gagaku* court music, *kabuki* theatre and Schifrin's (much later) soundtrack for *Enter the Dragon*. After some moments of Xenakis-style sliding atonality, the piece folds with ingenuous ease into a jazz ballad.

By contrast with such highbrow hybridisation, *Breeze From the East* is exploitation stripped naked. According to Paul de Barros's sleeve notes, Tjader thought the project was dumb. 'Creed . . . tried for a sound,' he told a *down beat* interviewer in 1966, 'and when I heard it, I went outside and vomited – figuratively, not literally.' Sadly for the nauseated Tjader, his dumb album has all the necessary sixties sparkle to appeal to our allegedly dumbed-down present world: brisk TV theme guitars, hustling bugalu backbeat, cool bossa-nova orientalisms, cappucino strings, coffee-bar organ, private-eye bass lines, up-up-and-away codas and the kind of smug Latin session percussion that yelps 'kitsch' and 'groovy' in the same slap. As de Barros says, '*Breeze* . . . has a sleaziness that appeals to the generation of musicians currently mining yesterday's "mood music" for gems of attitude and style today. Mood music was created in the Fifties as an anaesthetic. Though there is a campy cynicism attached to its cool, postmodern revival, some of the same social realities apply today. Escape is always appealing, so why not do it once in a while?'

Fusions of Cuban music with jazz were developing at the same time as the formation of the Modern Jazz Quartet. Untouched by Cuban rhythms, the MJQ – John Lewis, Milt Jackson, Percy Heath and Connie Kay – were more impressed by the exoticisms of Darius Milhaud (the first twentieth-century European composer to hear blues in Harlem) or the harmonic complexities and breathy rhythms of Brazilian bossa nova. Their elegantly interwoven chamber swing added another strand to the type of modern jazz that could reach an uncommitted audience.

The vibraphone was at the heart of many of these crossovers. Its seductive, lingering shimmer – like a burnished aluminium UFO hovering in desert heat haze – was constitutionally incapable of jarring or violent sounds; its burred, blurred attack – often compared to milk bottles falling down a flight of stairs – was sufficiently edged to carry a clear melody or driving riff above the volume of large ensembles.

• vibrating air

Before the solid-body electric guitar, the vibraphone was the ultimate modernist instrument, its technology of struck metal and vibrating air, percussion and melody, contrasting neatly with the 'primitivism' of mambo, jazz and exotica. Other exotics began in the piano-vibes quartet or quintet. Alice McCloud, for example, played piano (and occasionally vibes) with vibraphonist Terry Gibbs before she became Alice Coltrane and recorded Indian-influenced big-screen epics, organ fantasias and harp-led trios and quartets. Even in the deathly depths of lounge fuzak, the combination of piano, vibraphone and percussion presupposed some interest (no matter how faint or long departed) in the sound of music, as much as its structure and symbolism.

Alice Coltrane's explorations began conventionally enough, first playing organ in church in Detroit, then recording with Gibbs on straight-ahead albums such as *El Nutto*. After meeting John Coltrane in the early sixties, finally marrying him in 1966, she entered into the turbulent experimentation of his last groups, playing alongside Pharoah Sanders, Rashied Ali, Jimmy Garrison and a number of percussionists. Their music seemed to absorb the African and Indian influences that had taken John Coltrane so far (yet not so far) from hard-bop blowing sessions, sucking them into a maelstrom of sound that struggled to detach itself from worldliness.

After John's death in 1967, Alice Coltrane pursued this detachment further with meditation and music. First she recorded albums that mirrored the approach of tenor saxophonist Pharoah Sanders on his *Tauhid* album: a dense, amorphous swirl of cloud manufactured with shaken bells, bowed double bass, flowing piano arpeggios, tom-tom rolls and rapid guitar tremolando, followed by simple, compelling grooves and romantic melodies. Sanders's titles for *Tauhid* – 'Upper Egypt & Lower Egypt', 'Japan', 'Aum, Venus, Capricorn Rising' – demonstrate the exoticism surfacing in mid-sixties jazz at the cutting edge. 'Japan' was written after the John Coltrane group's visit in 1966. 'I was particularly impressed by the spiritual qualities of a lot of the people I met there, the respect they have for one another and for you,' Sanders told jazz writer Nat Hentoff. 'What I mean is that if you come from another culture, they accept you for what you are. They don't put down strangeness, but instead are open to what you have to offer them.'

Sanders's observations, spoken after experiencing the luxury of being treated well for his art, rather than being treated badly both for his skin colour *and* his art, are as wildly optimistic in their idealism as the publicity brochures for exotic holidays. They illustrate the connection between sixties utopianism and the expansion of musical references and resources. As with *Tauhid*, Alice Coltrane's *Ptah, The El Daoud* (1970) was divided equally between Egypt and the orient; *A Monastic Trio* (1968) explored Indian influences and African-American gospel, at times settling into a stormier version of the 'Wade in the Water' soul-jazz style taken into the pop charts by Ramsey Lewis; *Huntington Ashram Monastery* (1969) was a session of reflective grooves on which Alice used harp extensively, its brittle notes glittering like sunlight caught on the fractured wave tops of a placid sea.

With *Universal Consciousness* (1971), she went far beyond jazz. 'Having made the journey to the East,' she wrote in her sleeve notes, 'a most important part of my Sadhana (spiritual struggle) has been completed.' Playing organ and harp against ecstatic, restless soundstages of strings, *tanpura* drones, bass, drums and percussion, she conjures images of blazing light. Though lacking the fully realised global intensity of *Universal Consciousness*, later albums such as *Eternity* and *Transcendence* are interesting for their bizarre convergence of chamber settings, funky pitch-bend organ, Stravinsky, neo-Hindu chanting and African-American gospel. The adoption of a new spiritual identity seemed to allow Alice Coltrane the freedom to move unselfconsciously between the stages and settings of her life, moulding fantasy spirit worlds from the confrontation of previously incompatible musics.

● lotus land

Pacific (and Pacific-rim) exotica was a *tabula rasa* for fantasy, both sincere and ironic. The first signs that Martin Denny's exotica was not hermetically sealed and buried came from two very different sources. In 1978, Throbbing Gristle's *20 Jazz Funk Greats* included an instrumental track called 'Exotica', an ominous, fugitive vision, like an island glimpsed briefly through sea mist. Perhaps this was the island of Samburan, where Joseph Conrad sent his antihero, Heyst, in *Victory*. With the benevolent act of saving a damsel in distress, Heyst hoped to escape the world, only to be pursued by an unholy trio of villains, their grimacing, amoral misogynist of a leader greeting Heyst with, 'I am the world itself come to pay you a visit.'

A year after Throbbing Gristle's uncharacteristic bulletin from fantasy island, Yellow Magic Orchestra released their electro-pop version of Martin Denny's 'Firecracker' on their debut album. *Yellow Magic Orchestra* began and ended its first side with adaptations of two computer-game tunes, *The Circus* and *The Invader*, that factored the technological 'folk art' of arcade game soundtracks into the history of electronic music. According to YMO's Ryuichi Sakamoto, 'To me, Hawaii is very interesting. Hawaii is part of the United States of course, but many Asian people live there. They are all mixed – Asian people with original Hawaiians, Americans and Europeans. There's a strange culture there and a big misunderstanding, particularly for American sightseers. It's like a misunderstanding in Hollywood movies about Japanese or Asians – a typical stereotype or cliché misunderstanding like all Japanese people wear glasses, cameras and grey suits. Sometimes they wear Chinese costumes. In the beginning we pretended to be misunderstood Japanese.'

So Denny's exotica, transformed into electro-orientalism, was layered with ironic self-deprecation, introducing a new cliché of Japonisme, the technological, postmodern exotic who collapses ironic versions of traditionalism, orientalism, technocracy, privileged nomadism and consumerism into a single image. On the front cover of *Yellow Magic Orchestra*, that image was represented by a red-lipsticked geisha, dressed in a kimono, holding an open fan, her fingernails painted red and filed to points, her eyes eradicated by green-lensed sunglasses, her skull and brain sliced away and replaced by a Medusa's hairstyle of electric cables.

● exotica

Martin Denny's 'Exotica', recorded in or around 1958, was a slow, meandering bolero, a succession of florid arpeggios and trills played on piano, celeste, marimba and chimes. Bird calls trill and squawk. The impression is of a bamboo house in a clearing, the house hung with wind chimes that rattle together as the breeze quickens. Inside the house, we can picture two naked bodies, slick with sweat, sliding together in the torpid glue of afternoon heat.

This sultry imagined scene was typical of Denny's music, a version of George Shearing that reached into the pool of seductive images and drew exoticisms and eroticisms closer to the surface. Through their album covers, both Denny and Lyman drew constant attention to the role of their expanded sound palettes in this tropical fantasia, the array of Asian, Cuban and quasi-exotic percussion instruments that decorated their stage sets. These included tuned Burmese gongs, Chinese gong, Tahitian woodblock, Hawaiian gourd, piccolo xylophone, boobams, a new invention named the Magna-harp and non-percussion such as the Indian *sitar* and Japanese *koto* and *shamisen*.

'The cultures of the Orient have produced many musical instruments which, though they may sound strange to our ears, possess beautiful and exotic sounds,' wrote Denny for the sleeve notes to *Exotic Percussion*. 'It has long been one of my desires to apply these rare sounds to our own music.' Denny has been candid about the reasons for his purple patch of the late fifties. 'Part of the reason my records caught on was that *stereo* had just appeared on the market,' he told V. Vale for *Incredibly Strange Music*. 'People were interested in sound *per se* – and that included my so-called "exotic" sound. I guess I just happened to be there at the right time.'

Denny and Lyman used Asian percussion and similar unusual sound sources as embellishment. 'Actually, a lot of what I'm doing is just window-dressing,' he admitted to Vale. 'I can take a tune like "Flamingo" and give it a tropical feel, in my style. In my arrangement of a Japanese farewell song, "Sayonara", I included a Japanese three-stringed instrument, the *shamisen*. We distinguished each song by a different ethnic instrument, usually on top of a semi-jazz or Latin beat. Even though it remained familiar, each song would take on a strange, exotic character.'

Understandably, Denny's view was optimistic; the character of some of this ethnic window-dressing went beyond strange exoticism into crimson imperialist embarrassment. 'Softly, As in a Morning Sunrise', arranged for *shamisen*, Liberace piano, flute, celestette, bells and classical guitar sounds like the Ah-so-American vision of Okinawa portrayed by Marlon Brando in *The Teahouse of the August Moon*. As was the case with Lyman and Baxter, Denny's band book contained arrangements of show tunes, standards, bossa novas (by Tom Jobim and João Gilberto), international exotica, even the odd calypso, most of them miraculously resolving into imperious piano-bar jazz between the exotic intros and outros.

Drawn from sources both lofty and lowly, the international exotica included Ernesto Lecuona's 'Jungle Drums' and 'Malaguena', Margarita Lecuona's 'Tabou', Duke Ellington and Juan Tizol's 'Caravan', Rodgers and Hammerstein's 'Bali Ha'i', Bert Kaempfert's 'Tahitian Sunset', Cal Tjader's 'Black Orchid', Hoagy Carmichael's 'Hong Kong Blues' (as sung by Carmichael in *To Have and Have Not*) and Richard Rodgers's 'March of the Siamese Children'.

Denny enjoyed the patronage of American industrialist Henry J. Kaiser on Hawaii. Having built his Hawaiian Village resort on Waikiki, Kaiser poached personnel ranging from entertainers to cocktail shakers from Don the Beachcomber's. In 1956, Denny's group were booked into a creatively and financially fulfilling residency at Kaiser's Shell Bar. Kaiser became displeased with Denny's independent spirit, however. Notorious for his ruthlessness, he excommunicated Denny, seducing Arthur Lyman into a solo career with the same single-mindedness that he used to poach Denny. Feeling the pinch of sudden unemployment, along with new competition from his ex-sideman, Denny replaced Lyman with vibraphonist Julius Wechter. A very capable studio musician, Wechter played on Crystals and Ronettes sessions for Phil Spector. Later, he worked with Herb Alpert and formed the Baja Marimba Band. Though he lacked Lyman's ethereal touch, Wechter composed a number of tunes recorded by the Denny group. Including

'Aku Aku' and 'Mau Mau', lounge jazz tributes, respectively, to Thor Heyerdahl's trans-Pacific adventuring and the Kikuyu guerrillas of Kenya, these sat alongside Denny originals and a large number of Les Baxter compositions.

Even in 1966, after the Beach Boys had given up Hawaii for psychedelic drugs, this mix was standard for Hawaiiana. Henry Mancini's *Music of Hawaii* may have been titled like a French or German ethnographic record but the programme was steadfast. A brooding version of Baxter's 'Quiet Village' was played by Mancini on the solid-body electric harpsichord, probably as a consequence of Mancini's enthusiasm for Miles Davis. 'I was fascinated by the new Miles Davis album,' he told Leonard Feather of *Melody Maker* in January 1971. 'This was a nod to really what's happening with sound today. I particularly liked the electric keyboards. I'm a great one for imagery, which is such a vital element in Miles' music. You look at that title, "Bitches Brew", and you put the needle down and that's it!'

The other selections on *Music of Hawaii* are not quite 'Bitches Brew': Elmer Bernstein's cinema theme tune for *Hawaii*, adapted from James A. Michener's blockbuster novel; an ooohed and aaahed easy treatment (what Joseph Lanza called the wordless chorus of 'guardian seraphim') of 'The Moon of Manakoora'; one Mancini original, 'Driftwood and Dreams', an illustration of his winning tendency to spice easy-listening clichés with electric-guitar and bass-guitar effects more familiar on Beach Boys and Phil Spector records; plus, there was the usual filler of 'Beyond the Reef', 'Adventures in Paradise', 'Aloha Oe' and an arrangement of 'Blue Hawaii' that, in its introduction at least, sounds positively phosphorescent.

● feast of the mau mau

Thank you, it's nice to be here . . . (7 second silence, insert first question) . . . Yes, as a matter of fact I have. Through the early novelty stuff to rock and roll. Although the music that I've done, as you know, has continued about the same through all these trends. My record, 'April In Portugal', for example, with strings and the

Brazilian mandolin, ahh, was the forerunner of most of the, uh, records that I followed it with . . .

(16 second silence, insert second question) . . . Yes, I have been, uhh, in most of the world, picking up ideas from exotic music and so forth. Although it seems that most of my life I have had inclinations toward that kind of music – interesting, different music. I never like to do prosaic or the same thing that someone else has been doing before me. After 'April in Portugal' and 'Blue Tango', you know, we did the Yma Sumac album and *The Ritual of the Savage* exotic thing and *Tamboo*. Then we had, uhh, motion picture themes like 'Ruby', 'Unchained Melody'. 'I Love Paris' was an entirely different kind of record . . .

excerpted from *Open End Disc Jockey Interview with Les Baxter*

. . . I love Paris, why oh why do I love Paris? Because my love is here . . . How about Germany? Germany! Achtung, doogoozackazugu-zacky, mooiboohacka . . . and Chinese! Ahh Chinese, bingbong wingdong mickabongwickabong dingdongha . . . and Africa! I saw Mau Mau kissing Santa Claus . . . and Paris? Paris, Oui Oui, azure monsieur, ahuaca . . .

excerpted from 'I Love Paris', as recorded by Screamin' Jay Hawkins

The crunch for all of the exotica musicians was delivered by the rock machine. Already chastened by the failure of his folk-orientated Balladeers, Les Baxter tried electronics with *Moog Rock*, a heart-stopping attempt to apply Stylophone timbres and Latin *bugalú* drumming to classical themes by Borodin, Rachmaninoff, Greig, Bach and Chopin. Though valuable for posting advance warning of Emerson, Lake and Palmer, the album sounds uncannily like pre-set demonstrations on a cheap electronic keyboard. Baxter hated rock music and clearly felt that Robert Moog's synthesiser was no substitute for a roomful of violins.

Martin Denny's *Exotic Moog* album was inspired by Columbia Records' rock marketing of Walter Carlos's *Switched on Bach*. More vulgar than Baxter's *Moog Rock*, *Exotic Moog* oozes with grotesque charm. Opening with an ominously metallic new version of 'Quiet Village' (transformed, presumably, by the kind of changes that had turned quiet Hawaiian villages into American

tourist playgrounds), Denny revels in the Moog's strengths, aug-
menting its richly flatulent bass, pink noise spurts and petroleum
'gangsta rap' wail with fuzz guitar and bustling rock drums.
Clashes between the Moog's juiced viscidity and the cheesecloth
melancholy of themes such as 'Midnight Cowboy', 'Cast Your Fate
to the Wind' and 'A Taste of Honey' anticipate the methodology of
German, Italian and French soft-porn filmmakers of the seventies.

Arthur Lyman's response to the uprising of the counterculture
was to record Bob Dylan's 'Blowin' in the Wind' and Pete Seeger's
'Where Have All the Flowers Gone'. Recorded in the 'acoustically
near-perfect Aluminium Dome on the beautiful grounds of Conrad
Hilton's fabulous Hawaiian Village Hotel in Honolulu, where the
Arthur Lyman Group was appearing in the Shell Bar', Seeger's
pacifist message was rendered Pacific by being surrounded by
'Kamakani Kailio Aloha' and 'Hawaii Tattoo', not to mention a
swinging 6/8 cocktail version of 'Waltzing Matilda', recorded for
obscure reasons as a tribute to the recently deceased Winston
Churchill. Lyman's arrangements were less quirky than Denny's,
though leanings towards the Modern Jazz Quartet and Dave
Brubeck, expressed through tentative counterpoint and a chamber-
jazz feel, gave the group the virtue of a consistently gentle sound.

This consistency allowed Lyman to cover extraordinarily
diverse music without compromising his tiki bar integrity. *The
Colourful Percussions of Arthur Lyman* album, A&R directed by
Sonny Bono, managed to cross the gulf dividing the Bobby
Timmons-Jon Hendricks soul-jazz anthem, 'Moanin'', and a familiar, soon-to-be-famous folk tune, '(The Wreck of the) John B'.
Blowin' in the Wind went one step further, interpreting composers
as diverse as Bob Dylan, Darius Milhaud, Aaron Copland, Herbie
Hancock, Porter Waggoner and Eden Ahbez. The exotica genre
has been described as a precursor of so-called World Music or
World Beat. Mother of all synthesisers, exotica certainly anticipated the utopianism of a world without frontiers, a global
marketplace of glittering, miscegenating musics. At its most
anodyne, this search for a fantasy Esperanto sucked life out of the
world in order to feed its own deathly pallor.

12

apocalypse now

◆◆◆◆◆◆◆◆◆◆◆◆◆◆◆◆◆

The details of the place provide the timing, shape, resonance
and momentum of the associations; this is what makes them
echo. Through echoing, the *place* almost assumes the role of
psycho-analyst.

Peter Bishop, *The Myth of Shangri-La: Tibet, Travel Writing and
the Western Creation of Sacred Landscape*, 1989

A photograph: an overweight, puppy-faced young man,
dressed in a white T-shirt, hair outgrowing Beatle-styled, sits next
to a bearded, sunburned man in his late fifties, long centre-parted
hair, wearing a dark cardigan and smoking a pipe. They are leaning
against perforated baffleboard, in a recording studio. In all prob-
ability, the setting is the control room of Western Studios, Los
Angeles. The year is 1966. The work in progress is *Smile*, a Beach
Boys album that will never be released to the general public. The
young man is Brian Wilson; the older man is Eden Ahbez. Hands
in his lap, Wilson is open-mouthed, turned away from Ahbez, as
if distracted by a question directed to his good ear, listening to
two signals at once. On the deaf side of Wilson, Ahbez has that
sharp look about him that possesses people when they are really
listening hard to fine detail in music, head pointing down and
slightly cocked, eyes looking up and through. Had these two
aesthetic adventurers been talking, just a few moments before the
shutter clicked? Had Wilson been learning from Ahbez's exotic

sound paintings, recorded on *Eden's Island* in 1960? Were they discussing music, vegetarianism, world religions or the ups and downs of surf... or maybe exchanging their views of nature, listening to Brian's alchemical *Elements Suite*?

'*The Elements*,' explains Brad Elliot in his investigative discography of the Beach Boys, 'was a four-part suite of music representing the earth, air, water and fire. *Air* was a piano instrumental, according to Brian. The water section was called *I Love to Say Dada*, after the "da-da" vocals it featured. The fire section was titled *Mrs. O' Leary's Cow*, a reference to the great Chicago fire of 1871.'

At the suggestion of Beach Boy Al Jardine, the first song Brian Wilson ever considered recording was '(The Wreck of the) John B'. Also known as 'Sloop John B', this Caribbean song from the twenties was a hit for the Kingston Trio, a pop-folk trio whose American popularity embraced fashionable calypso-style material and anticipated the sixties folk boom. Dick Dale had also recorded a surf version. In his autobiography, *Wouldn't It Be Nice*, Brian Wilson remembers that the first incarnation of the Beach Boys, know as the Pendletons, failed to impress with 'Sloop John B' at their first record label audition. 'Unfortunately, our straightforward rendition of the traditional folk song did not elicit a positive response,' he wrote. The proprietors of Deck and X Records on LA's Melrose Avenue wanted to hear something new. What they got was 'Surfin''. Later, of course, Wilson returned to 'Sloop John B', creating an arrangement that went far beyond pop music conventions.

Awkwardly placed (and out of place) on *Pet Sounds*, 'Sloop John B' is two tracks: the turgid, irritating song that hit number 3 in the US *Billboard* charts in 1966 and the cascading tumult of sound – a sumptuous balance of delicacy and power, light and shade, pause and motion, high chimes and low brass – that can be heard on *Stack O' Tracks*, the album of Beach Boys backing tracks, stripped of their vocals.

'I listened to a lot of orchestral music,' Brian Wilson told me in 1986. 'I learned a lot of tricks too. Nelson Riddle taught me a lot about arranging.' Wilson had also come into direct contact with Les Baxter. Brad Elliot's research in *Surf's Up: The Beach*

Boys on Record, 1961–1981 unearths the connection. A number of songs – 'Muscle Beach Party', 'Muscle Bustle', 'My First Love', 'Runnin' Wild' and 'Surfer's Holiday' – had been written and produced by Gary Usher, Roger Christian and Brian Wilson for AIP's *Muscle Beach Party*, then turned over to Les Baxter.

'Since we had written the songs,' Usher told Elliot, 'we were concerned the tracks be cut right. We also supplied the background vocals.' Later, Dick Dale overdubbed guitar; then finally, lead vocals were added.

● nature boy

'Being allowed to listen to the Beach Boys (Acid rock was off limits),' Leslie Baxter Eaton wrote in a homage to her father in the sleeve notes to *The Exotic Moods of Les Baxter*. Les Baxter fan Skip Heller hears Baxter in Brian Wilson. Check out 'Diamond Head' and *Pet Sounds*, advises Skip. Wilson's vocal arrangements have their origins in the close harmony of doo-wop groups and the Four Freshmen, but sources for his instrumental arrangements remain unexplored. Improbably, they appeared to have emerged, fully formed, from the imagination of an inexperienced teenager whose main learning tool was his record collection. Since his father, Murry Wilson, was a frustrated easy-listening composer, it seems safe to assume that the Wilson household would have been well-stocked with Les Baxter records, racked up alongside the Frank Sinatras, the Phil Spectors, the Rosemary Clooneys. After all, Baxter, the Beach Boys and Murry Wilson were all signed to Capitol Records in Los Angeles, though *The Many Moods of Murry Wilson*, released in 1967, was a humiliatingly unsuccessful venture.

Released on the Beach Boys' *Friends* album in 1968, 'Diamond Head' is co-credited to Brian Wilson, though in his autobiography he claims that only two songs on *Friends* are his: a slacker existen-tialist's bossa nova for the late sixties, 'Busy Doin' Nothin'' and the wordlessly vocalised 'Passing By'. Besides, 'Diamond Head', named after a crater to the east of Waikiki Beach on Honolulu, is a peculiarly disjointed instrumental for Hawaiian guitar, ukulele and *Pet Sounds* water jug percussion. Co-credited to session bassist

Lyle Ritz, it was probably a vague idea, jammed in the studio and credited to the musicians hired for the session. With added surf sounds, 'Wipe Out' style crackle, birdsong effects and an experimental approach to slide guitar, the track sounds like a less virtuoso version of one of Speedy West's Polynesian tone poems, crossed with Arthur Lyman's studio Hawaiiana and Martin Denny's sound effects.

With his contributions to *Friends*, Wilson gave the impression of a man aiming for a level mood of mystical calm, as ambiguous in its maybe-profound, maybe-dumb aura as Peter Sellers in *Being There*. Although we may never know their intended conclusion, fragments from the abandoned *Smile* album suggest that Wilson began pursuing musical expressions of this plateau state immediately after *Pet Sounds*. 'Do You Like Worms' (also known as 'Do You Dig Worms'), recorded for *Smile* but never finished, overlaid an echoing music box harpsichord with intimately blissful, incomprehensible Hawaiian chants written by Van Dyke Parks: 'Wahhla loo lay, wahhlaloola, kee nee wakapoola'. Despite being sung by Mike Love, they sound like magic spells, sung to the accompaniment of breaking surf on a beach, a charm to lure mermaids out of the ocean into the arms of men. In 1986, I asked Wilson about the balance of power between sound and lyrics. 'The sound and the words both were important,' he said, his voice somehow flat and agitated at the same time. 'They're both important.' Had he ever considered writing an album of instrumentals, or wordless vocal tunes? Were words essential to his creative process? 'Words,' he replied, sounding impatient, losing focus, slipping away from me. 'Always vocal, yes.' Did he regret leaving these songs unfinished and unreleased? 'No, not really,' he answered, 'because they were all kinda contrived. They were contrived with no soul.'

At the beginning of the sixties, Brian Wilson was writing ecstatically romantic songs in celebration of heterosexual desire and homoerotic gang displays. 'We'll get the roughest and the toughest initiation we can find', written by Brian Wilson and Mike Love for 'Our Car Club', might be lines sung in Kenneth Anger's *Kustom Kar Kommandos*. This unfinished short film was described by Anger as 'an oneiric vision of a contemporary American (and specifically Californian) teenage phenomenon, the world of the hot rod and customised car'.

In fact, Anger used 'Dream Lover' by the Paris Sisters. He envisaged the cars as 'an eye-magnet of nacreous color and gleaming curvi-linear surfaces' while the customisers would be presented as 'shadowy, mysterious personages (priests or witch doctors)'. In his biography of Anger, Bill Landis quotes from an interview with *Spider* magazine. 'The cars,' said Anger, 'particularly the drag races – what they call the rail jobs – not only are obviously power symbols, terribly phallic and all this, but they're also an involvement in a controlled ordeal, in a controlled death-tempting ritual.' In a camp musical, ideally directed by Anger, we can imagine the Rommell-inspired attack battalions of Charles Manson and the Family singing the 'Our Car Club' lyrics in chorus, like *Seven Brides for Seven Brothers*, as they hurtle over the dirt fire roads of their helter-skelter escape route, heading for Death Valley in their customised dune-buggies, Manson firing Crowleyan magic at pursuing helicopters.

By 1966, Brian Wilson had moved from surf, cars and beauty queens to a less specific absorption in sensation, the magic of nonsense, the power of the elemental. Soulful or not, the *Smile* songs traced surfing's evolution from pagan simplicity and physicality through to a remote, introverted beatnik mysticism. The Hollywood pioneer of this latter lifestyle was Eden Ahbez. Born in Depression-era Brooklyn, Ahbez grew up in Kansas, where he learned to play piano. In 1943, he moved to California, where he changed his name from Alexander Aberle to Eden Ahbez. He and his wife, Anna Jacobsen, lived in the open air, riding bicycles, eating fruits, nuts and vegetables, practising yoga, subsisting on $3 a week. Looking like a time-out-of-joint Haight-Ashbury hippie in his jeans and bare feet, long hair and beard, Ahbez also played wooden flutes and composed songs. 'They were surprisingly comfortable in pre-70s Hollywood,' wrote Domenic Priore in his sleeve notes to *Eden's Island*. 'Once stopped by an officer for his esoteric appearance, Eden calmly explained "I look crazy, but I'm not. And the funny thing is that other people don't look crazy but they are." The cop thought it over and proclaimed "You know bud, you're right. If anyone gives you any trouble, just let me know." '

Then in 1948, Ahbez left one of his songs – 'Nature Boy' – at the Million Dollar Theatre where Nat 'King' Cole was singing. Ahbez left without leaving a contact number. When Cole decided to use the song, Ahbez had to be traced. 'Word was put out through Hollywood to find Eden,' wrote Priore, 'who had a street reputation in town as "the Hermit" or "the Yogi". When they finally found Ahbez, he was living beneath the first "L" in the HOLLYWOOD sign, spending nights in a sleeping bag and living off fruits, nuts and berries.'

In that same year, 'Nature Boy' turned out to be a huge hit for Nat 'King' Cole. Suddenly, Ahbez leaped from his $3-a-day existence to an annual royalty cheque of $30,000. Despite the sudden income, he refused to change his wandering lifestyle. 'In, fact,' wrote Priore, 'Eden may have been inspired to write "Nature Boy" on one of eight treks (by foot) across the United States. Ahbez was no poser. The strict vegetarian most often slept out-doors, whittling various sizes of wooden flutes and holding them up to the wind for audio pleasures.'

Ahbez began to release his own material, recording a 'Nature Boy Suite' for Olympic Records in 1955, singing on novelty rock'n'roll 45s such as 'Surfer John' by Nature Boy and Friends, even giving songs to Anita Ekberg. Then in 1960, Ahbez recorded *Eden's Island*, an album of exotic songs, recitations and atmos-pheric instrumentals. Released on Bob Keane's Del-Fi Records, one of the spiritual homes of surfing records, *Eden's Island* was recorded in one day with four jazz musicians: pianist Paul Moer, vibraphonist Larry Bunker, bassist Jimmie Bond, drummer Frank Butler. A female chorus added guardian seraphim noises and the architect of the project, Eden Ahbez, sang, rapped, recited poetry and played wooden flute.

'Martin Denny was real big at the time,' Bob Keane told Priore. 'He had all that – parrots in the background, and the birds and the tropical stuff – so I felt that *Eden's Island* would be a great album, because it was going along those lines. It was a suite to him. You kind of got the feeling like maybe he wanted to be a philosopher or something, but actually his lyrics were not philosophical. He was trying to paint pictures with his music, I think, which he did pretty well.'

Perhaps because of the quality of the musicians, or Ahbez's integrity, or even his experience of living a life relatively free from social conformism, *Eden's Island* is more affecting than the transparently commercial exotica of Denny or Lyman. 'Full Moon', a kind of *Astral Weeks* for the cocktail generation, is a good example of what Bob Keane pinpoints as picture painting. Very similar to Les Baxter's 'Sunken City', released the same year, 'Full Moon' rolls in a slow mist of expectant rising melodies and lulling resolutions. Frogs croak over the shimmer of Larry Bunker's vibraphone chords, marimba pulsations, the hiss of cymbals, the throb of double bass; Ahbez speaks his unashamedly naïve lyrics with conversational conviction, like a storyteller sitting in the glow of a driftwood fire.

'To live in an old shack by the sea,' he reads, 'and breathe the sweet salt air. To live with the dawn and the dusk, the new moon and the full moon, the tide, the wind, and the rain. To surf and comb the beach and gather seashells and driftwood, and know the thrill of loneliness, and lose all sense of time, and be free. To hike over the island to the village and visit the marketplace, and enjoy the music and the food and the people. And do a little trading and see the great ships come and go and man, have me a ball. And in the evening, when the sky is on fire, heaven and earth become a great open cathedral where all men are brothers, where all things are bound by law and crowned with love. Poor, alone and happy, I walk by the surf and make a fire on the beach, and as darkness covers the face of the deep, lie down in the wild grass and dream the dream that the dreamers dream. I am the wind, the sea, the evening star. I am everyone, anyone, no one.'

This urge to live as a voluntary Robinson Crusoe, or Thoreau at Walden Pond, shared the spirit of Colin McPhee's escapist fantasies: 'I once said all I asked of life was . . . the sociability of the village, a hut, and some savoury haunch broiling over the coals.' Most remarkable of all on *Eden's Island* is the final track, 'La Mar'. Slow and reflective, the piece begins with a stately, rather melancholy theme, played on French horn, piano, triangle and a muted drum, its soft, rounded attack identical to the water jug sound used by Brian Wilson on *Pet Sounds* five years later, then on 'Diamond Head', three years after that. Ahbez reads his story, a fantasy about seeing God during a shipwreck, and as he pauses, the drummer improvises a free duet with Ahbez's wooden flute (this short free passage created only two years after Ornette Coleman's debut recording), the storm image rounded off by a sound-effects disc of sea, wind and seagulls.

Having written an oddity in the canon of supper-club standards, an exotic, animistic song recorded by George Benson, Frank Sinatra, the Modern Jazz Quartet and John Coltrane among many others, Eden Ahbez proved the efficacy of his unfettered lifestyle by surviving to the age of eighty-six, living as a semi-recluse in Desert Hot Springs. Even then, it took a car accident, appropriately in Sky Valley, California, to finish him off.

● magic words

> The Symbolists gave [Gauguin] a farewell banquet at the Café Voltaire on 23 March, at which Mallarmé presided, proposing a toast in which he declared his admiration for Gauguin's search 'for renewal in distant lands and deep down into his own soul'. There were poems and more toasts, and further speeches and more toasts, and a recitation of parts of Mallarmé's translation of Poe's *The Raven* and more toasts.
>
> David Sweetman, *Paul Gauguin: A Complete Life*, 1995

In the sleeve notes of Les Baxter's 1970 soundtrack for Gordon Hessler's American International film, *Cry of the Banshee*, Baxter archly reported that one passage in the music had been reported by friends 'to cause an apparition to materialize. They thought that I, as the composer, should be warned of this. I had no idea, in my own writing, that such a thing was taking place, although every composer knows that sometimes when he is writing he will write things he doesn't remember, as if they come from an "outside" source.

'Whatever caused this, some said that during this particular passage they thought they saw Satan materialize – others were not sure just who the spiritual image was, but I feel I must warn those

who might have a fear of the supernatural of the possibility of
such an occurrence.'

In California, magic was in the air. Eden Ahbez, the spiritual
traveller, was in the vanguard of a trend towards the mystical, the
solitary traveller, the occult, the weird and the plain nasty. In San
Francisco there was Anton Szandor LaVey, self-styled High Priest
of Satan. A teenage runaway who joined the circus, LaVey played
the *William Tell Overture* on the calliope, then progressed to
Hammond Organ in carnie and grindhouse shows. In 1948, he
claimed to have played 'Slow Boat to China' for Marilyn Monroe
as she stripped at the Mayan Theatre in Los Angeles. LaVey also
played piano in the early fifties at a club called *Lost Weekend*,
presumably in homage to Billy Wilder's film portrayal of
alcoholism.

'Devil worship . . . was an excuse for exhibitionistic behaviour
and kinky sex,' concludes Bill Landis in *Anger*. Like exotica, and
exotic in its own way, occultism punched holes in the social fabric,
conjuring a parallel world, a self-contained externalisation of
fantasy. 'His music, his mannequins, his writings,' wrote Lawrence
Wright in a *Rolling Stone* study of Anton LaVey, 'the "total
environments" he attempts to create, his taste in just about everything, are reflections of this satanic pursuit of making his own
world.'

> I have just spoken of that morbid condition of the auditory nerve
> which rendered all music intolerable to the sufferer, with the excep-
> tion of certain effects of stringed instruments. It was, perhaps, the
> narrow limits to which he thus confined himself upon the guitar,
> which gave birth, in great measure, to the fantastic character of his
> performances.
>
> Edgar Allan Poe, *The Fall of the House of Usher*

Les Baxter's *Cry of the Banshee* soundtrack, along with his scores
for the AIP adaptations of Edgar Allen Poe (*The Pit and the
Pendulum, The Raven, Tales of Terror* and *House of Usher*),
the 1970 television special, *The Edgar Allan Poe Suite*, and the
H.P. Lovecraft adaptation, *The Dunwich Horror*, tapped into this
fascination with witchcraft, warlocks, apparitions, hauntings and

the occult. Starring Vincent Price and mostly written by novelist and screenwriter Richard Matheson, author of the chilling trapped-in-a-house-by-vampires novel, *I Am Legend*, the series elaborated Poe's claustrophobic minimalism, inflating the stories into camp narratives with a creepy psychological undertow.

'*Cry of the Banshee* is a veritable festival of gore and ghoulies, with copious amounts of blood-letting, burning and torturing,' wrote Tony Thomas for his sleeve notes to the vinyl release of Baxter's concert suite based on this score. 'Through it all Baxter's music pulsates, punctuates and sizzles, underlining the weird, frightening and occasionally romantic visuals. The Baxter score is, in fact, a textbook example of this particular kind – the kind in which the music is a greatly important factor in manipulating the sensibilities of the viewer ... his penchant for sound colors finds enormous opportunity in *Banshee* and other classic horror stories.'

Baxter confirmed his enjoyment of this freedom in *Soundtrack!* 'But horror films, in actual fact,' he said, 'present far *less* restrictions to a composer because of the extreme range or orchestral color at your disposal. The hardest films to score are those like *Born Again* where nobody turns into a monster or develops X-ray vision, where there are no ghostly houses sinking into the swamp.' But in his concert suites, Baxter was pulled away from exotic oddities, lured into symphonic pastiches by an aching desire for respectability, a faint hope for recognition as a 'serious' composer.

By the early eighties Les Baxter had converted, or rationalised, what some might consider a career decline into something positive, claiming that the lack of film work allowed him more time for serious composing. This serious thing had always been implicit, if not overt. 'Dad's secret dream, to see his symphony played at the Hollywood Bowl by the L.A. Philharmonic – conducted by Leonard Pennario,' revealed Leslie Eaton, his daughter, in her notes to *The Exotic Moods* compilation.

Despite the kitsch, Baxter was an ardent experimentalist, so long as the experiment fitted a commercial brief. In 1972, for example, his swampy score for another Ray Milland vehicle, *Frogs*, combined electronically treated frog vocalisations with his

own synthesiser playing. Baxter was proud of the fact that the
score was created by just him and the frogs, though doubtless this
concealed the stark reality of a rock-bottom budget. Important
though films such as *Frogs* may be in the archives of alternative
visions (or trash, depending on your point of view), they are a
poor way of establishing credentials in the worlds of music or
cinema. 'Fortunately, Les was enough of a name to always be able
to get a record deal,' wrote Skip Heller in his notes to Baxter's
Que Mango! 'As time marched on, the budgets got smaller –
which I am very sure Les noticed. I am no less certain his pride
suffered a bit for it, too. The glory days of Yma Sumac, the
Capitol Tower and his souped-up '57 T-Bird were over. Yes, he
still lived in Beverley Hills but he was no longer listed on the
Maps To The Movie Stars' Homes.'

Jealous of the superior quality of attention (scant though it
was), given to artists who starved for their integrity, Baxter lashed
out. 'I do feel that many so-called concert composers would dearly
like to pick up the revenue from films,' he told David Kraft and
Ronald Bohn for *Soundtrack!*, 'but in truth their avant-garde
music is totally unacceptable in *any* field: unlistenable, evasive,
unpalatable.'

● meshes

I believe that it is not altogether inappropriate to consider that the
peculiar and isolated position of the artist in Occidental culture might
arise from the fact that he, alone among professionals, does not –
by definition – accept certain beliefs which have so long been the
premises of Occidental thought.

Maya Deren, *Divine Horsemen: The Voodoo Gods of Haiti*, 1953

Living in a parallel universe to Baxter, composing exotic music
for film, theatre and ballet, was Teiji Ito. Unpalatable as they may
have been to Baxter and his audience, serious American exoticists
such as Henry Cowell, Alan Hovhaness, John Cage, Lou Harrison,
Ruth Crawford Seeger, Harry Partch, Moondog, Richard Max-
field, Steve Reich, Terry Riley, La Monte Young, Tony Conrad, Sun

Ra and Colin McPhee have become progressively better known as their innovations are seen to mirror changes in society at the end of the century.

The early works of composer, instrument inventor and theorist Harry Partch, for example, have been described by Danlee Mitchell as 'masterpieces of Americana, employing the language in a natural style uninfluenced by European traditions' (sleeve notes to *The World of Harry Partch*). Through Partch's search for integrated theatre, this Americana was enriched by more remote sources. 'The work that I have been doing these many years,' stated Partch, 'parallels much in the attitudes and actions of primitive man. He found sound-magic in the common materials around him. He then proceeded to make the vehicle, the instrument, as visually beautiful as he could. Finally, he involved the sound magic and the visual beauty in his everyday words and experiences, his ritual and drama, in order to lend greater meaning to his life. This is my trinity: sound-magic, visual beauty, experience-ritual.'

Partch found evidence of what he called Corporeal, tactile art, close to hand. 'Present-day Cantonese music-theatre,' he wrote in *Genesis of a Music*, 'which one can hear in San Francisco and New York if he can succeed in filtering the continuous percussion from his sense, is certainly a far cry from the classic Chinese type, yet even here there is frequent and illuminating evidence that the audience understands the words, despite the percussion and the tiresome cracking of peanut shells.' Partch claimed that he had been drawn, 'unconsciously and intuitively', to primitivism, 'in order to preserve my inner health – as a kind of spiritual restorative in the face of musical establishments clinging to habitual ways and philosophies'.

Although Teiji Ito's approach paralleled Partch's notion of primitivist drama, Ito remains an obscure character from the outer margins of synaesthetic, crosscultural arts. Born in Tokyo in 1935, he came from a Japanese family that worked in music and theatre, their combined work a heady mix of the exotic and phantasmagoric. Yuji Ito, his father, was a musician who became a costumier and set designer, working on films such as *The Wizard of Oz*. After the family had moved to New York City in 1941, his mother performed Japanese and Korean dances at the Museum of Natural

History, accompanied by the drumming of Teiji. 'I prefer to compose in reference to visible action or image,' Teiji said in 1953. 'When you write music this way – for the invisible part of something visible – you are creating a third effect . . . In a way it makes it possible for me to participate in the creation of something which is more than music, or more than music alone could achieve. It may be partly because I am Japanese and because this is the way oriental music functions. It is almost always part of a total in which all the other arts play a part.'

According to the sleeve notes of his first CD of compositions, *Meshes: Music for Films and Theatre* (released 1997), Ito studied clarinet and guitar, 'but quickly became interested in the music of other cultures, especially the percussion music of Asia, Africa and the Caribbean; in 1955 he studied with a master drummer in Haiti. His keen awareness of jazz, blues and flamenco infused his later music with a spontaneous, improvisational quality, and his knowledge of Buddhism, *vodun* and Native American beliefs added a mystical element. This eclecticism, along with his extended instrumental techniques and a kind of intentional 'neo-primitivism', anticipated many tendencies which have since become common in much contemporary music.'

In 1971, for example, he composed music for Jerome Robbins's ballet, *Watermill*. Premiered at the New York State Theatre in 1972, the ballet was based on lunar, calendar, seasonal and historical cycles. For its sources, it drew on Chinese, Japanese, Tibetan, African and Native American ceremonies. 'Some of the sounds are taken from nature very specifically,' wrote musician Mara Purl in a repertoire note. 'In the summer section, the little whistles represent crickets or cicadas, and are used in the Kabuki theatre to suggest just such a sound. I've seen audience members actually get hot during the summer section, and hearing those warm summer sounds is a part of what they feel. In the winter section, while Genji [Ito, Teiji's brother] is playing *shakuhachi* and I am singing, the others are making three distinct sounds – a sharp crack, a crisp bell, and a dull thud on the drum. These sounds are: a bamboo branch full of snow which finally cracks under the weight; the falling of the branch; the landing of the branch in snow.'

Teiji's *Axis Mundi* was recorded in the year of his death in 1982. According to Bebe Barron, interviewed in *Incredibly Strange Music*, Ito 'died in Haiti under very mysterious circumstances. Nobody knows what exactly happened, but he went swimming in a heavily voodoo-dominated area and then came out and died. He was only 47 years old.' *Axis Mundi* was made for Christopher Hampton's theatre piece, *Savages*. Composed of similar sound sources – flutters of dry gulch percussion, the unearthly howl of a bullroarer, trance drumming, the spirit wail of a flute – the piece evolves with remarkable coherence despite the looseness of its form.

● meditation on violence

'When the anthropologist arrives, the gods depart.' So declares, I am told, a Haitian proverb. Maya Deren, on the other hand, was an artist: therein, the secret of her ability to recognize 'facts of the mind' when presented through the 'fictions' of a mythology.

Joseph Campbell, introduction to Maya Deren's *Divine Horsemen*

As Clive Bell observed in *The Wire* magazine, *Axis Mundi* derives inspiration from 'shamanistic traditions of music without hysteria or embarrassment'. At the age of fifteen Teiji Ito met the Greenwich Village-based filmmaker (as well as priestess and student of *vodun*) Maya Deren. One of the most significant proselytisers and exponents of American underground film, Deren shot *Meshes of the Afternoon* over a two-and-a-half-week period in Los Angeles in 1942, collaborating with her new husband, Alexander Hammid. *Meshes* was originally released in a silent version, but in 1952 Maya Deren asked Teiji Ito to record music for *The Very Eye of Night*, her last completed film. Ito claimed that Deren was unaware that he was a musician; her decision was based on intuition. His music, a hypnotic, florescent, Balinese-influenced piece, overdubbed by Ito on flute, clarinet, Balinese *saron* metallophone, wooden xylophone and hand drums, was recorded by Louis and Bebe Barron, creators of the all-electronic soundtrack to MGM's 1956 film, *Forbidden Planet*.

Interviewed by Andrea Juno and V. Vale in 1989, three weeks after the death of Louis Barron, Bebe Barron recalled a voodoo ceremony, complete with fermenting tree-branch liqueur, staged by Maya Deren during Barron's pregnancy. 'There were all these primitive masks, drums and ritual objects everywhere, and led by Maya, everyone was swaying and doing this Haitian voodoo chanting and I started giving birth right on the spot, early!'

After nine years of living together, Deren and Ito married. Again, at her request, he added music to *Meshes of the Afternoon*, a score that lures the delicate, spiderweb formalism of classical guitar into the eerie spirit world of Japanese *gagaku* and Noh theatre. Ritualistic and dreamlike, Deren's films sought to place the humans within them, 'not as the source of the dramatic action,' as she wrote, 'but as a somewhat depersonalised element in a dramatic whole'. Her other films included *Meditation on Violence*, made in 1948, a study of Chinese Wu Tang and Shaolin boxing and Shaolin sword, enacted by Ch'ao Li Chi. Prescient in its anticipation of exotic montages of the near-future, Deren's soundtrack combined a recording of Chinese flute with her own tapes of *vodun* drumming, documented in Haiti. She moves between dream and dynamic action in her filming, the boxer gliding in slow motion, soundtrack silent, then exploding into the quick violence of drums and fists, the paradox resolved by flute and drum together. In his survey of American underground cinema, *Visionary Film*, P. Adams Sitney judges the film a failure: '*Meditation on Violence*, from a theoretical point of view, is a film overloaded by its philosophical burden.' In her schematic notes for the film, Deren maps the trajectory, a parabolic arc determined by music. 'The ultimate of an extreme becomes its opposite,' she wrote. 'Here the ultimate violence is paralysis after which the REVERSAL.'

This fascination with apparent paradoxes set up by music working against, and with, movement, is evident from a taped conversation between Deren and Teiji Ito, a conversation that illuminates both her films and his music. 'I remember seeing the Balinese dancers,' she says, 'sometimes they'd be standing on one leg, absolutely still –' Teiji interrupts, 'And the music would be going very fast –' and Deren finishes his thought, '– lickety split.'

Maya Deren had been influenced by an exhibition of South Seas ritual objects, curated for the New York Museum of Modern Art by anthropologists Margaret Mead and Gregory Bateson. This fascination with ritual was eventually fulfilled in 1947 when she travelled to Haiti to film voodoo rituals and dances. In her story, leading up to a sudden death in 1951, there are some parallels with the problems encountered by Colin McPhee in Bali. Having engaged in a version of anthropology, her films began to suffer from the problem highlighted by P. Adams Sitney. The practice of filmmaking became illustrative of theory; meanwhile, she dutifully documented voodoo practices, conscious of her unorthodox intrusion into the heavily guarded domain of social science.

As for the film footage shot in Haiti, she wrestled with it, unsuccessfully, until her death. Eventually, Ito and his second wife, Cherel, edited the material into a documentary, *Divine Horsemen: The Living Gods of Haiti*. In her book, she admits to a noble defeat. Humbled by the power of what she sees, hears and feels, Deren the artist capitulates and accepts a role as recordist. Even then, she feels a contradiction in this role. 'I have come to believe,' she wrote, 'that if history were recorded by the vanquished rather than by the victors, it would illuminate the real, rather than the theoretical, means to power; for it is the defeated who know best which of the opposing tactics were irresistible.'

But the book exists to counter her misgivings, an extraordinary document that brings together poetic gifts, empathy, sensitivity to the mythopoetic resonance of the events unfolding before her, a filmmaker's eye for detail, a music lover's ear for the power of sound. 'I have seen the sweat stream from a *houngan*'s face and heard his voice grow hoarse,' she wrote, 'as he labored to make some contact with a spiritual identity which he might bring forward into the body of the person.'

● I walked with a zombie

There were no mountains in Egypt so tourists climbed the Pyramids.

(Edmund Swinglehurst, *The Romantic Journey: The Story of Thomas Cook and Victorian Travel*, 1974)

Which was the advanced guard of exotica: highbrow or lowbrow? No matter how far anthropologists tried to distance themselves from the vulgarisation of their discoveries, the scholarly discipline of their observation and analysis of remote peoples simmered in the bowels of the melting pot, melting in popular imagination with *National Geographic*, highbrow orientalism, exotic art and fashion, exploitation films, travel books, tourist exploits, grindhouse pornography and natural-world television. Voodoo, for example, followed the same route as Jívaro shrunken heads: on the one hand, a serious study for Maya Deren and more conventional anthropologists; on the other hand, a terrific subject for horror films and cash-in exotica albums.

Naturally, Les Baxter was present at the feast with his soundtrack for a 1957 Boris Karloff vehicle called *Voodoo Island*, along with 'Voodoo Dreams', a zombie mambo recorded for the *Jungle Jazz* album, featuring the muscular saxophone of Plas Johnson. As for Martin Denny, he recorded 'Voodoo Love' – a wonderful slice of Sunset Strip hipsterism with no discernible connection to Haiti – for his 1967 *Exotic Love* album.

Compared with other musical portraits of *vodun*, Baxter and Denny seemed positively authentic. Don Tracy's *A Night with the Voodoo Family* was released in England in 1965 on Columbia's Studio 2 Stereo series. Produced by EMI A&R man Norman Newell, a familiar production credit from John Barry's early recordings, Tracy's voodoo was presented as the real thing by sleeve-note writer James Wynn: '*A Night with the Voodoo Family* is the brain child of Don Tracy – one of Britain's leading voices on the subject of Afro-Cuban music and also an authority on the voodoo cult. Years of study have enabled Don to present really authentic voodoo music, and this album is a fine representative cross-section of the sounds, melodies and rhythms associated with the cult.' The inclusion of Aaron Lerole's South African tune, 'Tom Hark', a huge international hit, alongside Xavier Cugat's 'Jungle Flute' and Ritchie Valens's Mexican-American hit, 'La Bamba', not to mention a choir of blue-eyed angels and some postwar march rhythms, did not reinforce this claim.

Issued by the Tops label, Robert Drasnin's *Voodoo* may have lacked the wall-of-drums sound of Tracy's concoction (played, no doubt, by the same London-based African percussionists who worked in Kenny Graham's Afro-Cubists in the early fifties or on John Barry's occasional Latin experiments in the late sixties) but the air-conditioned LA glide of Drasnin's version of a cult ceremony has proved more durable for students of kitsch. Drasnin's combination of alto flute, marimbas, bah-bah vocals, cocktail piano and Latin percussion is familiar enough, though he flies above the ordinary by smart deployment of Dorothy Remson's harp as an orientalist magic carpet motif.

A jazz saxophonist and soundtrack composer, Drasnin had contributed arrangements to Martin Denny's *Latin Village* album. For his reissue of the rare *Voodoo* album, Skip Heller's Damon Runyonesque sleeve notes describe the Drasnin trajectory. 'As Martin Denny's *Exotica* is sprinting up the charts,' he writes, 'every fly-by-night label is recording a Denny soundalike. Tops A&R chief Dave Pell – who is also the photographer for all the album covers – tells Drasnin to make a record in the Denny mold. I don't think Pell – who was and is a really great player and producer – thought twice about the session after it was finished. Exotica was not exactly something jazz musicians were striving for.'

As with all exotica, the piquancy (if it exists) lies in two conflicting responses: the immediate effect of the arrangements, which can be appreciated for their bizarre originality; followed by (or, in some cases, preceded by) a displaced reaction to the music's absurdity within a poisonous context. Loveable and detestable, arrogant and naïve, skilful and stupid, the nature of their kitsch leaves them saturated with levels of meaning that less controversial, more conventionally worthwhile musics often fail to deliver.

'*Kim* is a master work of imperialism,' Edward Said wrote in his 1987 introduction to Rudyard Kipling's novel. 'I mean this as an interpretation of a rich and absolutely fascinating, but nevertheless profoundly embarrassing novel.' Though Drasnin, Baxter, Denny, Lyman, Yma Sumac, Korla Pandit and Elizabeth Waldo were not the musical equivalent of Kipling, Said's ambivalence can be imposed on their compulsive, innovative, lush, ridiculous grotesqueries. Exotica is the art of ruins, the ruined world of enchantment laid waste in fervid imagination, the paradox of an imperial paradise liberated from colonial intervention, a Golden Age recreated through the lurid colours of a cocktail glass, illusory and remote zones of pleasure and peace dreamed after the bomb. Nothing is left, except for beaches, palm trees, tourist sites with their moss-covered monuments, shops stocked with native art made for tourists, beachcomber bars and an absurd perception of what may once have been.

'Ruins can be seen as fragments within the complex of absolute and imaginative time forming definite proof of past facts,' wrote architect Arata Isozaki in his essay, 'Ruins', 'facts broken and destroyed ... They have hidden effects on us, stimulating fantasies, visions and illusions. The elevated gardens of Babylon, Easter Island, the ancient Mayan pyramids, and the Celtic megalithic culture; the Pillars of Hercules, and the continent of Atlantis. It is no exaggeration to say that we live within endless series of such fantasies.'

And the dark-haired, voluptuous woman with the alluring smile, peering through a bamboo screen, or discovered waist deep in water, cupping her hands to give water to the voyeur who has surprised her, or lying in the midst of oriental instruments, a Japanese fish kite, a manly rifle, or simply posed in front of a Burmese gong, her bare breasts tantalisingly hidden just below the frame of the photograph?

'As a fantasy of erotic domination,' wrote Ali Behdad in *Belated Travellers*, 'the sexual relation with the native woman appeals to the colonizer's imagination because it combines erotic desire with the desire for mastery.' We can imagine the masculine den of the fifties, stocked with Denny, Baxter, Sinatra, Kenton, its lord and master, Mr Cool, flushed with the imminence of sexual freedom, dimly aware that the domination he craves may soon be under threat. 'We like our apartment,' wrote Hugh Hefner in 1953, setting the scene in his first *Playboy* editorial. 'We enjoy mixing up cocktails and an *hors d'oeuvre* or two, putting a little mood music on the phonograph and inviting in a female acquaintance for a quiet discussion on Picasso, Nietzsche, jazz, sex ... If we are able to give the American male a few extra laughs and a little diversion from the anxieties of the Atomic Age, we'll feel we've justified our existence.'

● ritual translations

> That was a time when words were like magic.
> The human mind had mysterious powers.
>
> Jerome Rothenberg, 'Magic Words' (after Nalungiaq), from *Shaking the Pumpkin*, 1972

'Starting with Georges Méliès, who was an illusionist by trade,' wrote Sheldon Renan in *An Introduction to the American Underground Film*, 'film has always had an attraction for those interested in magic and the supernatural. The reality that is created on film by the film maker is very real. To look at it is to believe it. On film one can do magical tricks and conjure apparitions that, if by chance they should exist, stay invisible in real life. Thus, film, the most science-and-technology-based of the arts, is the medium that gives most comfort to mystics and believers in magic.'

Artists were looking for new spiritual identities, using the influence of ritual and ceremony, as documented by travellers and anthropologists, to redirect their work. In 1966, for example, New York poet Jerome Rothenberg published *Ritual: A Book of Primitive Rites and Events*, a collection of performance pieces adapted from ethnographic documentation collected by Franz Boas, Bronislaw Malinowski, Alexandra David-Neel, Edward Sapir and others. There were echoes of the surrealists in this technique, their searches in ethnographic and psychoanalytic data for magic words and nonsense that might penetrate the unconscious and assault bourgeois conditioning. Rothenberg went on to compile two further collections of 'translations': *Technicians of the Sacred: A Range of Poetries from Africa, America, Asia and Oceania* and, in 1972, *Shaking the Pumpkin: Traditional Poetry of the Indian North Americas*, as well as *From a Shaman's Notebook*, an LP featuring readings by Rothenberg, David Antin, Jackson MacLow and Rochelle Owens of these 'primitive and archaic' texts, released on Moses Asch's Broadside label in 1967.

Links between artists and collectors of ethnographic music dated back to the eighteenth century. James Hewitt's opera, *Tammany*, with a libretto by Anne Julia Hatton, was premiered in New York in 1794. One song, 'Alknomook' (with the lengthy subtitle of 'The Death Song of the Cherokee Indians, An Original Air, brought from America by a gentleman long conversant with the Indian tribes and particularly with the Nation of the Cherokees. The words adapted to the Air by a Lady'), was originally published in London in 1784. The Lady in question was Anne Home Hunter, lyricist of Haydn's 'My Mother Bids Me Bind My Hair'.

Other women were more directly involved with the collection of Native American musics. Alice Cunningham-Fletcher, for example, lived among the Omaha Indians in 1881. In 1893 she published *Omaha Music*. 'The musical material Fletcher collected gave the American public its first glimpses of traditions and ceremonies never before witnessed by a white,' wrote Elsa Peterson in her essay, 'On the Trail of Red Sky Lady and Other Scholars'. Fletcher's studies inspired Frances Densmore, author of numerous papers on Native American music by the Teton Sioux, Chippewa, Pawnee, Cheyenne, Arapaho, Pueblo and others.

In *Nootka and Quileute Music*, published in 1939, Densmore quotes an earlier researcher, James G. Swan. A teacher and dispenser of medicines among the Makah Indians of Cape Flattery, Washington, Swan experienced the complex hybridisations of music already taking place in the nineteenth century. 'They are good imitators and readily learn the songs of the white men,' he wrote about the Makah in 1869, 'particularly the popular negro melodies. Some of their best tunes are a mixture of our popular airs with notes of their own, and of these they sing several bars, and while one is expecting to hear them finish as they began, they will suddenly change into a barbarous discord.'

Elsa Peterson documents the work of a succession of women whose ethnomusicology among Native Americans influenced modern composers. Born in 1875, Natalie Curtis was a concert pianist who collected songs from the Indians of Arizona, recording them with a portable phonograph at the turn of the century. One of her piano teachers was Ferruccio Busoni, an Italian composer who in his *Sketch for a New Esthetic of Music*, written in 1900, anticipated the stylistic mixtures, electronic instruments and microtonal and exotic scales that have become the common language of music at the end of the twentieth century. Although Busoni taught Curtis in Berlin, his travels to Helsingfors, Moscow and Boston led to another encounter with his pupil.

'After seven years of study in the Southwest,' Peterson wrote, 'she published *The Indians' Song* (1907), an annotated collection of some 200 songs, with considerable information about the accompanying customs, ceremonies, and religious beliefs. It was during the course of her work on this collection that her former teacher Busoni, now concertizing in the United States, learned of and began to share her interest in Native American music. Thus Curtis was responsible not only for her own publications and the pieces of pro-Indian legislation for which she lobbied, but also for Busoni's *Indian Fantasy* and other Indian inspired compositions.'

Even more intriguing is the story of Stella Prince Stocker, a nineteenth-century composer from Jacksonville, Illinois, who became a member of the Ojibway tribe. Given the name of O-mes-qua-wi-gi-shi-go-que, or Red Sky Lady (the subject of Peterson's search), Stocker not only lectured internationally on Indian music and legends, but also wrote two plays with music based on Indian melodies she had collected herself. Little more is known about her.

● the ascent to heaven

The Axis Mundi was the shamanic centre of the world, site of the cosmic tree from which the shaman made a drum, a painted drum that transformed into a flying horse as the shaman fell into trance and entered the invisible universe. 'By the fact that the shell of his drum is derived from the actual wood of the Cosmic Tree,' wrote Mircea Eliade in *Shamanism: Archaic Techniques of Ecstasy*, 'the shaman, through his drumming, is magically projected into the vicinity of the Tree; he is projected to the "Centre of the World," and thus can ascend to the sky.' After Maya Deren died, Teiji Ito became increasingly involved in a study of native American shamanism. His immersion in this alien world is apparent in works such as *Axis Mundi*, with its frame drumming, chant and bullroarer, and *Shaman*, a soundtrack used to accompany the early abstract films of Harry Smith.

Harry Smith was asked, by Arthur and Corinne Cantrill, why he started making films. 'Because an old woman with a bullroarer that had a snake drawn on it, swung it and I heard it,' he answered. Filmmaker, music anthologist, collector, occultist and crazy old coot, a resident of the Chelsea Hotel, Harry Smith claimed that his career of transforming the world began when his father, a cowboy theosophist, gave him a birthday present of a blacksmith's shop, ordering him to complete the alchemist's quest, transmute lead into gold. Smith was twelve years old. Born in Portland, Oregon, in 1923, raised in South Bellingham, near Seattle, he developed an early interest in the music and shamanism of Nootka, Kwakiutl and Lummi Indians. 'A photo in a 1941 issue of *The American Magazine*,' wrote Greil Marcus in *Invisible Republic*, 'shows a teenage Smith – with glasses, Pendleton shirt [the Beach Boys' favourite], and a look of calm concentration on his face as he sits before the feathered and horned elders of the Lummi tribe – "recording the drums and chants of the Lummis' annual pot-latch, or winter festival . . . Closest to the aboriginal form of any Indian dance in the U.S." '

In *Sing Out!* magazine, Smith told John Cohen that he was 'looking for exotic music. Exotic in relation to what was considered to be the world culture of high class music.' Despite that, he had a sardonic view of exoticism. 'I saw a picture of Dr. Boas taken in 1880 or 90,' he told Cohen. 'He looked exactly like a hippie – he had a pea coat and a beard. He was 24 or 25 when he first visited the Kwakuitl – I thought there might be a connection but there isn't – there always seems to be a recurrent romanticism regarding the Indians. It's due to the shortage of Buddhist headdresses. I've only occasionally run into any hippies who had much to say about the Indians. For a while they were naming cars after Indians – Pontiac, etc., and then there were Indian songs – Buell Kazee singing 'Little Mohee' . . . I'm pretty sure there have always been things like people dressing up in Indian clothes . . . I suppose that children dressed up like Saracens during the crusades, and when Genghis Khan was coming they all dressed up in Genghis Khan suits.'

Along with his interest in music, Harry Smith was a pioneer of American graphic film. Stills from his films look extraordinary. The earliest, made between 1939 and 1946, were hand painted or batiked directly onto celluloid. Later surrealist animations, shot between 1957 and 1962, were photographed from collages with titles such as 'The ascent to heaven on a dentist's chair', 'The descent from heaven in an elevator' and 'The skeleton juggling a baby in the central tableau of heaven'. Inspired by magick and music, they aimed at a synaesthesia of image and sound. Film *No. 4*, 'black and white abstractions of dots and grillworks made in a single night', began with a pan over a painting created to Dizzy Gillespie's recording of 'Manteca', a milestone of Cubop co-written by Gillespie and the great Cuban *conguero* Chano Pozo.

Pozo joined Dizzy Gillespie's band in 1947. 'Born Luciano Pozo y Gonzalez,' wrote John Storm Roberts, 'he was a member of the *abakwa* secret society, whose roots trace back to eastern Nigeria, and his singing and playing was strongly Afro-Cuban.' Machito's musical director, Mario Bauza, confirms this in Dizzy Gillespie's autobiography, *To Be Or Not To Bop*, written with Al Fraser. 'Chano had such a limited knowledge of our music,' Bauza told Fraser. 'He was really African, you know. He probably played when he was two and a half years old or something like that. All of the *Nañigo*, the *Santo*, the *Ararra*, all these different sects, the African things in Cuba, he knew, and he was well versed.'

Although 'Manteca' is two pieces stitched together, a climactic Afro-Cuban opening, smoothed out by Dizzy Gillespie's urbane jazz bridge, the tune was another example of African diasporic mysticism being absorbed into American popular music. Without knowing quite why, Smith may have responded to Pozo's magick, the complex legacy of African-Caribbean cult rhythms explored overtly thirty years later by salsa pianist Eddie Palmieri on his *Lucumi, Macumba, Voodoo* album.

'I had a really great illumination the first time I heard Dizzy Gillespie play,' Harry Smith told P. Adams Sitney. 'I had gone there very high, and I literally saw all kinds of color flashes. It was at that point that I realized music could be put to my films.'

According to Sitney, Smith then cut down his film *No. 2*, a batiked animation taking place 'either inside the sun or in Zurich, Switzerland', from its original length in order to synchronise it to Gillespie's 'Guacho Guaro' (the same Pozo-Gillespie collaboration recorded as 'Soul Sauce' by Cal Tjader).

Smith was acutely sensitive to music and sound, but he could be slapdash. The anthology of hand-painted films entitled *Early Abstractions*, now available on video with Teiji Ito's *Shaman* music, was distributed at one point with the Beatles' first album as its soundtrack; the Fugs also contributed music to one version, though this was destroyed during a fight between Smith and an audience member. 'It seems as if he wanted to obscure the monumentality of his achievement in painting and animating film,' wrote Sitney, 'by simply updating the soundtrack.' Another film, *No. 11*, also known as *Mirror Animations*, was synchronised to Thelonius Monk's 'Mysterioso'. According to Jack Sergeant's *Eyeball Head Poem: The Animated Worlds of Harry Smith*, Smith would show his film in clubs such as Jimbo's Bop City, 'where bebop jazz musicians would improvise to the projected images, "reading" the shifting colours and transforming shapes as music'.

Although his films were important in the development of American underground cinema, Smith is better known for the Folkways Records LPs that he compiled from his own record collection for Moses Asch. The three-volume, six-LP *Anthology of American Folk Music* (now reissued in CD form by Smithsonian Folkways, complete with interactive material about Smith himself) was released in 1953. It proved to be the catalyst for the American folk revival, which makes it one of the most important record sets of the century.

Among his deliberately decontextualised sequences of hillbilly tunes, blues and gospel singers, jug bands, Smith included one of the 'Indian songs' he spoke about: 'Indian War Whoop', by Floyd Ming and his Pep-Steppers. 'The effect of pre-Columbian America on contemporary music,' he wrote in his witty, eccentric notes to the anthology, 'has been chiefly to act as a catalyst between European and African musical elements. It is doubtful if this recording bears much real relation to Indian music; it is, rather, romanticism akin to that of "Western" movies.'

In *Invisible Republic*, Greil Marcus plots a direct line from the Folkways anthology to Bob Dylan's *Basement Tapes*. 'As Smith searched for the hillbilly classics and primitive blues made in the commercial half-light of the Jazz Age,' Marcus wrote, 'he found himself in the first years of his own childhood. He might have heard what people have always heard in strange music: the call of another life.'

Smith recorded material released as a triple-LP box entitled, somewhat misleadingly, *The Kiowa Peyote Meeting*. This latter release was typical of the man. The peyote songs, plus some lengthy narratives, were recorded by Smith during a visit to Anadarko, Oklahoma. His sleeve notes include some gems. 'I would like to make it clear that of the people I later worked with,' Smith wrote, 'none were met in the jail; the unfortunate victims of that place only provided the contacts. Also it would be only fair to say that while I was in Anadarko I was drinking heavily and it was only natural that some of the people I worked with also drank.'

At times, Smith claimed that his real father was Aleister Crowley, the English Magus. Perhaps it was this interest in Crowley that persuaded Smith to encourage Crowley disciple Kenneth Anger in the early stages of his filmmaking career. Whatever his motivations, he followed his own course through life. According to Bill Landis in *Anger*, 'Smith had a propensity for huge drug consumption: heroin, speed, acid, and, even in his sixties, smoking crack and huffing Liquid Paper with young apprentices. He cared not at all what people said about him – the more ominous the better – but, in general, everyone got along with him.'

That seems not quite the whole truth. In his biography of Allen Ginsberg, Barry Miles describes Smith coming to visit Ginsberg, hurting himself and staying a year. 'He took a perverse enjoyment in antagonizing Allen,' wrote Miles, 'who was once reduced to slapping him in frustration.' Bob Dylan dropped in, keen to meet this legendary archivist whose Folkways compilations of blues, folksongs and spirituals had given him most of his early material. Smith wouldn't get out of bed. Finally, Ginsberg's psychiatrist had to eject Smith, since his patient's blood pressure was threatening to shoot off the scale.

By the time he reached the end of his life, Harry Smith liked the idea that music could change the world. He didn't really like records, however. 'Any kind of popular trend is infinitely more wholesome than listening to old records,' he told John Cohen for *Sing Out!* magazine. 'It's more important that people know that some kind of pleasure can be derived from things that are around them – rather than to catalog more stuff – you can do that forever; and if people aren't going to have a reason to change, they're never going to change.' His final job before he died in 1991 was as shaman-in-residence at the Naropa Institute, Boulder, Colorado.

● towards the gleam of fires

The music came from the blind pig, heavy, thick, gummy like a quagmire; mud, the rich ancient soil of the Black-belt South with its climate, swamps, swarming with birds, snakes, bugs, wildflowers. Egypt of America, someone said.

Ishmael Reed, *Mumbo Jumbo*, 1988

One day, Brian Wilson showed up at Hal Blaine's house. He wanted Blaine to take his gold discs, just take them away, keep them. The past was another country; these framed golden discs were just so much lost luggage. Reluctantly, Blaine took some of them in. Better that than see them thrown in a ditch. After all, his cataclysmic drumming had contributed a whole lot to the Beach Boys sound: he, a veteran of Phil Spector sessions, along with Carole Kaye, Billy Strange, Glen Campbell, Julius Wechter (the same Wechter who took off to Hawaii to play vibraphone with Martin Denny), Barney Kessel, Leon Russell and all the others who concocted the Los Angeles voodoo for Spector and Wilson.

The ultimate in can-do session players, Blaine had played drums with everybody, on everything. The kind of 45s people describe as the greatest of all time were driven by the drum engine of Hal Blaine, making the biggest noise at the biggest moments. Like all drummers, Blaine was susceptible to the kind of skins/ bongo beat/let there be drums extravaganzas recorded by the likes of Gene Krupa, Sandy Nelson and Les Baxter. *Psychedelic Per-*

cussion was his version of Hollywood tribalism, recorded by Blaine with electric percussionist and vibraphonist Emil Richards, Paul Beaver (of Beaver and Krause) on electronic devices, Mike Lang on electronic keyboards and percussionist Gary Coleman. Even by psychedelic freak-out standards, *Psychedelic Percussion* was a sonic jungle, its acid-trip track titles – 'Flashes', 'Inner-Space', 'Love In' – illustrated by swooping electronic spurts, squeals and squirts, scrapers and cymbals, vibraphone, Japanese *sho*, Chinese gongs, Traumatonium, sub-bass canary, Tahitian *pooee lee* sticks, Klaxon horn, quarter-tone xylophone and Blaine's constant gravitation towards the Sunset Strip boogaloo, all of them slipping and sliding in a lake of echo. It was as if Martin Denny's band had dropped acid and fled into the primeval forest to beat bamboo.

Somewhere between Pharoah Sanders's *Tauhid*, the dark tunnel visions of Phil Spector and the percussive psychedelia of Hal Blaine, there was a night music, born out of the enclosed magic world of the recording studio. Mac Rebennack, better known as Dr. John, began his career in 1940 as a nine-month-old photo model for Ivory Soap detergent. Born in New Orleans, his early exposure to the music of Lightnin' Slim, T-Bone Walker, Professor Longhair and Fats Domino diverted him from electrical repairs to guitar. White, but moving in a black world, Rebennack worked his way into the fervid New Orleans R&B, rock'n'roll session scene. After being shot in the finger, he put aside blues guitar to take up keyboards, but with live work diminishing in New Orleans, temporarily flattened by the impact of Motown, Stax and Merseybeat, he moved to Los Angeles.

In LA, he was hired into Sonny & Cher's backing band on the recommendation of their New Orleans producer, Harold Battiste. It was in Harold Battiste's down time on a 1967 Sonny & Cher session at Gold Star studios, home of the Spector Wall of Sound, that Rebennack transformed, like the Loop Garou of legend who carried his head under his arm, into Dr. John, the Night Tripper. 'The original Dr. John claimed to be a West African prince,' wrote Jeff Hannusch in his notes to *The Dr. John Anthology*, 'and lived in New Orleans during the mid-1800s. He told fortunes, sold "gris-gris" potions, and held seances and voodoo ceremonies. Rebennack had long held a fascination for voodoo, especially after his sister gave him some books on Haitian voodoo she found at the antique store where she worked. Several musicians Rebennack hung with (particularly Jessie Hill) shared his interest and occasionally he'd visit Cracker Jack's drug store on South Rampart Street, which sold candles, love potions, good-luck floor wash, and incense.'

During the period of promoting his Dr. John persona to the rock press, Rebennack played up the voodoo, played down the R& B. 'I was afraid of voodoo, black magic,' he told Jacoba Atlas for *Melody Maker* in 1970, her transcription adding to the factionalis- ation, 'but when I got to the Temple of the Innocent Blood dey's all dese people groovin' around happy, no race differences, no hates. Dey wuz all one! And I could feel it all aroun' me. I say, dis is fo' me.'

Thick with percussion, the *Gris-Gris* sessions were created with a stellar group of New Orleans players: Jessie Hill, of 'Ooh Poo Pah Doo' fame, played tambourine; Ernest McLean, a guitarist who had been one of the cornerstones of the New Orleans sound, played mandolin; Harold Battiste played bass guitar and clarinet; drummer John Boudreaux had played with Art Neville and Professor Longhair. As for the backing vocalists, they were a cross-section of New Orleans R&B and deep soul, among them Shirley Goodman (of Shirley and Lee), Tami Lynn, Prince Ella Johnson and Jessie Hill.

The eerie descending melody of 'I Walk on Gilded Splinters', its whispers, snorts and threats, driven by Richard 'Didimus' Washington and Mo Pedido's mesmeric congas, made the tune something of a standard in post-psychedelic rock and pop. Rebe- nnack tried to persuade Washington and Pedido to solo on this track, but they refused. 'I got a little salty about it at first,' he told Jeff Hannusch, 'but that's the beauty about New Orleans musicians, they don't want to show off. But we had a lot of off-the- wall percussion things going on there.' In 1972, Johnny Jenkins recorded a boogie-soul version for his *Ton-Ton Macoute!* album. Somewhere between Captain Beefheart and the Allman Brothers, the track opened with a lengthy percussion jam; a few years later, this exotic intro became highly coveted by young DJs as one of the most obscure hip-hop breaks played in the South Bronx.

The most distinctive sound on *Gris-Gris* was a weird, sinuous, echoing horn, a breathy, buzzsaw oboe, vaguely Middle-Eastern but ultimately unidentifiable. In fact, the source of the sound was Plas Johnson, playing saxophones through what Rebennack called a 'condor box'. Having played with Johnny Otis, Etta James, Little Richard and Larry Williams, Johnny 'Guitar' Watson, Screamin' Jay Hawkins, the Coasters and Fats Domino, Johnson had become one of the leading session musicians in America. Although his late-fifties solo work for Capitol had leaned towards the big tenor sound of Lee Allan and Big Jay McNeely, Johnson had played 'The Pink Panther Theme' for Henry Mancini in 1966, contributed to the *Freak Out* of Frank Zappa's first Mothers of Invention album, thundered alongside Harold Battiste on Ike and Tina Turner's 'River Deep, Mountain High' and in 1958–9 soloed on tenor saxophone for Les Baxter's *African Jazz* and *Jungle Jazz* albums.

Despite its R&B pedigree, *Gris-Gris* became a psychedelic cult record, joining Santana's Latin-rock as a rare hippie excursion beyond blues, folk and Ravi Shankar. 'It was a mood thing,' Rebennack concluded with typical musicianly insouciance, 'that came out real nice.' But the catalysing effect of his Dr. John image was more special than that. 'The leader was obviously very much in charge, but his openness is such that you could imagine Miles Davis, Son House, Pablo Casals, or Segovia walking in and being able to find a place for themselves in what was going on,' Richard Williams observed in a 1970 *Melody Maker* man-on-the-spot report on Dr. John's *The Sun Moon & Herbs* London sessions. 'Truly, it was open music.'

With its strange timbres, its deep studio echo, its loose-limbed percussive clatter and throb, its ominous tales of charms and spells and nocturnal rituals, *Gris-Gris* conjured the secrets of African-American mythology and Louisiana magic, filtering them through phantasmagoric Hollywood and its technologies: old as the swamp, new as plastic, real and fake all at once.

● apocalypse now

> I tried to break the spell – the heavy, mute spell of the wilderness –
> that seemed to draw him to its pitiless breast by the awakening of
> forgotten and brutal instincts, by the memory of gratified and mon-
> strous passions. This alone, I was convinced, had driven him out to
> the edge of the forest, to the bush, towards the gleam of fires, the
> throb of drums, the drone of weird incantations; this alone had
> beguiled his unlawful soul beyond the bounds of permitted aspir-
> ations.
>
> Joseph Conrad, *Heart of Darkness*

Looking for the throb of drums and weird incantations, Francis
Ford Coppola allowed himself to be taken to a Grateful Dead
concert by promoter Bill Graham. The experience convinced him
to commission the Dead's drummers – Mickey Hart and Billy
Kreutzmann – to create a percussive underscore for his work-in-
progress, *Apocalypse Now*.

The Rhythm Devils, as they called themselves, assembled in
California in 1979 to record the percussive underscore. Along
with Hart and Kreutzmann there was Airto Moreira, Flora Purim,
Michael Hinton, Jim Loveless, Gregg Errico and Jordan Amar-
antha. They set up a labyrinth of percussion on the floor, threaded
with pathways so that they could move through the instruments.
'During the recording of the performance,' the album notes
explain, 'Coppola explained to the musicians that their task was
to conjure music not only relevant to Vietnam in the '60s, but
which also extends back to the first man at the origin of existence.
The essence of the film is the primal myth of the King being killed
and his assassin taking his place as the new King. The assignment
of the Rhythm Devils was to voyage upriver to the "Heart of
Darkness", and sound out the Apocalypse.'

They were asked to play 'the jungle river'. Not the jungle
river of Disneyland, the boat sprayed by elephants, menaced by
animatronic hippos, serenaded by Dennyesque parrots and
monkeys; their river was the Mekong, America's encounter with
the exotic, not as paradise but hell. Not soft vibraphone and
light Afro-Cuban percussion, but the yarling and moan of distant

wounded beasts, the resonance of the cave, the music of destruction, the atavistic terrors and fascinations of opposition and Otherness. The drumming is embedded in our fantasies anyway, so let it continue to signify the horror, the horror. 'The sound of the drums continued, without intermission, the whole day,' Herman Melville recorded in *Typee*, 'and falling continually upon my ear, caused me a sensation of horror which I am unable to describe.'

'All night they were disturbed by a lot of drumming in the villages,' wrote Conrad in an almost unreadably horrible little masterpiece of irony called 'An Outpost of Progress'. 'A deep, rapid roll near by would be followed by another far off – then all ceased. Soon short appeals would rattle out here and there, then all mingle together, increase, become vigorous and sustained, would spread out over the forest, roll through the night, unbroken and ceaseless, near and far, as if the whole land had been one immense drum booming out steadily an appeal to heaven. And through the deep and tremendous noise sudden yells that resembled snatches of song from a madhouse darted shrill and high in discordant jets of sound which seemed to rush far above the earth and drive all peace from under the stars.'

● short circuit

Near dark, carried on the bare back of a painted drum, I found myself sailing over blackened, smoking islands. Fires had been lit, and smoked for years until their oily haze cancelled the sun. Hovering for days, I watched the planes land and take off, some of them crashing into hillsides, erupting into fireballs that rolled down into the total darkness of the valleys. Strangely enough, tourists still came. They were fascinated by the apocalypse. Once they were sunburned. Now they clustered at night with soot-grimed faces, drinking *arak* spirit, eating contaminated fish served up on palm leaves in corrugated iron shacks, listening to apocalypse music, a short circuit, the globe in a circle, so exotic.

3

occidental/ oriental

case studies

13

outcasts of the islands

◆◆◆◆◆◆◆◆◆◆◆◆◆◆◆◆◆

the boo-yah t.r.i.b.e.

The day is 12 December 1989, and I find myself standing on a little suburban parking spot in Carson, Los Angeles. Balmy tranquillity hangs in the air like Valium fallout. Without warning, the peace is shattered by harsh alien sounds: RHHHUGGH, SMANG, GUHHHF, MROAGH, GHUA-GHUA-GHUA-GHUA-GHUA, PSHAANG, PSHA-PSHAANG, BUK-WANWANWANWAGA.

'King' Roscoe turns away from his labours on the bench press. Lines from Herman Melville's *Moby Dick* flash through my mind: 'I quaked to think of it. A peddler of heads too – perhaps the heads of his own brothers. He might take a fancy to mine – heavens! Look at that tomahawk!' And heavens! Look at those biceps! Were I to strap a couple of Vietnamese pigs to my upper arms, I would still rate as puny by comparison with the head of the Hit Squad, Va'a 'King' Roscoe Tufuga.

David Aveau Devoux, also trading under the very comprehensive nickname of E.K.A., or Every Known Attitude, is gentleman enough to allow me some self-esteem. Big guys don't worry us, he says, but guys of your build we stay away from if they make trouble. This is not as flattering as it seems, since within the Tombstone ethics of Los Angeles ganglands, it is the people who can't crush beer cans between two fingers or eat rusty nails who are most likely to pack a gun.

But as Sly Stone once sang, my only weapon is my pen. I had been forewarned about the Samoans of Carson by friends who had once had to play football against them, but what could be more restful than a day spent sheltered within the bosom of such an outwardly intimidating family?

Briefly, to explain: the Boo-Yaa T.r.i.b.e. were, and perhaps still are, a family group of Samoan rappers. The Hit Squad, engaged in their morning power lifts, were their outriders, their praetorian guard. For a short while, the Boo-Yaas were signed to Island Records; the association foundered, probably because their records failed to make a dent on the greater public awareness, though a better story was that the amount of high-class airline seatage required by this contingent of giants precluded a decent economic return on Island's investment.

Like the irritating full stops in their name, the Boo-Yah T.r.i.b.e. had a little too much going for them as a paper entity. Being a Samoan rap crew living in the heart of gangsta rap would be quite enough, but this extended family of brothers and cousins, some of them as awesomely enormous as sumo wrestlers, some of them ex-gang members with prison experience, had a story that overshadowed their music as it remorselessly unfolded.

The night before my morning in Carson, I had spoken with John O'Brian at the Sugar Shack, an exotic quasi-Polynesian bar that was serving as combined Boo-Yah launch pad and record company Bacchannal. O'Brian (a Boo-Yah producer, along with the more colourfully named Dust Brothers (the originals), Sugar Pop and Joe 'The Butcher' Nicolo) probably had sand kicked in his face before he met the Tribe. During the period when he was producing tracks on the crew's album, he gave them temporary custody of his keys. In the morning they would creep in to his apartment as he slept and clean up for him – a ferocious army locked in a silent Shake'n'Vac war on bohemian slovenliness.

This touching story returns to me as I stand in front of the open door of a garage, watching the Boo-Yah muscle engaged in their daily toning routine. Metallica thrash grinds out the sound-track as Roscoe, Gizmo and the identical Twins – John and Jake Tovio – pump huge weights in a steroid-free atmosphere of self-discipline. Iron echoes, metal on metal, pain and flesh, the bulge of veins; thunderous belches rip through the early afternoon silence of this drowsy outer sector of the LA sprawl.

Roscoe is taciturn, his grip like an alarm clock going off. He has just emerged from ten years in various jails, serving time for gang-related murder, and during that time he has become impressively 'yoked'. This means he has reinvented himself from humble beginnings as a mere human and is now closer, physically at least, to the stegosaurus. His attitude to his wasted years, as a youth spent in gang warfare, is as cast-iron as the perpetually malevolent mask of his face. 'Fuck that gangbanging shit,' he says. 'There's no future in that.'

What does anybody know about Samoans in Los Angeles, or Samoans in general, come to that? Virtually from the moment that Europeans came across these south-west Pacific islands in the eighteenth century, Samoa was strategic land, squabbled over and divided up successively by Germany, Britain, New Zealand and America, as well as being a spiritual battleground for contending Protestant and Catholic missionaries. Navigators Islands was the first name imposed by explorers, as if they existed purely for the convenience of ships. Robert Louis Stevenson, buried on Western Samoa in 1894, wrote: 'The handful of whites have everything; the natives walk in a foreign town.'

Stevenson took photographs of Samoan chiefs like Mataafa and Tamasese; these images, captured at the dawn of portable photography, portray men who seem carved out of granite. The Samoans may have been exploited but they were not passive, and while Stevenson and his family lived on the Islands there was civil warfare. Much later, Tom Wolfe portrayed Samoans as the ultimate urban nightmare in *Mau-Mauing the Flak Catchers*. In a dry run for his profoundly dubious 'ethnic terror' passages in *The Bonfire of the Vanities*, Wolfe wrote, 'You get the feeling that football players come from a whole other species of human, they're so big. Well, that will give you some idea of the Samoans, because they're bigger.'

'Boo Yah! That's the feedback when we go to a club,' says Paul 'Riddler' Devoux. 'Like "Boo-Yah!" Everyone looks at us like we killed someone. The way they look at us, it's like we're holding guns. But it's just us, just coming down to enjoy ourselves. Now, Boo-Yah is crack, but in our days when we were gangbanging, Boo-Yah was the sound of a shotgun.'

'Sawn-off shotgun going off,' cuts in Ted Devoux, 'and people just talking: "Last night, man, we went down the neighbourhood, took out the gang, Boo-Yah!" '

With their full contingent of rappers, musicians, bodyguards, soundmen and road crew, they stand in a long line in the parking lot behind the Sugar Shack. Perhaps twenty-strong, dramatised by the fading light of early evening, they could be waiting for direction from Sergio Leone, Akira Kurosawa or Ringo Lam. Queequegs of the smoggy urban plains, dressed to impress, they wear shiny boots big enough to be orthopaedic aids, skirts and aprons that give a sumo/samurai slant to the traditional Samoan *lava lava*, stud-encrusted dungarees with the bib turned down, long braided hair sprouting from a top hat like vines bursting through the roof, black shorts with razor creases, knee-high black socks, monkey boots, snaking ropes of pigtail, black bowler hats, weightlifting belts, leather gloves, customised dark glasses and tattooed necks and arms.

Tattooing is a Samoan custom, although less well known than other Polynesian examples, according to Robert Brain in *The Decorated Body*, 'because of the extreme reticence of those who practice tattooing and because the most elaborate markings are covered with the traditional loincloth.'

Ted 'Godfather' Devoux, the huge man who rules the Boo-Yah roost, was halfway through having an ambitious set of tattoos when the crew moved into a busy patch. Now he has to wait for things to calm down again before the torture can be resumed.

Torture, rather than calm, has shaped the status quo for Ted. Perhaps this is why he likes to listen to seventies soft-soul groups like the Temprees and the Escorts. Standing in the back yard of his auntie's house in Carson, he is leafing through a book of family photographs and reminiscing. In the middle of the yard a tangerine tree and a lemon tree hang with fruit. Over to one side, chicken is cooking on the barbecue and on the decks Brenda Holloway has just finished singing 'Every Little Bit Hurts'. Now Martha Reeves is singing 'My Baby Loves Me'. Ted is propped up against the bar, looming over a dustbin packed with beers, soda and Perrier, all submerged under iced water. Also in attendance is Sam

'Sambo' Niko, the crew's minder and Ted's partner in survival since childhood.

The Devoux family moved to Los Angeles in the fifties. 'My dad was in the navy, the army and the coastguard, and he got kicked out of all of them,' says Ted. 'Pops was a Hell's Angel. That's why everybody trips out, that he's a minister now, preaching the gospel.'

'He's still got his tattoos,' says Sam. 'He has a donkey right in the middle of his chest.'

'What he did is,' says Ted, 'when he was with the Hell's Angels, he moved up in rank through the Chapters. He went around knocking out all the leaders of the Chapters. He was into this thing where, if we go one on one, we fight, I win, you come with me. So there was at least six or eight of them and they called themselves the Jackasses.

'Back then they thought he was a Mexican. They called him different names like Coconut or Pancho. They really didn't know what he was, but I guess the thing of him being so crazy, he was down for anything, and they couldn't understand that. He was a hardhead that they loved. He rode a Harley and he was heavily into a lotta stuff. A lot into drugs and the Syndicate, but he just got tired of that stuff. They say that I took him to church when I was little. I was going to church with my auntie. One day I told him, when I was a little kid, to come with her, and the next you know, it changed his life.'

We look at photographs: Christmas in Tokyo Disneyland. A Los Angeles club. Wives and girlfriends, nieces and nephews. The invitation to a funeral. Ted in Japan with his cousin, Konishiki, the breathtakingly gigantic sumo wrestler also known as Sally. Another young Devoux brother, known as Rook, then wrestling in Japan on the sumo circuit. A newspaper clipping about death. A coffin. On the decks, Billy Paul has just finished 'Me and Mrs Jones' and now Lou Rawls is starting up with 'You'll Never Find Another Love Like Mine'.

When the brothers were growing up, their father and mother became Christians. 'Church was first and then us,' says Ted. 'It would get to the point where there was no food in the house and he was taking people from the church out to eat. I had to make a way for my brothers, to make it better for them. We didn't have much money, we had a lot of mouths to feed. We would go and rob houses, rob gas stations, strong-arm robbery, everything. Me and him used to do it just to feed my brothers and keep good clothes on them. Then we got heavily into the gang life. Man, here we go again, the gang fights. And the thing that I learned was that all the guys of our age, they had younger brothers. They were in and out of jail and the younger ones would follow. So I had to set an example and do something different 'cause I didn't want that to happen to my brothers. I used to get so stressed out. I tried to commit suicide. Me, having no one to run to, I had a problem.'

Family snaps: here is their brother, Robert 'Youngman' Devoux, being buried, and here is the newspaper clipping about the way he died, shot after somebody threw a bottle at a car. Here, too, is their uncle Sulu Devoux being buried that same year. He was shot six times in the back while watering his lawn.

'That happened,' says Ted, 'and I said, man, what next? Then I lost one of my best friends. He's smoking that dope, you know, and his heart stopped. He died when we were doing my uncle's funeral.' He coughs hard, like a gun. 'Man, this is one thing after another. And I was like looking up to the man upstairs, saying, "Hey, whaddyou want us to do, man? Are you trying to push us back into this gang life that we worked so hard to get out of?" '

In the world of anthropology, a skirmish broke out between rival supporters of Margaret Mead's *Coming of Age in Samoa* and Derek Freeman's *Margaret Mead and Samoa: The Making and Unmaking of an Anthropological Myth*. Commenting on this opposition, James Clifford has written: 'One is left with a stark contrast: Mead's attractive, sexually liberated, calm Pacific world, and now Freeman's Samoa of seething tensions, strict controls, and violent outbursts. Indeed Mead and Freeman form a kind of diptych, whose opposing panels signify a recurrent Western ambivalence about the "primitive". One is reminded of Melville's *Typee*, a sensuous paradise woven through with dread, the threat of violence.'

The younger members of the Devoux family may never have set foot in Samoa, but to an outsider, allowed into the family circle for a few days, their life seems to fit this contradictory pattern to perfection. For every expression of loving closeness, there is a glimpse of the perpetual paranoia of their existence. 'We don't even let the girls go out,' says Ted. 'The boys go and do the shopping, just because of that fear.'

The extended families common to Samoans can also be war battalions. 'Our family's known here in the city,' says Ted. 'We're one family you don't fuck with. The thing about Samoan families, it's not just a handful of people, 'cause my dad has six brothers, two sisters. Within that six brothers, the least sons they have is three. In my family I have eight brothers. My dad's brother, Larry, he's got six boys and one girl. My auntie, here, she has three boys, and my other uncle, he has five boys and one girl. That's why we're so close-knitted. You mess with one, you mess with all of us. You're talking about an army.'

The day draws on and we move to the front of the house, past the side window lined with trophies for football and weightlifting. Just by the front door of the cream painted bungalow is a patio with a glass-topped table and four tubular steel chairs. The cars are parked in front, along with the Boo-Yah white Chevrolet van, equipped with $3,000 tyres, their air caps topped with tiny dice. Killer Daytons, they called these wheels, because people would hijack you on the LA freeways and shoot you for them. Or so they said.

The Riddler is present at the table, along with Roscoe, the Godfather, E.K.A., Don-L, and, briefly, the quiet bass player of the crew, Danny Boy. Riddler is the Boo-Yah lyricist and main rapper. 'I've been writing since I was in the seventh grade,' he says, 'about twelve, and it was funny, 'cause it started off with this girl in school. I used to write poems that rhyme. When the Sugarhill Gang came out, from then on I wrote lyrics and kept them.'

Roscoe supplies Riddler with the hard-core prison slang. The rough vocal harmonies, too, are derived from the same source. 'That's where a lotta that music comes from,' says Roscoe. 'The jailhouse. You never know, you might be sitting in your cell. You might be humming something. He might say, "Damn, I didn't know you could sing." But when that person comes out from the jailhouse, he's gotta find somebody to hook up with. Like myself, for instance, I've been gone for years and here we are now.'

As long as they are members of the Boo-Yah T.r.i.b.e., the brothers will not be cutting their hair. Of that, they assure me. Call it the Samson complex, or an externalised sign of the bonds that hold together their fragile identity as armoured outsiders. With a basement full of guns and a daily routine that is close to red alert, the Boo-Yahs inevitably express joy, pleasure, identity and emergence through metaphors of death, intimidation, fear and imprisonment. Their music carries traces of California's pan-ethnic utopianism of the early seventies, when bands like Mandrill, War and Jorge Santana's Malo mixed funk with jazz, post-psychedelic rock, African and Latin elements. But they are only traces. As time runs out for the century, optimism runs with it.

A helicopter passes close overhead. 'I say the first album is like an introduction,' says Riddler. 'It's the new funk. It's Samoans doing it. Music was always ours anyway. Now if we were born on the islands, huh, we wouldn't be hip. We wouldn't know what was up. We were born down here in Los Angeles. We just lived in the darkness, man.'

14

black night and the whooping sounds of alarm

◆◆◆◆◆◆◆◆◆◆◆◆◆◆◆◆◆

bill laswell

On 21 October 1994, in a quiet courtyard in St Germain, leaves flutter down the face of a high wall of ivy, falling in scrapes and whispers into a stone water basin at the wall's foot. A bird, or maybe a dropping twig, splashes loudly. Muted evidence of a vacuum cleaner; bursts of heavy metal construction work. Warm sun for autumn but the duration of this two-hour conversation is determined by a gradual drop in temperature.

Black beret, long hair, some streaks of white now, matted dreadlocks at the back. 'This is the longest year I've ever experienced,' says Bill Laswell, 'and it's not over yet.' A bass player, producer, fixer of hybrid experience and what Ornette Coleman calls 'a monitoring system', Laswell has developed an unusual mode of operation. Since the first Material albums, released at the beginning of the eighties, his New York-based operation has specialised in convening musicians, vocalists and writers from extremely diverse cultural backgrounds. For the successful projects that arise out of these collaborations, the meaning of exotica shifts to suggest a zone of discovery through unfamiliarity.

In the year that I met him in Paris he had worked on more than thirty albums of productions and/or collaborations. A random shuffle through the deck: funk bassist Bootsy Collins, the late Eddie 'Maggot Brain' Hazel, various Last Poets (and all the controversies that follow in their wake), James Blood Ulmer singing Schoolly-D's 'I Wanna Get Dusted', Jonah Sharp, Jah Wobble, Blind Idiot God's Andy Hawkins, a rendition by painter

Julian Schnabel of Tammy Wynette's 'Apartment Number Nine', accompanied by Ornette Coleman. In the next two months he was planning a trip to Kansas to record William Burroughs for a collaboration with Ornette Coleman; a trio improvisation album with Tony Williams and Buckethead; then a tour of Japan with the Painkiller trio of Laswell, John Zorn and ex-Napalm Death drummer Mick Harris. 'If I ever have to pull out all the stops,' he says, 'I've got some back catalogue.'

telematic nomads . . . Soon to New York, then Kansas, but here in Paris, direct from Pete Namlook's studio in Frankfurt where the fruits of another trip are absorbed into the retrieval system. 'I actually went to Mongolia two months ago. I had a big tour from the Japan Foundation. It was all Japanese traditional and classical and jazz musicians and musicians from West Africa and America. The idea was to travel, create a film, a CD and collaborate with musicians from these areas. In some cases there was interesting music and in some cases the government would pick the musicians. So in Uzbekistan you had guys looking like the Village People and they're singing to a backing tape, or a heavy metal band that only played ballads. That was pretty great, actually.'

drones 'We went to Uzbekistan, to Ulan Bator in Mongolia, to Hohat, which is Inner Mongolia. It's really Chinese but a lot of Mongolians are living there. In Ulan Bator I recorded a lot of singers and instrument players, but actually told them it was for a recording and could they just make drones and play long tones and I would mix them with something else. I made a record with Pete Namlook using that recording. So it's all **bass**, with bass feedback, loops of bass and no rhythm, except for the repetitive bass sounds with this Mongolian stuff.

'**Words** become especially interesting; things interesting or things even just abstract that give quick images of things. I did this thing where William Burroughs spoke [Material: *Seven Souls*, 1989] and the only reason I was thinking of Burroughs was because I was looking through this book – *The Western Lands* – and I realised how powerful some of the things were he was saying. People always looked at Burroughs as some kind of a subversive, or a hip guy. That it's very dark and sarcastic. I always

thought the opposite and that book was really about freedom.
There's a lot of hope in that writing and I thought it was amazing
also to connect with the Egyptian Book of the Dead and the Story
of the Souls. I thought, this is great information.'

behind the curtain . . . 'real music, sound. The work Burroughs did with Gysin, which wasn't really known at the time
they were doing it, was all about deconstructing language and
form. The only way to arrive at some new way was by deconstructing or changing – by the cut-up method or by erasing the
word, rub out the word – all that is incredibly valuable for
the musician.

'I won't even say musician, because normally musicians are
no different from sports people. But let's say an artist. That's
pretentious too. A person that's trying to be creative. I think all
that is vital information and you can **cut that up** too. That's the
stuff that really opens up a lot of doors that people didn't even
recognise as doors. It makes you think and then not think. It's
really to bypass the brain and get to the knowing of something
by direct contact and not always taking the maze of the learning
experience which is, for the most part, systems based on other
people's discoveries which might have been random.'

'Collaborations – that's the key.' **an archaeology** of figures
who have warped consensus reality. Curating, retrieving, con-
necting fragile links between a graphic here, a text there, a sound,
a lost soul, a smothered history, or a recorded moment which
disabuses the notion that we are all on the same path. Creating
what Burroughs and Gysin called *The Third Mind*.

Listen to **spoken word** as manifesto: Hakim Bey's *T.A.Z.*
(Axiom 1994): 'Chaos comes before all principles of order &
entropy, it's neither a god nor a maggot, its idiotic desires
encompass & define every possible choreography, all meaningless
aethers & phologistons.' Then look. Front cover image a James
Koehnline shrine for late-twentieth century hoodoo; back cover
the rippled reality photography of Ira Cohen (poet, imagist, traveller, trance archaeologist).

building a **temporary autonomous zone** . . . 'I liked that text
[Hakim Bey's *T.A.Z.*] when I read it. It had a humour – the way
it was also looking at systems and form and religion and every-

thing. It can also be attacking in an encouraging way as well. In fact, when I saw that book I didn't know anything about Hakim Bey or who he was. I'd seen the name a little bit and I assumed it was probably a Muslim from the Middle East, or maybe it's an African guy living in America. But whoever it is, it's obviously a terrorist or anarchist of some kind. And then you go on to find other things . . .

'I was attracted by the cover when I first saw it. James Koehnline – who had made that cover – I immediately contacted him before I had any contact with Hakim Bey, and started licensing things and getting him to create images. His way is all very primitive collage. No different than **cutting up** words or tape and it's all done with paper. I thought it was computer art, 'cause I was obsessed with Tadanori Yokoo, the guy that used to do those Miles covers. He did *Agharta* and *Pangaea* and those weird collages, very colourful. When I saw Koenline's thing it related to this Tadanori Yokoo work. Recently in Japan I started to work with Yokoo finally.'

Then make another **connection**, to Mati Klarwein whose paintings have been used by Jon Hassell for three albums. 'I'd been licensing some of his old stuff and he did one for the Last Poets. I think we've done three. He lives in Majorca. He's lived there since the seventies. He's a strange guy. He was born, I think, in Israel. He was really pro-Arab but his family was Jewish. They were pro-Arab and pro-Palestinian so they had a hard time, in their way in those territories and then they moved to New York when he was young. There's a few books that are impossible to find. Most people don't know his work except for *Bitches' Brew* and a few other things.

'I finally got to see some of the older stuff he had done. A lot of things for and about Hendrix. Alan Douglas, who was at the time helping to introduce Hendrix to a lot of things, some good . . . all kinda things, but he was responsible for turning him on to a lot of music. Especially the connections with Miles, Tony Williams and Larry Young. He introduced Hendrix to Mati Klarwein, I believe. There was a whole scene around Hendrix of women who were connected to Mati. Alan's wife, Stella, was very much part of that scene. They used to have a store, like a boutique. She's

Moroccan. They would fly to Marrakech and buy all these weird coats that Hendrix and Brian Jones used to wear, and they'd bring 'em back and sell them to like Miles and Santana and people buying hippie stuff at the time. So there was this little clique around Hendrix.

'Ira Cohen was a writer and a really strange photographer, 'cause he did Mylar photography. He did the cover of *Devotion* [John McLaughlin with Buddy Miles, Larry Young and Billy Rich, released on Douglas]. He just recently found some stuff of Hendrix that he had done. It's exactly what people are doing now with computers.'

hidden webs 'That's the network that will leave a shape, I think. A pattern. The rest of it will come and go. Those points connect. They've always been connected and we're forever just discovering that is connected to that, but they've been there the whole time. Ira had a magazine. He printed it in Marrakech in the sixties, called *Gnawa*, and that magazine was the first to publish any poetry by Paul Bowles. Gysin as well, they had a big connection.'

He starts to talk with enthusiasm about Peter Lamborne Wilson's history of Islam in America, and the Ron Sakolsky and James Koehnline edited anthology – *Gone to Croatan* – about the multiracial nomadic isolated **tribes** which formed during the early settlement of America. 'This goes back as far as Sir Walter Raleigh, when they established a village or a city in Virginia. They went back to England to bring more people and when they came back, the people they had left had gone and joined the Indians and they had left this message: Gone to Croatan, which was a tribe.

'I see a connection even today with that. Like I have a studio where I'm seeing everyone's trying to get away from a certain way of thinking into a more **autonomous** space. Into an independence and into a way out of racism and judging people. Everyone's working together and it gets beyond the structure of what you're supposed to be, racially. Where your place is because of colour or how you've been educated.'

'Plagiarism as a cultural tactic should be directed at putrid capitalists,' writes Hakim Bey, 'not potential comrades . . . There is **no exotic other**.' Laswell concurs, but offers another angle. 'I appropriate music from everywhere. I don't think it's possible to own a piece of music. To me, we're all playing the same stuff. It's just combinations that make it new. And there is such a thing as someone who has a voice, that plays a certain way and has a style. I think everyone does that to a certain degree and to me, it's all available. If I did something and it was a piece of music and it had a beat and a theme and even a word or something and if somebody took the exact same thing and put it out and made a million dollars I know that I wouldn't contact them. I know that I wouldn't try to sue them because I don't believe you can own a sequence. I think we're all trapped into playing sequences unless it's totally experimental and then you're doing something else. And that's where it gets interesting. Only then. The rest of it is we're all playing somebody else's stuff. To me, it's chord-changes music.'

Music without chord changes: **Cymatic Scan** (Fax) . . . 'That was done really quickly. I don't think he [Tetsu Inoue] realised we were doing it. I set up a bunch of guitars and stuff, like with E-Bows. He works all analogue, so it's like Electro Harmonix pedals and a bunch of keyboards. You just set it all up and because of the effect of the pedals, they all start talking to each another. And that's incredible. It's always different. I'd set up the same with string instruments, which I never touched this way [mimics normal playing position] but I'd just do stuff with them when they were down flat. Because I had a volume pedal and primitive pedals, the pedals were doing all the talking. We did that for like an hour and then I said, "We got it." He's like, "OK, I think I'm ready." And I said, "No, we shouldn't mess with that. That was really good." '

The third Painkiller album – *Execution Ground* – reworks loud live performances by the trio into studio-processed volcanic **landscapes**. 'I was kinda stressing that I didn't think it was possible for me to be interested in music that people played any more. That if five people came into a room, knowing their influences, knowing their backgrounds, knowing maybe what they had for dinner, it's not interesting. It's been done a million times. I thought maybe if you change that even slightly, then I would be interested, whether by processing it, whether it was by killing one of the guys while they were playing. Anything, but just make it different. Find another way to determine a creation of something.'

the black night and whooping sounds of alarm . . . On the morning of guitarist Sonny Sharrock's funeral, Bill Laswell and Pharoah Sanders boarded a plane for Morocco. After *Gnawa Music of Marrakesh: Night Spirit Masters*, Axiom recordings of Morocco's trance music brotherhoods, came *The Trance of Seven Colors*, by Gnawa master Maleem Mahmoud Ghania with Pharoah Sanders.

'Mahmoud Ghania is really strong. He's also a guy I always tried to get to and people would always say, "No, you don't wanna mess with those guys." Finally, I had a connection in Canada with a guy who had lived in Essaouira and he said he could make that connection with this guy. When I went to Marrakesh I bought all of his cassettes – he had made about thirty of them. It was the heaviest bass stuff. I would always say, "What about this guy?" No, you don't want them. They're doing something bad. It's evil. It's **the dark side**. But this guy had the connection and we went and met his family and his father, who was about seventy something and was still alive.

'Basically, they came from Guinea, which means all that *sintir* (*guimbri*) playing is rooted in *doussou n'goni* playing. But in that Gnawa, they play seven trances, seven styles of playing songs, and dances and narration, **colour and scent**, seven times go into seven sections. And of those seven sections of colour, one is black. In the black it's very heavy. People can do performances where people crawl inside of a skin, a bag, and as they play, that person can decide if they wanna live or if they wanna give themselves to that music. And it's said with that music, they can lift them into a better way of living. They can also take them out.

'There's also mutilation. Like his mother was an adept who would take a spear or sword, somehow stick it through her and they swallow needles and shit like this. It's like in Brazil, Bahia, people do that, and drink boiling stuff and just go out, **completely outside**.' I think of a recording by Paul Bowles and Brion Gysin in Tangier in 1961, made for Ira Cohen ('Allah Moulana Jilala', released on *The Poetry of Ira Cohen*, Sub Rosa), during which Farato the fire-eater drank a kettle of boiling water.

'Mahmoud Ghania's sister, I think, is learning that way even now. The mother died. She was very scary. That's why, when you mention that with people about the real thing – they don't want to risk being around the real thing. That's heavy. You'll hear it in the way he hits his strings.

'I wanted to bring something from our end of it which I thought would be a **spiritual** contribution, which is Pharaoh's presence. I think when we got there everybody was suspicious. These Gnawa don't like jazz. To them, it's confused music. So the guy came to Pharoah and said, "I'm a little worried that the master doesn't like jazz." And Pharoah said, "I don't play jazz. I'm playing avant-garde." And the guy said, "OK, I guess that'll be fine." I was not encouraging him to play crazy. I thought it was more about the experience of hearing that music. I said, if you want to bring a phrase, maybe everybody can play; they're all playing repetitive cycles on layers of phrases. He played this riff and I said, that's cool, where'd you get that? He said, "I think I learned this when I was a kid from the Seminole Indians." It sounded good, and then they started playing the same riff without discussing it. Then they had a vocal already prepared for it. When he stopped he said, "How you guys know stuff like that?" And they said, "This is the name of that song," and this song is like two thousand years old.

trance & the funk 'Playing stable phrases with feeling and every time you play a cycle it's as important as the first cycle you play. Same with dub. I could listen to one bass line for years. To me, it's all different. Somebody say, no, this is a loop, it's all the same. It's not the same.'

funk 'n' trance 'I think it's always been there, any time we're doing repetitive music, that quality is there. I think it's a real force and it's a thing that can get into a dimension that we're not aware of how to navigate inside of, but we all bring that to sound, on different degrees or levels. We all have that. Inside of that, if you have any kind of power, it's laying in there. And this kind of repetitive thing, call it trance or call it whatever, can be inside of that without realising you've changed spaces. I think that's a real thing and very few people have experienced what it feels like to go into a trance while experiencing music. We don't get to do that with the kind of music we hear.

'In **Joujouka** [see *Apocalypse Across the Sky: The Master Musicians of Jajouka*, Axiom] it happened to me twice and I realised what the feeling was. It's like if you're in this chair and you lean back a little too far and you catch yourself. That's when you're flipping into it. I've seen people possessed by it, by listening to that music in Marrakech. I know what the feeling is now and I know how powerful it can be and I know it has nothing to do with the experience that we're getting from listening or what people are saying about trance. They're way off. Like this woman who did this thing with the spear – that's like complete removal. That's like the real thing.

'Yeah, **the eye goes up**. I've seen that in sanctified churches, like circus tents in the south. I used to play in churches. My friend was an organ player in a black church and we would play in a rhythm and blues band. I would go on a Sunday when there was no bass player and I would play in this church. People would lose it completely in exactly the same way – not as intense or aggressive as the experience with these Gnawa – but they would go somewhere else. And that's the real magic.

'There's mutilation **ceremonies** where people are so far in trance that they play rhythms with really sharp knives all over themselves. They don't feel anything. Then they'll just fall out and the next day they'll be fine. In some cases they'll be hardly even scarred. That's got everything to do with something we don't know about and rightfully so. Those things you can't know. That's the energy and the mystery and the power of it. You can't know that. That's why it's worth being there. That's why it's worth pursuing. That's why it's all possible. The rest of it is just already figured out and already been done and you're just rearranging the words so that it can fit the occasion.'

Both shivering now, we go inside.

15

body piercing, civilisation, the cave

◆◆◆◆◆◆◆◆◆◆◆◆◆◆◆◆◆◆

ornette coleman,
the modern jazz quartet

On 13 September 1995, we knock on the door of a room in a west London hotel. The man who answers to the knock is wearing a white shirt, splashed with large coloured spots, a grey waistcoat and grey trousers. He bends graciously to shake hands with my daughter, greeting her in a soft lisping voice.

She leaves to wait downstairs in the lobby. I enter the room to talk to this man, who is Ornette Coleman. From his momentous Los Angeles recording debut in 1958 up until the present, Ornette Coleman has been labelled as a difficult musician, a revolutionary, even a charlatan. Yet for Coleman, a saxophonist, later violinist and trumpeter, who shattered the jazz establishment, the priorities of life and art have always felt less dramatic than revolution suggests. Now in his mid-sixties, he struggles to shake off the tiredness induced by constant travelling and explain in notoriously elliptical manner his unique contribution to music.

'When there's a certain inspiration that a person is being inspired by,' he says, 'without that person having an audience, then someone will say, "You're way ahead of your time" or "You play far out." ' For me, none of those titles were what I had in my mind. What I thought I was doing was trying to play a music that would not sound repetitious, that would not sound clichéd, but would have meaning to everyone who would enjoy it. That's the same goal I am heading towards at this moment."

To see Coleman's exuberantly electric Prime Time band play live is to realise the sincerity of that intent to entertain. Many jazz musicians make their mark early in life; few have continued to reinvent themselves past middle age. Coleman still changes and moves, but as he does so he searches for better means of communication. Certain key phrases emerge from time to time, signposts to the core of Coleman's theory and method. There is tone dialling, for example, and then there is harmolodics. *Tone Dialing* was the title of Coleman's 1995 album. Influenced by both hip-hop and J.S. Bach, which is not unusual these days, it included a fragment of telephone tones. I assume there is more to tone dialling than just a few bleeps.

'When you ask me a question, I'm answering and you're listening, you're receiving,' he answers. 'So that's tone dialling. The tone is the most important part of the body because it takes on the shape of what you don't want somebody to know and what you do want someone to know. It also tells them that you've lost control of what you think it is. Tones from your mouth tell you that. Lots of music, whether it's folk music or African music or Chinese music, the more it becomes political the less it stays true to what it is.'

So Coleman is talking about the essential character of a person, the essence of sound and the nature of communication more than he is talking about musical tone. Understanding the depth of his theories and their application to his music requires intuitive leaps rather than intellectual analysis. His harmolodic theory, for example, continues to spread bafflement. As I understand it, I say to him, harmolodics is a method that allows harmonious, independent improvising yet creates an expressive environment in which one player's contribution will not obscure any of the others.

'That's exactly right,' he responds, his enthusiasm catching me off guard. 'Oh man, I'm so glad you expressed that to me because that's what I am trying to say. It could be applied to any form of expression without the loss of someone else's position. You have the television, the radio, you have all kinds of signals going out there trying to receive and pick up things for their own environment. But the more people depend on someone else to express what they're feeling, the less success they're going to have in the environment, because behaviour doesn't respond in the same direction.'

For Coleman, harmolodics is a principle that can extend beyond music into all forms of expression. In November 1994, he caused controversy and walk-outs in San Francisco by staging a performance that included dance, video, readings by a theologian and a demonstration of the ritual body piercing of Fakir Musafar. 'That concert, for me,' he says, 'was really heading towards civilisation. The civilisation that I grew up with was a caste civilisation. The civilisation that I hope to see exist one day is where every person, regardless of their race, creed or colour, or their ability, or their knowledge, or their sexual preference, will find a way to be an individual and make a contribution to each other's relationship. That, I think, will raise the consciousness of why human beings exist to relate to each other.'

Simple enough to comprehend, but why body piercing?

'Well, I had read a book called *Searching for Miracles*,' he explains. 'It was about an Ethiopian or some tribe that had got in contact with their own forces. And in that book, on the cover, there were Indonesian people piercing their own jaws, piercing everywhere, and they were also walking on fire. I said, Oh my goodness, if I could get these guys on the bandstand before I played everybody would probably be very interested in what I'm going to play, what kind of music we're going to play, because they'd be so stimulated from watching these people. So I set out to look for them. I found out they live in Paris, on the outskirts in some kind of monastery.'

Coleman continues to maintain an unshakeable, if often unfounded, belief in the higher qualities and aspirations of his potential audience. Born in Fort Worth, Texas, in 1930, he took up saxophone playing at a young age in order to help support his family. 'My father died when I was seven,' he says, 'and my mother was only interested in the church.' So he played gruelling stints in R&B bands and touring carnivals, face to face with the realities of entertainment in segregated America.

A meeting with Charlie Parker brought two eras together. 'I met Charlie Parker at the Watkins Hotel on Fifth Avenue and

Western in Los Angeles,' he recalls. 'He was playing at the Tiffany
Club. He came out at intermission because they put me out of the
club. I couldn't buy a peanut. I had no money. I said, "I love those
left-handed songs you're writing." He started smiling and then I
went round to his room and he was too busy. But he said, "I heard
you play the saxophone." I said, "Yeah, I try," but I knew that he
knew there was no other saxophone playing but me. I was playing
the same way I'm playing now. But I had such a respect for his
tradition and what he stood for that I wasn't going to try and say,
"Well you know I have something I'm doing, I want you to hear
it." '

Blues inflections remain a central component of Ornette's
crying saxophone sound, even in his striking collaboration with
Howard Shore on the soundtrack to David Cronenberg's *Naked
Lunch*, but the term 'jazz' has become problematic. 'Jazz to lots
of people means black,' he says. 'Like classical to lots of people
means white. But music in general does not have any colour or
gender. So there are white people who think that if something
doesn't remind them of their concept of who they are then they're
losing identity, and vice versa for black people.'

In the sixties, Coleman spoke out against the club environment
that was a naturally assumed home to jazz. The musicians might
as well step up on the bandstand with a hard-on, he claimed. The
setting revolved around sex and a musician who had something
to speak of, other than sex, was disadvantaged by this imposed
context. In this sense, Coleman shared common ground with the
Modern Jazz Quartet, though they also encouraged him in his
early days, sharing the stand with Coleman and Don Cherry in
San Francisco in 1959.

The attitude towards the presentation of jazz at the conclusion
of the sixties was summed up by Frank Kofsky in his book, *Black
Nationalism and the Revolution in Music*. Referring to the white
musicians of the cool school and their attempt to bleach jazz
whiter, Kofsky wrote, 'usually this is done under the shibboleth
of making the music more "legitimate", which translates as
"respectable to white middle-class audiences", which in turn translated as "more like European concert music" '.

The Modern Jazz Quartet grew out of Dizzy Gillespie's big

band of the late forties. Pianist John Lewis, who had studied anthropology and music at the University of New Mexico, played on Gillespie's recording of 'Manteca', along with the original MJQ drummer, Kenny Clarke. From the original quartet of Lewis, Clarke, Milt Jackson and Percy Heath, formed in 1951, Lewis became leader and Clarke was succeeded by Connie Kay, a veteran of the Atlantic Records house band. In *Blues People*, Leroi Jones (now Amira Baraka), though full of praise for the Modern Jazz Quartet and the pianistic abilities of John Lewis, wrote, 'Lewis's attempts to "combine" classical music and jazz have more often than not been frightening examples of what the *final* dilution of Afro-American musical tradition might be.'

This fear of miscegenation still lingers, though in a rather upturned form, in the desire for a jazz past that is black, tough, masculine, physical, danceable and underground, a collection of attributes that objectifies 'blackness' just as surely as the white, cool school, 'third stream' jazz that sought to achieve legitimacy by supposedly distancing itself from the African-American foundations of the music.

The idea of underground has a physical counterpart in the club milieu of jazz. Speaking in 1989 to Percy Heath and Milt Jackson of the MJQ, I raised this issue. 'In the sixties,' Heath responded, 'blacks were trying to get some identity. Our music was never as ethnic as other musics. We were trying to present the music from the cultural aspect and break the associations with smoky nightclubs.' He talked angrily about a Dutch critic who had recently taken the MJQ to task for playing in a concert hall. 'He thinks we should still be playing in the caves,' said Heath. 'He couldn't understand that we were playing to a hall full of people sitting down dressed up, not in their jogging suits, for crying out loud. They get sharp and go to a concert. You didn't necessarily have to go to a jazz club or brothel. We were trying to correct that attitude.'

For Ornette Coleman, identity is more closely related to the conditions in which people live rather than their racial origins. In the middle of explaining this, he falls asleep. 'Mmmmh,' he says, waking after a few seconds. 'Yes, I'm very tired. I was actually thinking of something but when you woke me up it went.'

'Instrumental music doesn't need words for it to have meaning,' he says, 'but sometimes a word needs meaning for it to become a word. For me, I've always been interested in the instrumental part of sound because you don't have to think of race, you don't have to think of style, you don't have to think of the quality of someone else doing something. You don't have to join anything. You don't have to conform. All you have to do is see if what you're doing has any value or validity to your environment. I have been working on that for twenty-five or thirty years and I find that it is still intact to this very moment.'

He falls asleep again.

16

lost horizon

◆◆◆◆◆◆◆◆◆◆◆◆◆◆◆◆

burt bacharach

In his descriptions of formative musical experiences, [Darius] Milhaud alluded frequently to the values of diversity and simultaneity. His account of a trip with Claudel in 1918, for example, portrays in glowing terms the musical simultaneity of Puerto Rico, where American influences merged with traces of Spanish colonization. Milhaud was particularly struck by the presence, at any given moment, of Spanish couples dancing the tango, an American military band performing Sousa marches and foxtrots, and the Cuban composer Romeo playing dances in which 'Bach-like allegro themes' were combined with the 'sharp, syncopated rhythms of popular music' and the 'emphatic grinding rhythm of the *guitcharo*'. For Milhaud's young ears, this juxtaposition of musics from different nationalities and the coexistence of popular and classical idioms within a single dance piece was fascinating and exotic rather than discordant.

Nancy Perloff, *Art and the Everyday: Popular Entertainment and the Circle of Erik Satie*, 1993

In an overheated room of London's Mayfair Interconti-
nental hotel, I am sitting waiting to meet a man whose music
continues to be unfathomably exotic, despite its beguiling famili-
arity. The date is 20 March 1996.

More than thirty-five years ago I first heard the Shirelles sing
Bacharach's 'Baby, It's You'. Dionne Warwick's incredible run of
Bacharach/David interpretations followed – 'Don't Make Me
Over', 'Anyone Who Had a Heart', 'Walk On By', 'I Say a Little

Prayer', 'Alfie' – alongside recordings by Aretha Franklin, the Carpenters and Dusty Springfield that epitomised the great potential of popular songwriting. The collaborations between lyricist Hal David and composer Burt Bacharach ended, appropriately, with their music for the 1972 film version of James Hilton's orientalist novel, *Lost Horizon*.

Finally, he joins me. He is wearing a sweatshirt, BURT BACHARACH printed on the right breast, just so we know who he is. Tired, his voice quiet and hoarse, speaking in a kind of shorthand, he is relaxed and friendly.

But something bothers me here, a too-eager desire to fit Bacharach into cocktail kitsch. What I always heard was an exoticist, a composer so ingenious that he could condense a hybrid of soul and pop, Brazilian, Mexican and bebop, something as fugitive and impressionistic as Ravel yet as strong and immediate as rhythm and blues. All of those contradictory elements, melted together by a love of sound, seethed under the surface of perfect pop without ever disturbing the emotional impact of Hal David's lyrics.

Before his career in pop began, Bacharach studied in New York with three composers: Bohuslav Martinu, Darius Milhaud and Henry Cowell. Martinu was a Czechoslovakian exile who had been expelled from Prague Conservatory for 'incorrigible negligence'; Darius Milhaud, born in Aix-en-Provence, was a Parisian associate of Erik Satie, Jean Cocteau and Blaise Cendrars, and a member of the group of composers known as Les Six. In 1923, he collaborated with Cendrars and Fernand Léger on a ballet called *La Création du Monde*. Milhaud had started work on the ballet on his return to France from a trip to the USA, which included his musical excursions to Harlem, where he had enjoyed Noble Sissie and Eubie Blake's *Shuffle Along* and Maceo Pinkard's *Liza*.

'Cendrars had travelled to Africa and South America,' wrote Nancy Perloff in *Art and the Everyday*, 'and in 1921 had published a "Negro" anthology in which he translated a book of "Negro" songs and poems. A serious and enthusiastic proponent of Africana and jazz, he intended to write a scenario narrating the creation of the world according to African folklore. It was exactly the kind of exotic subject that appealed to Milhaud, and it fitted

well with the jazz score he wished to write based on the music he
had heard in the United States.'

Milhaud had also travelled to Brazil and mixed melodies from
Brazil, Argentina and Portugal. His *Saudades do Brasil* were,
according to James Harding, 'a characteristic mixture of tender-
ness and truculence, of gaiety and an undercurrent of sadness. He
never forgot the glittering splendour of the bay that opened out
before the city, nor the palm trees etched against a pearl-coloured
sky.'

As for Henry Cowell, his passion for Asian music influenced
many younger American composers. 'Cowell claimed to have
heard Japanese *shakuhachi* music before he knew Brahms,' wrote
Carol J. Oja in her biography of Colin McPhee, 'and beginning
in the late 1920s taught a course at the New School for Social
Research entitled "Music of the World's Peoples." ' This was the
course on which John Cage, substituting for Cowell, played a
recording of Buddhist chant to the class and, to his delight, pro-
voked diametrically opposed reactions: 'Take it off. I can't bear
it any longer', and 'Why'd you take it off? I was just getting
interested.'

Born in Menlo Park, California, in 1897, Cowell had grown
up in California, Kansas, Oklahoma and Iowa. Influenced by the
folk music he heard in these areas, he studied non-European music
in Berlin in the early thirties, later travelling to Turkey, Lebanon,
Pakistan, India, Japan and Iran. Between 1937 and 1941 he was
imprisoned (with hard labour) in San Quentin prison for engaging
in homosexual sex. On his release he moved to New York, where
he began publishing new scores, proselytising and teaching. Along
with Bacharach, his students had included John Cage, Lou Harrison and George Gershwin (another American exotic, Gershwin
composed his *Cuban Overture* after spending the spring of 1932
in Cuba). Cowell also encouraged Colin McPhee, writing in
response to a radio performance of McPhee's *Tabuh-Tabuhan*: 'It
seems to me certain that future progress in creative music for
composers of the Western world must inevitably go towards the
exploration and integration of elements drawn from more than
one of the world's cultures.'

Cowell's innovations included the tone-clusters, made with a fist, a forearm or the palm of his hand, scored into piano pieces such as *The Tides of Manaunaun* and *Advertisement*, and his percussive exploitation of the piano interior in *The Banshee*, *The Aeolian Harp* and *Sinister Resonance*. Impressed by the way Cowell had run a darning egg up and down the piano strings while trilling on the keyboard, John Cage developed the principle into his pieces for prepared piano.

While touring as an accompanist to Marlene Dietrich in 1961, Burt Bacharach saw one of his earliest songs, 'Baby It's You' taken into the charts by the Shirelles. This conjunction of musical cultures somehow seems entirely apt for a musician who had experienced the exoticisms of Milhaud and Cowell. This was how I was thinking, in the face of the lounge revival.

So we began to talk.

The thing that strikes me about the Burt Bacharach revival is that you're being called Easy Listening. I'm old enough to remember when your records first came out. In England, at least, a lot of them were considered to be R&B.

I thought so. I don't think it's easy listening. There's a general umbrella that a lot of music is falling under from that time period. I wouldn't qualify my music as easy listening. I think it's sophisticated, urbane, a little bit urban, sometimes difficult, sometimes complex. Easy listening to me would connotate no changes in metre, no bar changes. And I use a lot of bar changes. So I'm really OK with whatever you wanna call it as long as there's attention called to it and people are listening.

If 'Make It Easy on Yourself' by the Walker Brothers is easy listening, then so be it. When I was first successful here they always referred to 'the Bacharach sound'. I thought, what is 'the Bacharach sound'? People asked me and I didn't know, because I thought a song like 'Walk On By' was as opposed to 'Wives and Lovers' or 'What's New Pussycat?' as a song could be.

Before Oasis appeared as Bacharach devotees there was a fashion in this country for taking your songs and putting hard beats underneath, contrasting beautiful melodies and those sentiments with the beats. In a way, Soul II Soul grew out of that trend.

But to come back to this R&B thing. The period when you

and Hal David wrote all those songs was an incredible time for songwriters. In America you had the Brill Building teams, Goffin and King, Leiber and Stoller, Holland Dozier Holland, Brian Wilson. Most of those people, yourself included, were working on the cusp of pop and R&B. It seemed a very fruitful area. Now you look back, were you conscious at the time of working in that zone?

As I look back, I think that was one of the interesting corners I was working in, because I had a three-cornered situation. I was writing R&B stuff for Chuck Jackson, the Shirelles, Jerry Butler and, of course, Dionne Warwick. That felt very comfortable for me. I had another side which was Gene Pitney, Bobby Vinton, Bobby Vee. You know? More vanilla songs, more like straight pop songs. Then I had this third corner which was travelling around the world conducting for Marlene Deitrich and writing orchestrations for her, which is as far as you can get from R&B. The common thing is music. It's all music.

The best, the guy that I just worshipped when I thought about sheer brilliance and doing a couple of things at the same time was Leonard Bernstein. It takes my breath away. Man goes in in the afternoon and conducts Bach, Brahms, new works, with the New York Philharmonic. In the morning or later on that night he's writing West Side Story. Fancy free. That punctured my belief system that if you were a serious conductor you lived like one life, the way you ate breakfast or brushed your teeth. You see someone like Leonard Bernstein shift gears, change his clothes. Amazing.

So it's a kind of social fluidity.

A lot of people can't do that.

But in a way, you had the same thing. On the one hand you were writing R&B for the Sceptre/Wand labels; on the other hand you were studying with Darius Milhaud. It's kind of a jump and kind of not a jump, because it's what the twentieth century is all about.

Uhh-huh. You could take Dave Brubeck as another example. He studied with Milhaud and he's playing jazz.

Something that characterised that period, the fifties and sixties particularly, was that a lot of the singers were black and a lot of what you might call the backroom people – the songwriters, the

*entrepreneurs, the producers, the arrangers – were Jewish. That
was a very fruitful but problematic relationship. With hindsight,
how do you feel about that now?*

I haven't thought a lot about that but it's very interesting. I'm
not sure I know why it happened but you had Gerry Goffin,
Carole King, Leiber and Stoller, Jerry Wexler, Phil Spector, Sid
Bernstein. There were always Jewish men and women, mostly men
at that time, who were always in the forefront of the entertainment
world, the music world, running publishing companies. There was
a gravitation towards it. I don't know, it's an interesting concept.
Until you spoke about it I hadn't thought much about it but
now that you do, looking back, absolutely. Look no further than
Florence Greenberg running Scepter Records. There's an example
that's always blown me away. This sorta like normal, heavy, white
woman from Brooklyn or New Jersey, I dunno which. As Jewish
as you can get, running a hard-core R&B record company and
crazy in love with Luther Dixon. Interesting.

*Now there are a lot of tensions associated with that relation-
ship. At the time were there tensions? I'm not talking about the
outrageous entrepreneurs who we all know ripped everybody off;
I'm talking about the creative people. How did it work?*

Were they shaky at the time? I never was conscious that there
was anything going on. You know, I had a sense that some of the
acts had gotten imprisoned, or imprisoned themselves or been
taken advantage of, whether it was the Drifters, the Coasters,
replaceable people in the group. I don't know whether they were
being paid properly or not. We were just making music and not
into the social consciousness.

I used to hang out a lot with Jerry Leiber, who was one of my
best friends at the time. We'd always go out and have a drink or
something in New York and talk about writing a song. I just
found him terrific to be around, and funny, and brilliant. Those
two guys in the studio together were the best I'd ever seen. They
could nail two or three songs in a three-hour call. 'Stand By Me',
that's an amazing piece, when you hear it now. No overdubs that
I know of.

*There was a production style, arrangement style and I guess
you were one of the pioneers. It was associated with the crossover*

between pop and soul: the choked guitar chops playing the back-beat, that kind of thing. Can you remember where that started?

I went to a lot of Leiber and Stoller dates, just because they were great events. I'm sure I learned stuff gradually.

You don't get a lot of credit for your arranging.

I think you do backwards on your arranging because it comes in as part of what we used to call the background sound. But I don't know if arrangers were ever supposed to get so much credit as the songwriter or the record producer. Record producing has never been something that I sought out to do. I'm not very good at working on things I haven't written. The times that I've done it I've not done so well. I just don't get it like I get it on my own material. I started producing out of self-defence. My songs were getting ruined, so I said, hold on, let me just do this.

Do you think a good song should be able to come through, even if it's a bad singer just playing it on a box of matches?

I think that's highly questionable. I think some good songs have been lost both in the performance and the production. Now, it's hard for good songs to come through. You gotta have all stops pulled out. Like if I was writing what I was writing then, now, I think it'd be much harder to make standards, established songs. Radio in the States, R&B radio, was a very different format. You had the people that could really establish a good song: Aretha [Franklin], Gladys Knight, Dionne [Warwick], Patti LaBelle, could sing an R&B pop song, start it there and then spill it over. There's no guarantee with any of those artists any more. It's crowded with Snoop Doggy Snoop or whatever his name is, or Dr Dre. It's not a knock on those records because some of those records are very brilliant but what it does is close the access to radio for softer songs.

You were born in Kansas City, weren't you, and moved to New York. They're both jazz towns.

Well, I left Kansas City when I was one, so I didn't go to too many jazz clubs then.

Not like one-year-olds now?

Heh, lined up queuing outside the door.

Did you listen to a lot of bebop?

At a certain point it's all I listened to. You gotta know, as a kid growing up and you're listening to Harry James, the Dorsey Brothers, then somebody opens the door for you and lets you hear this music that's thirty years in front. You never heard anything like that. Tadd Dameron's big band, Dizzy Gillespie's big band, Bud Powell, Thelonious Monk. Amazing.

Tadd Dameron's Fontainbleu, those pieces, the Gil Evans things –

Gil Evans was great . . .

– do you see some of the roots of your interest in arranging and chords and so on in some of that material?

I think it's possible. If it's acquired, it's subliminal. At an unconscious level it's just what you perceive and take in. There's an influence with the classical music tradition, there's an influence from Brazilian music.

Do you mean bossa-nova, Tom Jobim?

Not so much Jobim. More Djavan, Milton Nascimento and what they were doing on the hillsides. You go in a club in Brazil, in Rio, and there are ordinary people, like somebody who works in a bank, business person, they're sitting in this club, they've got a cocktail stick, playing the most complicated percussion patterns on their glass while the band's playing. Man, how do they do that? It's great. Very sophisticated music. Way over the bar line but they all know where they are. They know it by the heart.

I guess you have the same balance of earthy and sophisticated in Brazilian music that we were talking about with R&B. You had gospel with the sophisticated chords. There seems to me to be a parallel there.

Mmmhmm. Once I could really do what I felt like without somebody, some A&R man, saying, 'Everybody's dancing and you've got to make it all 4/4', or 'You can't have a three-bar phrase.' I thought, they're on top of the world, they're running this company. They're probably right and I'm wrong. Then you ruin the song.

I was listening to the Walker Brothers, 'Make It Easy on Yourself' and thinking you would use four chords where somebody else would use one. Every chord seems to build the emotional weight of the song as you move towards the climax.

Right, that was the hope, the plan. To also get some drama

in the songs. You know, I don't know how much comes from being able to stand back and get away from your central instrument. Being able to hear in your head and write it down on paper. If you're writing at the piano, you tend to be writing bar by bar by bar. Great songs, they're written every day on somebody's central instrument but for me, I wouldn't really know how to stand back and get the long picture, sitting at a keyboard. You play pretty chords and you're MIDId to three synthesisers. I mean, it's a magnificent sound. You can dupe yourself. It's gorgeous, but when you strip it all back you'd better have a melody underneath it. So I find, I've gotta get away from my working instrument. I've gotta hear it in my head and then I can hear all kinds of proportions, and, shall we say ups and downs of where it should go, drama points.

Is that an obsession with sound?

Obsession for me with sound? I don't know if it's any more of an obsession than anything else in my life. Yeah, I tend to try and make it go a hundred per cent. Do I get obsessive with my music? Yeah. Am I as obsessive now with my music as I was? Maybe not. It's hard to sustain something like that.

That ability to visualise is a very intense mental and emotional process, isn't it?

It's exciting. It's so comfortable for me to do; it's not like I had to call on deep high powers to reach that stage. It's just a natural process. It's like the more I've learned about orchestration, the more I hear the accuracy of what instruments really sound like. I make mistakes still.

Very often in great partnerships, when they're really firing, there's a tension which can either be out in the open or underlying. Sometimes it seems that stuff comes out of that friction and then the relationship falls apart.

Yeah. It was a long period with Hal David and a long period with my ex-wife, Carole Bayer Sager and now I kinda like writing with a lot of people. I equate it to being married, being married to Hal, being married to Carole, a long-term marriage. Now I'm dating a lot. I used to be a little anxious about sitting down with somebody else sitting in the room. Would I be comfortable? What if I didn't come up with anything? Would I find it tolerable? I find it's much better to be in a room with somebody that you kinda like, I really do, than somebody who's really, a real pain in the ass. You could say life is too short but there are other people to write with. I don't think it has to be adversarial, you don't talk to each other.

When I say tension, I don't necessarily mean adversarial. It can be just difference. With two very different people, that difference can produce something really interesting.

Yeah, I think for me, I shied away from writing with a woman.

Why is that?

Maybe that scared me. Maybe that's too much like my mother. The other writer had, maybe, power, was strong, and I just didn't need to be in a room with somebody who in any way would call any of this stuff in that made it change back into a mother–son relationship. That's just a guess, without anybody saying that's what happened, but I think it's possible.

It's a very intimate process, isn't it? You're dealing with very intimate emotions.

It can be. My best way, of course, is to do a lot of that work by myself. Let me get away, I'll see you tomorrow, I'll call you, play something on the phone, 'cause when it gets right down to it – I don't like that, that's not good – I don't want to subject somebody else to that.

A lot of Hal David's lyrics were about vulnerability and vulnerability, particularly in the sixties, was a difficult subject for men to deal with. This is one of the things that makes those songs so interesting. The music is vulnerable as well. It's taking risks, it's shifting, it's ambiguous. It demands attention.

[long pause]

That's not a question.

You made a statement. It sounds right on to me.

So vulnerability being a different area for men at that time, was that something you would ever discuss with him as an aim of what you were doing?

No. Hal was kinda like a person who'd look one way and then he'd deliver these clever lyrics. It was always a surprise to see what he'd written. I think 'Alfie' is one of the greatest lyrics ever written, by anybody. There's an example where you've got a whole lyric and you set it. I just had to sit down and write a melody about what I thought the film was about. It's more restricted, boxes you in more.

Do you think there's a problem of dealing with maturity in songwriting if you've begun in a teenage field?

So much of what I'm writing is music rather than words, but I don't know that it's different either. I think what I'm writing from is the sponge part of my heart that sees and feels what my life is and has been and might be. So that's what I sit down and write. You're calling it from afar but it has everything to do with who you are. Not direct stuff. Not like trouble with my girlfriend. I think it's much more subtle than that. It just comes from a stockpile of what you experience. I'm lucky enough to have a way of expressing it.

I guess there's a reason why there's not a whole lot of up-tempo, taa-ta-ta-taa-ta songs in my catalogue. I'm not a forward, in-your-face kind of person. So if I can just be OK with that. That's how I am. That's why I was good at hosting those Lew Grade television shows I used to do over here. I think it was very low key, you could get away with that, soft, not in-your-face. They were tolerable for the viewer to take over a long period of time. I'd kinda forgotten about that.

I've always enjoyed your performances of your own songs but you're obviously not Dionne Warwick. It's interesting hearing Brian Wilson now, having been through every trauma in the book. You hear this mature man with a cracked voice. It doesn't have that angelic purity but it has something interesting, which is about life. Why have you felt the need to perform your own songs?

I'm very careful when I perform my own things. When Dionne and I do concerts together I wind up singing a total of five minutes. I'm very self-conscious about my singing, just about all the time. I'm used to beating myself up so I don't beat myself up about my singing any more. I think there's a certain licence. Hey, I wrote the song, I'm not trying to compete. I'm a songwriter and this is how I feel the song.

Given your connection to Darius Milhaud, your interest in Tadd Dameron and so on, I'm surprised you haven't worked in more impressionistic, instrumental areas.

Well, I think my one departure was the Houston Symphony album I did [*Women*]. It really was all-encompassing. It was all my life. It wasn't successful at all. What happens is that if you really wanna do something then you do it. If you have a burning desire and it's really important to you. I studied with Milhaud and Martinu and Henry Cowell. Back in that period I was studying with Henry Cowell down at the New School at the same time I was studying with Bohuslav Martinu at the Maddox Music School. I did recognise this was a hard way to make a living. Maybe somewhere down the line I'd be teaching at a small university to support this while I write something. Maybe copy all the parts out for a symphony orchestra to play. How badly do I want it?

I know my mother's disappointment was huge. It was a very peak time in my life when Leopold Stokowski with the New American Symphony came with a commission, a grand, for me to write something for the orchestra. I think one of the biggest turn-offs for me was the way symphony orchestras plan. They plan like, you're booked to conduct them two years from . . . next February. Ummm, the idea of developing a work and delivering it to them two years hence. Oh man, if they'd said three months from now they debut my piece I might have done it. I might have pushed it over the top. And I turned it down. My mother, I think it hurt her a lot. It was something, in retrospect, I should have done. But I didn't.

Maybe that's why you had a problem writing with women. You thought they might say, "Let's write something like Ravel.'

Very possible – it makes a link in with my mother. Sure, yeah, I see it.

Did you ever meet John Cage when you were studying with Henry Cowell?

Uh-huh, sure, sure. I used to hang out a little with him and Lou Harrison. Go to some of their concerts. I remember going to the Macmillan Theater up at Columbia University when John Cage was presenting his work for twelve radios and twenty-four players with Cage conducting [Imaginary Landscape No. 4, 1951]. It was like two people to a radio, one of them changing the station, one had the volume. I thought, this is nuts, this is really nuts.

Maybe that's where those muted guitar chops on the backbeat come from, it comes from Henry Cowell.

Well if it comes from Henry it comes from the fist on the keyboard. You know a great story about him, when he did a concert in Paris they sent the boxing critic to review his concert because he was the fist, plucking inside the piano, smashing with his elbows.

Boxing writers are usually better than music writers, in my opinion, but that's another story. Do you think this whole thing is particularly to do with the American experience? On the one hand you've got the Shirelles; on the other hand you've got John Cage, Leonard Bernstein, show tunes. It's mixing up and making something that really captures people's imaginations because it condenses the whole experience.

I don't know about that. I think a person that's tapping into 'Baby It's You', the Shirelles, doesn't have a clue who wrote it, doesn't have clue that person is out conducting for Marlene Dietrich in Warsaw as the song is climbing up the charts. Are they drawn to the music in that way or is it what I'm able to put in the melting pot?

Maybe 'Baby It's You' is not a good example of what I'm talking about. Something like 'What's New Pussycat', it's a very experimental song. It hits you right where a pop song hits you but you listen to it dispassionately and it's a very experimental song.

Tom Jones never knew what hit him when I played him that song. All he wanted to do was just wail. It was a waltz. This song was way out there.

It'd be nice to think there was a little bit of John Cage in 'What's New Pussycat', or Gil Evans.

Yeah, you know, or Kurt Weill. To be able to move in that available space, to have the musical vocabulary, that's back to being able to write music down, to learn the rules, to be able to break the rules. It's about having learned and studied and having enough ammunition coming from different places. I think 'What's New Pussycat?' came from scoring that film and watching Peter Sellers's craziness. That German thing that he had, that German accent, and that wife. That melody came right off his craziness, the eighty-third watching of that scene with Peter Sellers, I got it.

One reason I didn't do a lot of films back then, you know. After *Butch Cassidy*, that was a hard film to follow, because that was so great and so great to watch. In the way I watch a film, if I get a dog, the fourth time I'm running it I say, no, why did I do this? I could have used this time to write maybe three important pieces of music.

Mentioning Kurt Weill is interesting. It makes me think of songs like 'Surubaya Johnny' which had that bitter-sweet feel. They were quite lush. Did you listen to him a lot?

No, but you know you just hear as you go along. I've never been one to be playing music. I think and hear music when I'm really writing. It just chews up so much of my available time. You know the costliest things I've ever done? Do things like go to see a play, working on a song at the same time in the daytime, carry it with me into the theatre, not being able to lose it. I either finish the problem area of the song in my head in the theatre but my attention has gone there so it's deprived me of what I saw in the theatre, so I never got what was going on onstage and I never got what was going on in my head. Both got unresolved.

I don't wanna listen to a lot of music. If I get a massage and the massage lady brings along some music that's disruptive, turn off the music. I could never make love to music because I'm not into the woman, I'm into, wait, what did the saxophone play in the sixth bar? Oh man, Jesus, that was not good!

There's a theory that music that really speaks to people emotionally is often produced by people who are very isolated. Has that been true of you?

Oh I'm sure, it's good company. It's a great companion. You can split off. I've always used it. Sorry, you can't stay tonight, I have to write an orchestration. So you can separate yourself, go into music, which is a private thing, and close the door. I don't want the maid to hear what I'm playing. That is a form of isolation. I think it goes way back to when I entered a radio jazz-piano scholarship competition in New York. I sent in my application when I was in second-year high school. They went from 150 down to fifteen and the fifteen they sent telegrams, but I never told my family. My mother and father, they saw this telegram: 'Congratulations, you're in the final fifteen.' 'What is this?', and I had to tell 'em. I didn't want anybody to know, I was so sure I wouldn't win. It's mostly rooted in, you won't succeed. You'll fail. It's like keeping the horse in the barn. If he doesn't run then he won't lose. All right.

The stuff comes up through the cracks anyway.

Always does, always does.

17

from the outer limits

◆◆◆◆◆◆◆◆◆◆◆◆◆◆◆◆

nusrat fateh ali khan

To really appreciate a cartoon like *The Jetsons* – fundamentally the Suburbans in a possible future as opposed to *The Flintstones*, who are the Suburbans in a prehistoric past – you have to be somewhere modern. So my daughter, Juliette, and I were resting in our Lahore hotel, Juliette watching *The Jetsons*, and I was considering this fantastic idea of late fifties rock'n'roll, the generation gap, undomesticated husbands, smart housewives, labour-saving devices, the bad-tempered boss and all that American stuff, transposed to a place in outer space, and of course, comparing the present reality to that imagined future.

What the future turned out to be, a little later on, was hearing the *Home and Away* theme, via satellite, invaded sidelong by prayers for the Holy Prophet, broadcast from brutal sound-shredder Tannoy speakers mounted on the roof of a mosque across the street. With their tonal malleability and melismas, Muslim prayers, like whale songs, have become the unforgivable cliché of rave sampling; it came as a shock, then, to hear a chance hybrid so harmonically incompatible, so like talons scraping slowly down a blackboard.

Our second evening in Pakistan; the date was 22 February 1996. I was standing surrounded by poverty, mud, noise and dead animals, on a Lahore street in the old part of the city. Over by a tangle of bare wires was Michael Brook, producer of *Night Song*, Nusrat Fateh Ali Khan's then-current album release on Peter

Gabriel's Real World label. Juliette was studying a metal rack hung with skinned chickens. Rain poured down, the drains were awash. Across the road, the shop fronts were festooned with strings of fairy lights, like all-seasons Christmas, and a vivid reminder that this conjunction of wet weather and improvised electric wiring demanded constant vigilance.

Without thinking about it too much, Brook had just pointed his video camera at some meat-chopping activity outside an adjacent restaurant. The proprietor of the restaurant where we had just eaten insisted that Michael video *his* meat, particularly the huge metal dish of mysterious internal organs laid out at the edge of the traffic. Literally drumming up custom, our meat chopper clattered the edge of his iron guts display in a ringing paradiddle, Brook's home video threatening to look like a scene from *Blood Feast*, soundtrack by Bow Gamelan. Not for the last time, I was relieved to be vegetarian.

Racing through the streets, our driver's gangsta rap tape playing in the van, mothafucka this, mothafucka that (who knows what a full understanding of such lyrics might lead to in Pakistan), the visual impressions strobed, flicking one on top of another, too numerous and too rich to absorb. A ram standing in the rain, mud-spattered and forlorn. Bullocks, donkeys, a horse painted with henna patterns for the Eid festival, all pulling carts that groaned under steel rods, wooden benches, every kind of cargo, ploughing remorselessly through the choking blue air chaos of two-strokes, overloaded kamikaze buses, painted trucks, bicycles, death-trap taxis, scooters, motorbikes loaded with whole families, wife riding sidesaddle with the baby in her arms, son squeezed in the middle.

A disturbance. A small child knocked down by a motorcycle, milk splashed in the road like a jet of white blood. Flashing by to vanish in the dust, a car sticker celebrating MEN AT THEIR BEST – THE PAKISTAN ARMY. A jet fighter plane perching nose skywards on a traffic roundabout. Film posters – *Tough and Deadly* and *Tai Chi* – delirious images of knives, pistols, rifles, seductive women, moustached bandits, Chinese martial artists. In Hall Road, strawberry sellers, their soggy fruit laid out in baskets balanced on bicycles, trudged through communications alley;

Tannoy speakers hanging like dried fungi, mountains of boxed TV sets, a giant satellite dish wired to the lamppost outside Tahir Electronics, mounted on top of a small black hatchback saloon. Every few hours, the constant blare of car horns mixing with prayers from the mosques, a brass section from the outer limits.

That night we drove at speed through the dark serpentine streets of the old quarter of Lahore, the red area as our driver described it, finally pulling up in front of the decrepit City Cinema. For the first time during this trip, Juliette was nervous. Shadowed figures stared down at us from balconies, soldiers armed with stun sticks and machine guns lined the front of the building. People too poor to pay were forced to hang off spiked railings surrounding the forecourt. Their concert would blast out of wardrobe-sized loudspeakers set up by the doors.

Finally, Nusrat arrived in the custom-painted *Qawwali* land cruiser, a regal entrance for a shy man. On our first evening in Lahore, Juliette and I had taken tea, the warm milky stuff that prohibition Pakistan runs on, with Nusrat and two of his aides. Imperious characters with mobiles at the ready, these two made no attempt to ease an uncomfortable situation in which my attempts at conversation freeze-dried on utterance. Of all the musicians I have met, Nusrat seemed the most clearly focused, even single-minded. He would sit very still, whether surrounded in a room full of people or face to face, looking uncomfortable, withdrawn, nervous.

I had been warned in advance by Michael Brook. 'There's not a lot of small talk,' he had said when asked about his working relationship with Nusrat. But if the talk turned to serious matters of musical techniques and history, or the spiritual purpose and poetry of Qawwali, and if he could speak in his own language, he would smile, his eyes would flash; he spoke with authority, knowledge and excitement.

That sense of mission creates a strangeness about people, a remoteness from the world. In the musical domain, Nusrat had a quickness about him that belied the resistance of his body. As he sang, his hands cut through the air in rapid and complex arabesques, shooting notes to heaven. He moved at speed through musical genres: making music for such films as *Natural Born*

Killers and *Passion*; working with Pearl Jam's Eddie Vedder, Massive Attack, Peter Gabriel, Michael Brook or Bally Sagoo; writing Bollywood soundtracks; playing at holy shrines and pagan rock festivals; and as a musical ambassador, trying to close the gulf between Pakistan and India.

When singing, the change that came over him was dramatic. The ungainly, awkward physical presence transformed into a channel for spirit, emotion, inspiration, otherworldly visitation, call it what you like.

There are certain musicians whose early death is expected; musicians who court demons, who drive themselves too hard, who mend their listeners, perhaps their own turbulent souls, in each act of making music and then find that these intense healing sessions collect payback in the form of a shortened life span. I think of John Coltrane, Otis Redding, Jimi Hendrix, that sense of working with volatile forces, of taming the dragon and articulating its energy, channelling a tornado of emotion and experience through their musical gifts, cramming it all in while there was still time.

At the City Cinema, I watched Nusrat clamber onto the stage. Supported by one of his aides, he could barely handle the climb. Hugely overweight, short of breath, suffering from kidney problems, he looked as though he should be home in bed. Settled in front of his group – lead vocalists, support singers who clap rhythms, two harmoniums and percussion – he slowly unwound the first song of a lengthy, invigorating evening. The vacant mask of his face melted, the suffering body came alive, the power switched on to full force. From this point, the transformation was total, the commitment absolute. His voice swooped and hovered, rising through the octaves then narrowing to a knife blade of feeling so sharp that it cut through to the spirit. In this session, he sang for hours, leaving fitter people exhausted.

Two nights later we were at the open-air Qaddafi Stadium, a bear pit of a venue, up onstage with the VIPs and TV cameras, ringed by the home crowd, 10,000 strong. Nusrat was headlining, but first came a powerful performance by Abida Parveen. A religious folk, *ghazal* and pop singer from the highly unstable Sind region around Karachi and Hyderabad, she delivered with frightening authority. 'Is that a man or a lady?' Juliette whispered. Dry ice rolled over the awesome Parveen; a woman showered us with scented rose petals. All around, members of the audience were chanting 'Ali, Ali', in response to Parveen, some falling into trance, twitching, collapsing, attracting vulture flocks of photographers. The most ostentatious dancers were carried off by soldiers.

The Nusrat build-up was hardly what you would expect, given the devotional core of his music. After a lot of speeches in which 'Pakistan!' and 'Discipline!' were repeated with alarming verve, the MC bawled his introduction: '*Last Temptation of Christ*, *Dead Man Walking*, *Bandit Queen*, *Natural Born Killers*'. In this atmosphere of near-hysteria, despite problems with microphone stands and amplification, Nusrat delivered with fiery, concentrated intensity, hands swooping in parabolas, corkscrews and wild twisting bat flights that gave outward shape to his melodic improvisations. The set was short but punchy. With 'Musst Musst', customarily the last song of the night, still racing towards a conclusion, the audience jumped to its collective feet and exited at speed, leaving an empty arena and an eerie feeling that the whole event may have been an illusion.

The following day, still reeling from the power of the concert, I attempted to find some logic in the many contradictions raised by the congenial, reserved Khansahib. Nusrat lived in the exclusive Lahore suburb of Faisal Town. Like any other wealthy celebrity, he employed a uniformed private security guard, armed with a machine gun, to watch the front gate, day and night. Twice, Faisal Town's power failed and during these moments of utter darkness in Nusrat's music room I felt an acute sense of reaching across a void of incomprehension.

Expressions of Sufi liberalism, such as poetry ostensibly about alcohol and women, trance states and the musical ecstasy of Qawwali, are not easy to reconcile with the censoriousness of the mullahs. In certain areas of Pakistan, adultery can lead to the condoned murder of a woman. Yet sex still appears in exquisitely erotic packages, via satellite TV transmissions of Indian film clips and pop videos. 'I can't work this out,' I said to Muhammad Yasin

Malik, an independent television producer whom I met in Nusrat's music room. 'What is the reaction in Pakistan to these sexy clips?'

'There's no reaction,' he answered, 'because the people who see them, the ones who can afford satellite TV, already know and accept these things. The people in the villages don't have satellite.' We talk a lot about transcontinental information flow, conveniently forgetting that, in the past and now, physical journeys have formed the basis of cultural diversity: trade in goods and people, wars, imperialism, religious missions, migration, exploration, economic or political flight, colonial plunder. What I hear in *Qawwali* is a wildness that suggests the fiercely independent peoples of the North-West Frontier. This may be romantic conjecture, yet I found my instincts partially confirmed when I probed into Nusrat's family tree.

'My history starts six hundred years ago when my ancestors migrated from Afghanistan to India,' he said. He followed this with information that gave me quite a surprise. 'When they came to India they became disciples of two families in music. One was called Dagar, they only sang *Dhrupad*. They learned *Dhrupad*, then they learned *Khayal*. Then one of my forefathers learned *Qawwali* from another family. The education of these two families has been passed on.' So *Dhrupad*, the austere, palpably ancient vocal style of Moinuddin and Aminuddin Dagar that I heard performed in Golders Green and Hampstead in the mid-seventies, is entwined, along with the gorgeously elaborated *Khayal* style, around the distinctly rougher, outwardly more ecstatic group improvising of *Qawwali*.

I asked him how he negotiated the differing demands of so many hybridised, sometimes unfamiliar musical forms. 'Because I have the basic knowledge of classical music and I have learnt all styles,' he answered, 'there is no difficulty in adjusting. This is part of my family tradition.' Not completely satisfied with this answer, I asked Brook for his impression.

'I think we can't map our idea of the sacred and profane on the way he thinks about it,' Brook said. 'He's not exactly spreading the word, but he's spreading the sacred music. There's no such thing as bad publicity.'

Perhaps one of the keys to this versatility is the Sufi religion itself. Qawwali is a musical and poetic expression of Sufism, the mystical and, in certain respects, relatively liberal branch of Islam. The aim of the music is to elevate the audience to a spiritual plane. Sufi also gives one resolution of the contradiction raised whenever religious musics are performed to people of other faiths or no faith at all. What can the music possibly mean when it is plucked out of its natural context?

'The message of Qawwali is not only for Muslims,' said Nusrat. 'There have been very great people in all religions. Christians, Hindus, Sikhs, they all had good Sufis. The message of the Sufis is the same – how to reach to God – but they all have different ways.'

What seems to be implied, both musically and spiritually, is an infinite relativism through which all forms blur into each other. But for Nusrat, limits did exist. The full-time job of his life was devoted to the exploration of these limits. 'What I have to do is ensure that the beauty of the work does not get destroyed,' he said, 'but at the same time the new generation gets the message too. That is a lot of work.' It was, indeed, a lot of work. Eighteen months later, he died. He was forty-eight years old.

On a final day in Pakistan, the infinite complications of the region's history became apparent when we took a rapid guided tour around Lahore Fort and the adjacent Badshahi Mosque. Our guide was skilful, not just in synthesising a convoluted narrative into coherent précis, but in sparing our postcolonial blushes by emphasising Sikh vandalism in order to downplay the sadism, destructiveness and plunder of the British. Within this vast complex of ornate, crumbling buildings, pools and courtyards the ceiling of one small tower is covered with glass, its surface bubbled into inverted, translucent cobblestones blackened by the dirt of centuries. A flaming torch lit in the gloom set off a liquid shower of reflections.

A feeling lingers, of past and present holding up accusative mirrors to each other (with the future making faces at the pair of them). This is not peculiar or particular to Pakistan. We breathe a similar air wherever we are in the world. Mix *The Jetsons* with *The Flintstones* and there you have the contemporary experience. Inside the Mosque, Juliette and I stood facing into one corner.

Michael Brook stood far off in another and whispered to Juliette. Thoroughly spooked, she refused to say a word. So Michael and I conversed at a distance and, with far more clarity than the present day Pakistani telephone system, sound moved across space as if by magic.

18
tropical dandies

◆◆◆◆◆◆◆◆◆◆◆◆◆◆◆◆◆◆

haruomi hosono, willie colón

In 1860, Count Eulenberg, the first ambassador of
Prussia in Japan, took office in a style that hinted at world events
to follow. Eulenberg marched forty marines behind a military
brass band from the Yokohama pier to his new home in Akabane.
According to Eta Harich-Schneider, in *A History of Japanese
Music*, 'the Edo people were stunned.'

Six years later, the *daimyo* of Fukui petitioned the French
embassy to appoint a French officer to teach French military music
to the band in his private army, and by 1874, following a suggestion from the Japanese Emperor, there were moves to include
Western music in the repertoire of the *gakunin*, the musicians who
played Japan's ancient *gagaku* court music. The reasoning behind
this flawed, faltering step towards a fusion of East/West pomposity
and nationalism lay in a report drawn up after ministry consul-
tation. It read: 'We have repeatedly adopted music from other
countries. This was a natural human development. Now the situation is the same with respect to European music. Not only in the
army and navy, but also at court ceremonies and banquets we
need the music of the West.'

sample # 1

Exotica, a book of musical illustrations by Yosuke Kawamura.
Images: like a barrage balloon drifting in the sky, a fiery red chilli
pepper carries salsa *conguero* Ray Barretto through a small swarm

of flies. If G. Cabrera Infante's hothouse novel of pre-revolutionary Havana, *Three Trapped Tigers*, was to burst into life in Tokyo, it would share the spirit of these drawings. Surrounded by copies of *Latin N.Y.* magazine, Yosuke poured out exquisite and disturbing exotica inspired by exotic places, salsa stars (Barretto, Hector Lavoe and Eddie Palmieri), and legends of Cuban music such as Arsenio Rodriguez.

Another book, *La Tierra de la Salsa*, is devoted to his love affair with Nueva Yorican salsa: black and white sketches, hacked out quickly with broad, dancing lines to capture the vitality, speed and heat of the music, snapshots of Latin musicians, street scenes, magical products from *santeria* shops in the Bronx. 'This popular music which was raised on the air in the streets is very contemporary, was improved by Willie Colón and his associates, and it has the smell of a bracing sea breeze blowing in the city. The kiss and the trouble between the lovers on the corner. Tamarind syrup ready to drip off a Sno-Cone. The sound of the subway. The radio news drifting out of some open apartment window. The smell of the market where sugar cane and green bananas are lined up on display.

'The summer sunset shrinks in the distance. One's shadow melts beneath the lights of the city. The night skyscrapers, looking like a chandelier growing out of the earth, twinkle to life. Car horns and the driving sound of a cowbell sound like the rumbling of the sea. The neon lights sway in the wind.'

Willie Colón, alias El Malo o el Hustler!! con Hector Lavoe (canta), painted by Yosuke in 1974, shows these two salsa greats in their gangster personae, both smoking exploding cigars, behind them, screaming across a pale blue sky, a plane trailing fire and smoke. Yosuke's writing and drawing make me think of Willie Colón's 'Neuva York', the hurtling pressure of its Latin percussion, the grandiose urban romanticism of its Cinemascope strings punctuated by the sounds of helicopters, sirens and road drills. I remembered speaking to Willie Colón, salsa trombonist, bandleader, record producer and native New Yorker, in 1986.

Colón was born in 1950. As a seventeen-year-old he recorded his first album – *El Malo* – in the Latin soul style known as *bugalú*. Later records combined salsa's rhythmic complexity and drive

with edgy, lush urban atmospherics. His production and arrangement for the late Hector Lavoe's epic 'El Cantante', for example,
soared on a exhilarating wave of violins yet still crackled and
flared with nervous energy. In 1986 Colón had recorded a club
hit called 'Set Fire to Me'. We talked about the New York musical
mix. 'It's kinda like tribal things,' he said. 'I'm very comfortable
with it because it's like from my home turf. Most of that music is
coming from the South Bronx where I was born and raised. It's
part of that street culture. Basically, all the music that I've ever
done comes from that street culture. We were just second-generation Puerto Rican sons of the immigrants, mostly like sweatshop
workers and things like that. We were like little enclaves. It would
look like a little Latin American town in the Bronx – everything
from the radio stations to the signs on the stores. Rumbas out on
the streets. People playing dominoes in the streets. In the summer
it would be hard to tell it from Caracas or San Juan or Panama.'

Yosuke Kawamura's drawings portrayed the globalisation of
culture: on the front cover of *La Tierra de la Salsa*, a Latin woman
dressed in a *kimono*, holding up maracas; his *Living in the Jungle
Land* from 1976, the profile of a man smoking a Lucky Strike, a
fly buzzing by his nose, propped up on a shelf by the aquarium,
a postcard – Stranded in the Jungle – an explorer waist deep in
water, each arm disappearing in exotic crucifixion into the mouth
of a crocodile. Other paintings depict occupied Japan through
couples – Steve and Sachiko, Kimiko and Bobby – or through
anachronisms – like a scene from a samurai film, two retainers
and their sword-toting master pause in a journey to drink bottles
of Coca-Cola from a vending machine.

sample # 2

The paintings of Masami Teraoka. 'I now live in Hawaii,' wrote
Masami Teraoka, 'a great place to observe both Americans and
Japanese. Although Japanese tourists look Westernized, they think
very differently from Americans. In my paintings, I often depict
Japanese with samurai-era hairstyles to symbolize their traditional
attitudes. When such people come into contact with Westerners
on the beach in Hawaii, they face culture shock, unsure whether

to be seduced or repelled by American excesses and freedom.' His *Christine at Hanauma Bay* shows two Japanese men on the beach, one a samurai, one a punk, staring at a Western woman wearing a bikini. 'Both are male chauvinists,' writes Teraoka, 'or perhaps they are just in awe of American women.'

Alexandra Munroe compares Teraoka to artists such as Jean-Michel Basquiat, Pepón Osorio and Hung Liu. 'These artists render the exotic stereotypes of their respective Otherness or minorities,' wrote Munroe, 'precisely so as to upend them... Unlike the work of artists whose passions are informed by multi-culturalism or identity politics, Teraoka's elaborate narratives about the ways in which the East and West collide in a post-modern, highly consumerist society are constructed from an essentially detached, nonpartisan vantage point. His conflicts are fantastic in order not to be specific, and they are not specific in order to be about broad human pathos.'

sample #3

Tadanori Yokoo, graphic art innovator and lead actor in Oshima's *Diary of a Shinjuku Thief*. 'Sometimes, looking through his catalogues,' wrote Mark Holborn in *Beyond Japan*, 'one could feel the absorption and recycling of art as if by an alien intelligence... In 1887, three years before his death, Van Gogh took his *Japonisme* to an extreme by painting a *kabuki* actor, surrounded by Oriental motifs of bamboo, lotus flowers, and cranes, as if he had borrowed Utamaro quite literally... A hundred years after Van Gogh, Yokoo has reversed the process and pointed the telescope back at the tradition of Western art, which he has lifted, cropped and reinvented, collaging the fragments of his dreams, the details of half-remembered movies, with all his graphic brilliance.'

Paintings and silkscreen prints by Tadanori Yokoo: *Green Horizon*, from 1981, a Tarzan and Jane couple in the forest, like matinee idols, Jane in her red and white flower-print dress, a protective hand resting on the fur of the perplexed tiger who stands beside her. *An Impression of Tahiti* from 1973, naked Western women, cut out and pasted on exotic backgrounds. *Shambara*, from 1974, a Tantric adept meditating on a tiger-skin rug that seems to hover a few metres above a deep blue beach; in the background a red sunset over the ocean; at the top and bottom of the print, Indian advertisements for soap.

sample # 4

1964, *The Peanuts Hit Parade*. On the front cover, the Peanuts singing duo pose in kimonos, umbrellas at the ready in case of a spring shower. The distant ancestors of Pizzicato Five, Frank Chickens, DJ Towa Towa, Melon, Sandii, and other Japanese exotics, the Peanuts are accompanied for this record by the Six Jones and the Tokyo Cuban Boys. Their repertoire forges New World compounds in the white heat of exotica: a French song, 'Papa Aime Maman', arranged as a mambo and sung in Japanese, for example; 'Tintarella di Luna' arranged as rock'n'roll hovering on the edge of *chachacha* but held in check by a bass line borrowed from Little Richard's 'Lucille'; 'More than Anything', adapted from Tchaikovsky's *Swan Lake* and arranged as a Latin bolero; 'Yellow Bird', arranged in classic Martin Denny/Arthur Lyman exotica style, the bird song trilled on unison piccolo and xylophone; Gene Pitney's 'Hello Marylou Goodbye Heart' arranged in Hawaiian country pop style.

sample # 5

Jungle-Da (subtitled ... *not primitive* ...), released in 1985 by S-ken, *alter ego* of Tokyo resident Tadashi Tanaka, a guiding light in Japan's exotica movement. An ex-computer engineer, Tanaka spent three years soaking up New York atmosphere in the mid-seventies, returning to Japan to stage lowlife cabaret (*Nipponese Night*) in Tsubaki House, a well-established Tokyo discotheque. *Nipponese Night* was part of a move to revive the spirit of Japan's *Taisho* period, a short-lived hedonistic period between the two World Wars when foreign influences ranging from Charleston dresses and jazz to Dada and Surrealism were greedily absorbed into Japanese élite society.

S-ken portrayed himself as a parody of Eno-ken, a stand-up comic of the *Taisho* period who merged traditional *rakugo* comedy with elements of American vaudeville. S-ken's fabrications were rooted in nostalgia for the Japanese urban culture of *Taisho* cabaret. In similar fashion, Stony Browder Jr. and August Darnell's fantasies of Dr. Buzzard and Kid Creole (particularly on *Dr. Buzzard's Original Savannah Band* and *Dr. Buzzard's Original Savannah Band Meets King Penett*) disinterred Caribbean, African and forties American music for the late disco period in New York.

'What we did on the *King Penett* LP,' Browder told Carol Cooper in 1982, 'was use the triangle on the top end and the high-hat played the syncopation to the triangle. So we gave it an African kind of ring. And it's a tribal thing. Most of the Savannah band rhythms we color with a little Latin, but it's also colored more on the theory of the three cult drums from Africa. So we use that primal rhythm most times against a more continental feeling. Then you color it even more continental with strings. But we're not playing disco fills, we're playing almost classical strings, from a Hollywood, yesteryear perspective. It's a romantic, Hollywood interpretation of European classical things; never strictly Schubert, but that Hollywood interpretation of Schubert. Then, when you put the blues into those five-part harmonies – you know, the saxophones – when Duke Ellington and the 'A' train get put in along with the Latin horns, you start to lean more into the street sounds, the kind of African and Puerto Rican dance music you hear in the parks here.'

sample # 6

'Riot in Lagos' by Ryuichi Sakamoto, released in 1980 on *B-2 Unit*, a buzzing, microtonal electro-ceremony, the spectral Japanese megalopolis mapped onto the disjunctions, stresses and cultural dynamism of a West African city. 'I have a problem with the West,' said Ryuichi Sakamoto. 'I hate to divide the world, East and West, where is the edge?' In an essay entitled 'Finally, I Reach to Africa: Ryuichi Sakamoto and Sounding Japan(ese)', Brian Currid wrote, 'Sakamoto's music is key to understanding the 1980s in Japan primarily for its play with the inter-cultural space of the recording and film industries, and his use of the recording studio as a symbolic "crucible" for the internationalization (as opposed to "Westernization") of Japan.'

sample # 7

Prior to the formation of Yellow Magic Orchestra, Haruomi Hosono, adopting the persona of Harry 'The Crown' Hosono, records a series of exotica albums in the 1970s: *Tropical Dandy* in 1975, *Bon Voyage Co.* in 1976 and *Paraiso* in 1978. Pictured on the covers as the captain of an ocean liner, a pensive playboy, a dandified island-hopper, he filtered a *mélange* of American and tropical influences – Okinawan folk music, calypso, big band swing, Hoagy Carmichael's 'Hong Kong Blues', Martin Denny, the New Orleans R&B of Allan Toussaint, Frankie Ford and Dr. John, western boogie, Little Feat, the singer/songwriting of James Taylor, the Hollywoodland exoticisms of Van Dyke Parks's *Song Cycle* and *Discover America*, the orientalist musical motifs of American cinema – through his skewed, highly original Japanese aesthetic. Dripping with tropical languor, popping with lovehearts, the songs conjured the image of a wanderer, gambling and romancing his way through Louisiana and the Florida Keys, Trinidad, Hawaii, Okinawa, Bali, all the ports of pleasure.

In 1973, Hosono's first band, Happy End, travelled to Los Angeles to work with Van Dyke Parks. Mutual admiration for each other's exoticas grew out of the meeting. The son of a Jungian psychiatrist, Parks was born in 1941 in Massachusetts. His first two careers were child actor and Disney songwriter, the perfect apprenticeship for his *Smile* collaborations with Brian Wilson (particularly the sumptuous word layers, elephant trumpet brass and jewellery percussion of 'Surf's Up'), then his solo albums of Americana, calypso and late-twentieth-century trade war Japonisme: *Song Cycle* in 1968, followed by *Discover America*, *The Clang of the Yankee Reaper*, *Jump!* and, in 1989, *Tokyo Rose*. Drawing verbal and musical connections between Californian beach culture, Hollywood image voodoo and the realities of so-called paradise, Parks explored the mythical overlays that had accrued in American history, the factions of pioneer past replayed in the fictions of the screen. 'I was there to support his "dream-escape",' Parks told Beach Boys authority David Leaf, speaking of Brian Wilson, 'he wanted to make the American saga a legitimate currency in this new global music market that had just defined itself since 1964.' Parks's final line for *Song Cycle* was 'Dust off Pearl Harbour time'. 'Yankee go home,' he sang on *Tokyo Rose*.

'For me, a turning point in the growth of Japanese self-confidence came with the realisation that South-East Asia is just down the road,' wrote Clive Bell in *The Wire*. 'Listen to the way Hosono's "Shambala Signal" (on *Paraiso*, 1978), fashions a Balinese-style workout for tinkling gamelan and synth played through a wah-wah pedal. The album also features an Okinawan folk song ("Asadoya Yunta") sung by a woman with all the correct folk inflections over pop strings and a disco bass. And "Fujiyama Mama" is arranged for marimbas redolent of Thai classical music. In sum, the Hosono trilogy constitutes a fascinating melding of fake Orientalism with a burgeoning Japanese sensibility.'

Hosono recordings in the nineties returned to various versions of his seventies exoticisms, contrasting what Clive Bell called 'retro-lounge' with ambient electro-globalism, alchemised in the 'crucible' of the studio, the kind of hyperdub montages predicted by Jon Hassell's Fourth World recordings. Representing the retro-lounge was his *Swing Slow* album with vocalist Miharu Koshi, particularly 'Voo Doo Surfer', 'Disappeared' and a dreamy 'Paradise ver. 2', the latter with its 'Quiet Village' bird calls, all featuring Hosono on Korla Pandit-style cheese organ. Representing the hyperdub were tracks such as 'Quiet Lodge Edit', like Javanese music in an electronic lung, or 'Aiwoiwaiaou', in which Super Mario plumbs the intricate junctions of Nigerian *juju*. His *Interspecies Organisation* collaboration with Bill Laswell maps a colour-saturated view of the spectral megalopolis onto Willie Colón's tribal city. Like Wong Kar-Wai's Hong Kong, this place could be another place, in some other time, or many places, in all times, to many people, mutating identity.

Appropriately, my communication with Haruomi Hosono was relayed through electronic mail. Hosono's answers were translated by Haruna Ito with the assistance of Michiko Yamamoto.

Did Japanese exotic acts like the Peanuts, Shizuko Kasagi or the Tokyo Cuban Boys, I asked, make any impression on you in the early 1960s?

At the time, the Peanuts and the Cuban Boys were not perceived as exotic; on the contrary, they were swept up in the everyday ordinariness of television. Kasagi Shizuko was a star from before the age of television, and her boogie-woogie beat, certainly exotic at the time, did indeed liven up people during that post-World War recovery period, I believe. I also recall as a child being excited by that 'Tokyo Boogie-Woogie.'

Was their 'exoticism' any more 'exotic' than American rock and roll or folk music?

Kasagi Shizuko's boogie-woogie actually had a Japanese sensibility in its rhythms and its melodies, so it did seem a different thing from the authentic boogie-woogie. Still, that was because, for Japanese people of that time, that meant having accessibility by being 'traditional Japanese music'-like, and in this sense, the jazz feel and such from America was the real exoticism. In other words, for those of us post-World War generations, traditional Japanese music was nothing more than common and stale music, and all manner of culture that was desired and admired was from abroad. This, however, is the complete opposite today.

What was more exotic to you as a child and a teenager: Japanese folk music, traditional theatre music (Noh) and court music, or American swing and country & western?

If rock and R&B are also to be included within the scope of folk music, then all of these I think have developed in a quite straightforward, healthy manner. Things I perceived as exotic were, for example, films from Hollywood in the 1950s where the picture of Japan was occasionally represented in an extremely warped way, and the twisted, surreal mood that they exuded. And, the cheerful senselessness which can just be laughed off and forgotten was also essential. Examples: Jerry Lewis's comedy movies, *Around the World in Eighty Days,* Roy Rogers's cowboy outfit, the impression of Chinatown in Hawaii. (The Asia depicted in Francis Ford Coppola's *Apocalypse Now* – that was not funny.)

When you presented yourself as Harry 'The Crown' Hosono, did you imagine a life story for this character? Was he influenced by stereotypes from Japanese film or fiction?

Japanese names like 'Tanaka' and 'Suzuki', written in their Chinese characters (as we do in Japan) are somehow directly linked to the archetypical image of the square, serious Japanese.

But the moment you decide to add an American name, Tony or Frankie, for example, to that square surname, you get a mysterious sort of second-generation comedian which had never existed before in Japan. I'd been intrigued by such comedians' names since I was a child, and in my mind it overlapped with my own aspect of a musical trickster. Examples: Frankie Sakai, Tony Tani.

Japanese orientalism seems unique in Asia as being an orientalism that denies, or distances itself, from its own place in orientalist depictions.

Japanese exotica seems as highly developed as American or European, in its way. Was your use of Martin Denny with YMO [Yellow Magic Orchestra] an ironic comment on this?

Japanese people can never be true orientalists. This is because we are trapped within what Westerners term 'the Far East'. I would say that my own orientalism is a mind's eye view which I arrived at through taking a roundabout, Hollywood-esque perspective. I practised what Brecht mentioned, 'See as through the eyes of a stranger.'

The adaptations of computer-game melodies with YMO, plus your compilation – Video Game Music – seem to suggest that computer game music is a new kind of electronic folk music, also exotic in its way, yet communal, like folk. Is that close to your ideas of computer game music.

Computer music is a tremendous and terrible creative method in that it is not mediated by 'cultural disposition' such as skill and technique, but is a possibility for directly expressing the musical imagination. Looking at the origins of computer music, you might say that the origins of music itself can be seen there too. In other words, this is a process of creating a form of music by the input of three elements, PITCH, STEP and GATE. After the demise of YMO, I delved into such activities for a long while, and it was as though it were a dialogue with my own ego. If you take that as far as it will go, then music can depart from its 'cultural disposition' and come in contact with the internal world of individuality. On the other hand, this also means that one comes into contact with the DNA within ethnicity at the same time.

I hear a lot of Alan Toussaint and Dr. John in your solo albums of the 1970s, mixed with the postwar occupation soundtrack of jazz swing, some Van Dyke Parks, some Western Swing and country boogie, Hoagy Carmichael, Lee Dorsey, Little Feat, Van Morrison, Latin music – incredible in fact! What does all this mean in terms of Japanese culture?

Its the first time anyone has ever said to me that it was 'incredible', and this makes me very glad, of course, but it is work that I did twenty-five years ago. Fellow musicians who knew that I was making that curious music would say, 'What in the world has gone wrong with him?'

That is how little I was understood. In this way my musical tastes showed a certain tendency, and that tendency was 'boundaries'. It was for me the place where different things collide, like on a shoreline, which in literature is sometimes discussed as a universal kind of ideology, but in music it is simply the phenomenon of music itself, and I feel that just as some animal life begins on the shore, jazz and rock music also came to be. And appreciation of this sensation is personal potential, and there are such people in any country, so I myself am not able to view it within the paradigm of 'Japanese culture'.

But if I am to point something out, it would be that because Japan did meet defeat in the war, the experience of a cultural schism in generations such as my own led me to take this manner of approach. As a tendency world wide, the energy of the sense of contest between boundaries is diminishing. Japanese pop music is certainly very uninteresting, but American pop music is about as uninteresting, too.

Were you influenced by film and television music when you were growing up?

Until I was age ten, none of the middle-class homes in Japan owned television sets. So my childhood was like Woody Allen's *Radio Days*. So influences on me would be mainly from radio. A tune that came on the air every morning was a song from very far away (and exotic) that I most loved and still cannot obtain, a tune by Francis Lemarc with just human whistle and musette called 'À Paris'.

In the evening, the Three Suns' 'The Touch (Le Grisbi)' beckoned my heart towards far away, dark, and lonely places. It was this sensation that has long domineered in my consciousness, and continues to live vividly still inside me.

Is there a relationship between your 'exotica' phase and more recent albums, such as Interspecies Organisation, *with its melting of Mongolian song into electronics?*

In a previous question I mentioned that computer music contacted with ethnicity. It is an important point that the computer is an extremely standardised musical tool. Through the use of a Macintosh computer, music software like Performer or Cubase, and MIDI and GM sound modules, mutual exchanges can be achieved between people anywhere in the world. Within those electronic sound sources, there are sounds of traditional instruments such as the *shamisen*, the bouzouki, the lute, the *shakuhachi*, and anyone may use them freely.

In this way, now that borders in the world have been basically rendered meaningless, the question of ethnicity on a deeper, more serious level within people arises. It will come to relate also with ideas of shamanism. It may also be an occasion for a new understanding or respect to rise between the self and the other. I do think that, if music were to be the intermediary vessel, then ethnic wars possibly would end . . .

Were you aware of other exotica composers in the 1970s, such as Arthur Lyman and Les Baxter?

Their music developed a unique 'incognito' sensation of 'strange land' that had existed nowhere, and for that I have much respect. They probably have no need for tales of plantations that are always in the background of exoticism. Martin Denny's 'Sake Rock', Arthur Lyman's 'Otome-san' (it's actually 'Otomi-san') had a ridiculous liveliness to it that completely turned over the way I viewed Japan. Perhaps Hawaii is the true other-world on the border between West and East?

Was psychedelia a kind of exotica to you?

Just like there is a place like India ahead of Hawaii, there is psychedelia up ahead of exoticism. Likewise there is Don Juan Matius, there are UFOs, and the earth begins and spreads out from the aboriginal.

4

pink noir

adventures in
paradise

19

a civilised song

◆◆◆◆◆◆◆◆◆◆◆◆◆◆◆◆◆◆

And the white man's canoe, advancing up stream in the short-
lived disturbance of its own making, seemed to enter the portals
of a land from which the very memory of motion had forever
departed . . . Astern of the boat the repeated call of some bird,
a cry discordant and feeble, skipped along over the smooth
water and lost itself, before it could reach the other shore, in
the breathless silence of the world.

Joseph Conrad, 'The Lagoon'

My invitation to speak at a conference concerning
sound culture and nationalism was welcome. The place and time
hardly matter. These holiday conferences being the soft option
that they are, the ambience was familiar to the point of being
soporific. We were committed to discussing the nature of identity
in the late twentieth century but for the majority of delegates, our
setting – a resort hotel in late season – was conducive to late-night
drinking in improbable discos rather than intellectual rigour.

We had reached the second evening without any serious chal-
lenge to the status quo; the character who joined us for dinner
that night called himself Marlow. None of us knew him and in
conversation the following day we discovered a mutual ignorance
of his work. Did he spell his name Marlowe or Marlow? My
memory fails me on that insignificant point. What I remember
with forceful clarity is the intensity with which he delivered his

story, recounted at a point in the proceedings when the wine had relaxed us sufficiently to grant us forgetfulness, or forgiveness, regarding his haunted demeanour and odd speech. He described the incident three times, taking a long pause for a drink before embarking upon the next version in a different dialect. In his mind, he might have been addressing three distinct audiences, though our company regarded itself as being quite uniform, considering our placement in the turmoil of history, not to mention the disputatious nature of academic practice. He began, however, in the language that he had used, somewhat fitfully, throughout the evening . . .

'Listen! At Mamba Point, three soldiers stop me.

'Wall-eye, ragged-arse bazooka crazies . . . On my knees I sniff their gunpowder and tremble, hearing a tale of sneaking out of the desert shimmer, them wearin' aprons and scarves, golden wigs, wedding veils, swim suits and horror masks, eyes shining wires of radiance through smoke as black as ash.

'That's how they came, they said. Metal heavy.

'I listened as they told me how the smoke rolled back, slow and lazy.

'Nervous, they said, noses running, muscles on a constant tic, so when the smoke rolled back and a sugar-pink neon light flooded the scene their fingers took command, impacting shells into what they truly believed was the ghost light of enemy witchcraft spells, laid at the border crossing, flarin' and jumpin'.

'But the spells were phantoms in the smoke and sand and dust; it all clear and they see just a little mall of shops selling underwear, patisseries, pet houses and garden furniture. A woman is walking a poodle, the dog's hair dyed green, cut into cloud shapes and stars, and two steps behind her is a muscle guy, walkie talkie and cute little hi-velocity auto in ready mode.

'So poom! Now just glass and little shreds of rayon, plastic bamboo, some flecks of pastry, synthetic cream, twisted coconut and a floating dust of dog hairs.

'There were limbs, too. Pink spray in black snow.'

Here Marlow laughed, a chilling laugh that seemed to battle its way out of his throat.

'Washed in blood, the sugar-pink neon had lost its frosted charm.

'When their eardrums settled, they heard a pretty tune circling in the hush.

'Still spooked, they detonated that sound with grenades originally made in England, transacted in beautiful rooms by a Mister Chen and a Mister Henderson, sold in car boots and mountain pass markets, ending up on the edge of white desert at Mamba Point, blowing this little mirage to shit.'

He paused, emptied his glass, then resumed . . .

'You no fit hear! Na Maimbah Point three soldiers dey stop me. Wall-eyed, ragged-arse bazooka crazies . . . Wen ah butu for ground on my knees, I dey smell gun powder and I dey biggin for tremble, hearing a tale of sneaking out of the desert shimmer, de soldiers dem dey wear apron and scarves, golden wigs, wedding veils, swim suits and horror masks, dem eyes dey shine wit wire of radiance through smoke as black as ash.

'Na so dem come, them dey say, heavy metal.

'I dey listen as dey fit explain how the smoke rolled back, slow en lazy. Nervous, they said, dem nose dey run, dem muscle dey timap en shake, so when the smoke dey roll back and a sugar-pink neon light flooded the scene, dem finga take command, de bom dem dey fordom pan thing wey dem beeleeve sey for true true be the ghost light of de enemy im witchcraft, juju wey dem don put for border crossing, flarin and jumpin.

'But the spells were phantoms in the smoke and sand and dust: wen all don clear dem jos see little shops wey dey sell underwear, akara, pet houses and garden furniture, wan woman wey carry im little dog go for waka, e dye de dog im hair green, cut into cloud shapes and stars, and two steps behind her is a muscle guy, walkie talkie en wan pan dem small gangster automatic ready for shoot na big wahala dey take place.

'So poom! Now some glass and little shreds of rayon, plastic bamboo, some flecks of pastry, synthetic cream, twisted coconut en dog hair de float for dust.

'There were limbs too. Pink spray in black snow.

'Washed in blood, the sugar-pink neon had lost its frosted

charm, wen dem eardrum don stop for ring, dem hear fine fine tune circling in the hush.

'Still dey be fearful, they detonated that soun' with grenades originally made in England, Henderson and Chen talking porcelain, then them sold in car boots and mountain pass markets, ending up on the edge of white desert na Maimbah Point, blowing this little mirage to shit.'

Staring at each of us in turn, Marlow gulped from his replenished glass. Anticipating my interruption, he began again . . .

'Yehri! Na Maimbah Point three sojah dem stop me.

'Wall eyed, ragged arse bazooka crazies . . . wen ah butu pan me knee.

'Ah smell gun powder ah biggin for trimble, hearing a tale of sneaking out of the desert shimmer, dem wehr apron en scaff, golden wig, wedding dress, swimsuit and plastic mask, dem yai bin dey shine wit wire of radiance through smoke as black as ash.

'Na so dem kam, they said, metal haybee.

'I listened as they told me how the smoke rolled back, slow and lacee. Nervous, they said, dem nos dey run, tranga musool de ben, so when the smoke rolled back and a sugar-pink neon light flooded the scene, dem finga take command, de bom dem fordom pan weytin dem beeleeve sey for true true was the ghost light of enemy witchcraft. Fangadama wey dem don put nar de border, flarin and jumpin.

'But the spells were phantoms in the smoke and sand and dust: wen all don clear den jos see lili shop wey dey sell pioto underwear, patisseries, pet houses and garden furniture, wan ooman wey kerr im kaykayray dog go waka, e dye de dog im iyar green, cut into cloud shapes and stars, and two steps behind her is a muscle guy, walkie talkie en wan pan dem small dombolo automatic ready for shoot na konkoroma dey take place.

'So poom! Now just glass and little shreds of rayon, plastic bamboo, some flecks of pastry, synthetic cream, twis twis kokenat and a floating dust of dog hairs.

'There were limbs too. Pink spray in black snow.

'Washed in blood, the sugar-pink neon had lost its frosted charm. Wen da drum na dem yase don stop for ring, den yehri fine fine tune circling in the hush.

'Still spooked, they detonated that sound . . . '

Here Marlow paused again, clearly exhausted by his reminiscence and the strange impulse that had compelled him to
translate his own words. He seemed to be listening, perhaps
hearing the circling tune, then the explosion that had brought
silence. Suddenly agitated, he pulled two newspaper cuttings from
a pocket of his sweat-ringed shirt and pushed them across the
table, knocking a half-empty wine bottle on to the floor. Passing
these clippings around, we studied the photographs, which seemed
to come from some hell of the furthest imaginings.

What we now knew for certain was that this man, though
apparently deranged, had not invented his narrative. Slumped deep
in his chair, Marlow took the scraps of newspaper back, folding
them neatly, then finished in a barely articulate mumble.

'. . . blowing this little mirage to shit.'

We sat, the subdued pack of us, in a bubble of silence. Marlow
burst the wretched thing. 'I have heard tapes, you see,' he said,
his voice now steady. 'Concluding their transaction with the sale
of electronic torture instruments and illegal land mines, Mr Chen
and Mr Henderson took tea and discussed Chinese porcelain. Mr
Henderson asked to hear the famous singing voice of Mr Chen's
concubine. Mr Chen ordered the woman to sing one of his own
compositions.

'I cook my pink dark heart for you
I burn and eat my pink dark heart for you

'She concluded with a monologue of her own.

My child, sleeping on traffic islands, breathing transparent blue
poison, stands up to see the fireworks she thinks she hears, is
caught in the crossfire of a gun battle, falls and lies like a sleeping
child.

'The sentiments appeared to displease Mr Chen, who expressed
his displeasure by demonstrating one of his electric stun sticks on
the unfortunate woman. When the show was over, Mr Henderson
showed his pleasure with a gift that matched the cruelty of Mr
Chen's words and deeds.

20

pink fluffy cubicle on mercurius port

◆◆◆◆◆◆◆◆◆◆◆◆◆◆◆◆

As our ship, the *Lord Jim*, heaved to in the violet glow of Alpha Mercurius, wave officer Olmeijer's sensors picked up static-spiked wisps of Muzak songs. Or were they? Perhaps they were fine and rare examples of ambient crooning. How could we know? Muzak had been banned on Earth-One for more than two hundred years, yet the sound (or our fantasised speculations) lived on in collective memory, scuttling in the shadows of the digital archives. Old-timers such as myself had been tempered in the noise vats of our homeland planet, yet we shared the fascinations of our juvenile crew members, fascinations with that mysterious place where human desires shatter and reformulate as they enter the consciousness of machines and retrieval systems.

We had entertained no thoughts of berthing on this exotic and dangerous planet. Mournful and repetitious, a signal from deep space had transmitted cries that refused to be ignored. Within physical sight of the planet I discovered that my role as a Lay Magistrate was the reason for our enforced diversion; some obscure problem of a refugee ship fragmenting on incoming with great loss of life yet the uncanny survival of a chief mate leaving questions of culpability and responsibility to be resolved and inter-planetary legal knots to be unravelled.

So here we were, on the brink of entering the flesh pots and strangeness, the digitised Tru-Life clubs with their post-sentient karaoke and other wonders, the Monologue clubs where prurience met twelve-step absolution in equal measures, the Dream Fluid laboratories with their onanistic vaccination programmes. The crew's desires divided neatly into fleshpots and Zen digi-installation temples. As for me, once my duties were discharged I would investigate a little place footnoted in my Rough Guide. Principally, I longed for sunset.

Hidden in the dark Batavia district of Mercurius Port, Crooning On Venus was distinguished by a fascia caught in the grip of architectural delirium. Not so much post-retro as pre-discernment, the club signalled loudly to every tormented soul in the universe. Momentarily discouraged, though not keen to linger on this frankly threatening pavement of vermin and slinking shadows, I entered.

Whatever my fears, they dispersed as soon as I soaked up the perfume of the room. The Mercurians were nothing if not experts in the art of manipulating moods. Issued on entry with a mood template, I was required to enter my preferences on the spectrum, along with their estimated intensities. Melancholy, loss, romance, lust, violence, tranquillity, disturbance, surrealism, hallucination and nightmare were my chosen stimulants. I ticked the karaoke option as an afterthought, knowing that liquor had a disarming tendency to convince me of my skills as a crooner as the evening progressed. Having already divested myself of most of my portside allowance on this incontinent mood selection, I could barely begrudge one more expense.

To my chagrin, I found myself seated in a fluffy and rather risqué cubicle in company with the *Lord Jim*'s anthropologist, Dr Malinowski. A bluff character who was well known to Mr Olmeijer as a consumer of electronic pornography, Malinowski shared my interest in song as an expression of the tenacity of human beliefs, failings and aspirations. Nonetheless, he was not a man with whom I wished to relax. Given to pontification, he never missed an opportunity to impose his erudition, even when all around him were reduced to an undignified chemical stupor.

Yet there was no avoiding the situation without unpleasantness. I resigned myself to an evening of mixed pleasure and pain. 'Shall we compare templates, Doctor?' I asked. Behind that unhygienic beard of his, he blushed. Malinowski's preferences were well known to anybody who wished to hack into his service profile, yet he still contrived a sanctimonious façade. 'Never mind then,' I said, papering over the awkwardness. 'We can sing together later.' He nodded and busied himself in his private gloom. No club demanded shared experience in this day and age. Green-lighted, I motioned my sequence into initiation phase, kicked off my shoes and sank back into the pink fluff.

21

sugar & poison

◆◆◆◆◆◆◆◆◆◆◆◆◆◆◆◆◆◆

Dr Horse, Wild Turkey mooded, bootlegged, heats tobacco tip, sucks coronary smoke inward, illicit minded.

Awake as if snakebit, a torrent of sweats, heart's motion a drum 'n' bass breakbeat, he had fallen headfirst out of a dream.

Set in Mexican motel room, his own shaped shadow blocking hall light yet sufficient luminescence for nightmare glimpse of fishnet serpent writhing by satin shrouded alterbed where groin's desire lay only one hour in past time.

Whispers at the dark end of the street. Radio came on with a blast – an Acapulco disco bump groove – the fat man at the desk lip-zipped on psychosexual manifestations.

Just stepped out for worm's liquor and narcotic plant after three straight shifts.

'Taxi,' yells Horse, 'Take me to another part of town.'

Dozed in Chimpera noodle shop. Now faced with life's upset. Club managing in Mercurius Port – interplanetary satellite mail booking – like clock's tick an eternal circle.

Waking life's admin little different to nightmare's dark messages. Tired of programming music's background lull for dull-witted cerebralists. Meet 'n' greet Earthside coach parties and corporate champagning with drive-by shooting thoughts masked by shit-eater's grin and glad hand.

Horse, doctor in audio destabilisation, prescriptions punishable, assignations dubious, marginal tasks variable, turns to Earthside remedies now available on Offworld media.

Like beer's stomach settler boon in moderation, nerve's calming not always sourced in volumes of mellow.

The Doctor's blue desires – notorious back home – emotion's bizarre cuisine of sweet and bitter.

Jack, that cat was clean, he murmurs realistically.

'Baby I love you I want you I need you for ever come on back to me let me pump you all nite long' not rich or strange enough for Dr Horse's overloaded blood.

Too lowered in life's humpbacks. Too much rising to the top.

Horse needed slow songs about murder, despair, life's injustice, financial vacuum, cross-dressing, flesh texture, foreplay and sleep as much as the planet's other half needed songs about groin's requirements after candlelit supper for two.

Dr Horse accessed his collection – music called soul once upon a time in a far off country – found items not available or deleted for irritant reasons of corporate withdrawal.

Made impatient by absences in source material, Horse punched in switchback selection for emotion's in-depth exploration of sound-word-feeling-rhythms.

He cut them from a timeslice notable for uptown mood's contrast of urbane sensuality and identity rehab leavening despair's pit of dashed aspirations after FBI's trickeries, war's end and economic downturn.

Cool as the next fool, Horse enjoyed a disco bump 'n' hustle but found trenchant pleasures in narcotic reversions to infant state, agonised urban fear cries heard on disco's downside, sensual skin touch after the boom-boom stops, melting into sleep states, dried tears clarity, hybrid tropic languor, machine sex and long distance love's longing.

Planetside and disengaged, Dr Horse felt veins open, flooded by gush of aliveness.

Caught up in complex emotions, chasing a dream, glad to be unhappy, remembering who he was and what he was to himself.

Far inside the vibrations of a silent scream.

By imagination's implant, sonic concentrating, Earthside recall, he followed Al Green around a vocal booth in Royal

Recording Studios, 1320 South Lauderdale, Memphis, Tennessee. Heavy-lidded, Green lifts himself out of this world, circles in a trance of confusion and loss, walks away from the microphone, claps in ecstasy. Dr Horse is absorbed in the words. 'Grains of time,' he ponders. 'What the mothership are grains of time?'

Whispering in the aether talk, he thinks he hears a faint reply . . . 'you're a fish, I'm a water sign . . .'

'Float on,' he tells himself. Some questions, only a ballad can answer.

22

curios from the museum: part 1

◆◆◆◆◆◆◆◆◆◆◆◆◆◆◆◆◆

We were in New York City, a weekend of torrential rain and freezing winds. Charles Keil, author of *Urban Blues*, *Tiv Song*, co-author of *Music Grooves*, had spoken of many things, accompanying his talk with a *dumbek* drum and a couple of percussive assistants, one of them a regular drummer at New York *santeria* ceremonies. In passing, Keil recalled blues singer J.B. Lenoir; how he had arrived at Mister Lenoir's house in Chicago in the sixties and Lenoir had been amazed. The British, the French and the Belgians had all made their journeys downriver but Keil was the first American white man to walk through his front door. I asked Charlie if he had found out what possessed Lenoir to record an extraordinary single called 'I Sing Um the Way I Feel'. Keil didn't know the record but he said Lenoir had told him of a dream about an elephant playing the saxophone. Later, after a Cuban lunch, after we had listened to whistlers from space and the aquatic sounds of Weddell seals recorded under Antarctic ice by Doug Quin, after we had drunk beer together, Keil posed a question. 'What's the most exotic thing you've found?'

I couldn't answer at the time, except to say that nothing is really exotic any more. Later, I considered the question again and decided that there were two items that stood out from all the rest. One was 'I Sing Um the Way I Feel'. Back home in London, I dug it out from a cardboard box full of 7-inch vinyl singles, stared at the yellow and red Sue Records label, remembering times and places, music like smoke in the air.

Miraculously, the record was playable. I dropped needle to plastic, relished the nostalgia of crackle, instantly remembered every last detail of Lenoir's strange groove, played by what he called his African Hunch Rhythm: a light rustle of brushes on a snare drum, swishing a jazzy shik-a-tik *shik*-a-tik zhik-zhik tip-u-tik, like a cat dancing in dry leaves; bongos, clear and sparse, hit with a nice little flamming double note on the high drum; Lenoir's riffing acoustic guitar, clean, beautifully melodic, quietly propulsive, dropping out to leave space for the clip-clop and hustle of the African Hunch Rhythm; nothing else, other than the voice, high, strained and singing words so condensed in their meaning, sometimes so strangely enunciated, that they leave themselves open to fabulous misinterpretation. Nothing but the silence of the world.

What were these words? What could they be about? I can only approximate, and the first two phrases are clearly in need of a second opinion: 'Got me mad, office unwell, that's why I sing my blues, I sing zem the way I feel. You love your babe, I love mine. You may have her if you want to but I'm going to take my time. Take your time, take your time. Your girl look good and it takes my breath, the way my baby love me, oh I just can't help myself. Ooo-weee. I love these gal, like a baby chile and if they take my life I'm goin' give it wif a smile.' Just two minutes and thirty seconds of music from some other magical dimension.

I consulted Paul Oliver's book, *The Story of the Blues*. There was J.B. Lenoir, photographed at a recording session with bassist Willie Dixon, a big man filling every inch of a dark suit, set up with his double bass on a raised platform. Lafayette Lake, also wearing a dark suit and tie, played piano, alongside a saxophonist and drummer, both unidentified. At the front was Lenoir, head raised and cocked to one side as if keening in that taut voice of his, playing a white, solid-body electric guitar and wearing black trousers, black shoes and a zebra patterned tail coat that stretched down to below his knees.

Paul Oliver, one of the most eloquent of all blues scholars, had visited Lenoir in 1960, recording their conversation on a heavy EMI tape recorder that disintegrated when he journeyed south into the humid summer heat. Lenoir talked to him about dreams: the dream of an old devil, 'somethin' with a bukka tail and a shape of a bull but he could talk', that made his father quit singing the blues; a dream his mother sent him, giving him numbers for the lottery; the musical inspiration that came to him, 'like through a dream, as I be sittin' down, or while I be sleepin''. Oliver spoke affectionately about Lenoir, sketching the profile of a kind, contemplative man, somewhat eccentric but afflicted by bouts of sadness. 'He has a fondness for Zebra-striped, yellow velvet or similarly bright jackets and wears a small earring,' he wrote in *Conversations with the Blues*. He also noted that he had been christened J.B., never given the names that would have filled out the sound of those initials.

J.B. died from a heart attack as a result of car crash injuries in 1967. Unlike his guitar playing, which grooved and swung with impeccable precision, death was timed all wrong. A few more years to play with and he might have reaped some benefit from his status as a hip bluesman in England. 'I Sing Um the Way I Feel' was included more than once on blues albums compiled by Guy Stevens, released by Chris Blackwell on Island Records. As for the single, recorded in Chicago in 1963, shipped in London in January 1965, this was a rarity for being a blues on Sue, a label primarily devoted to examples of soul and R&B that would pass the mod fashion test of the mid-sixties.

I remember John Mayall, one of the pioneers of British blues, along with Cyril Davies and Alexis Korner, covering Lenoir material and borrowing certain aspects of his style. J.B. was an odd choice for a white English bluesman to emulate. Some of his material was topical and political – he sang about the Korean War, the Vietnam War, President Eisenhower, racial discrimination, drinking, debt and voodoo – and his approach was quirky, innovative, lighter and quieter than the emotional turbulence or outright aggression of Otis Rush, Elmore James, Buddy Guy, Muddy Waters, John Lee Hooker, Albert King and B.B. King, the artists whose influence shaped British blues. He looked outwards, into the world, disliked what he saw and commented on it. The others

seemed more self-obsessed, their music a churning pain driven
down inside and then regurgitated with a force that was shocking.

In Britain, where such externalised suffering was repressed,
the early blues underground took inspiration from these qualities
of mystery, emotional profligacy and exoticism, the Otherness of
blues origins. In the eighties, this exoticisation of poverty and
racial segregation was transferred to advertising, presumably to
appeal to British men, something (though not entirely) like myself.
We had listened to blues in our teens, the theory went; now we
spent our disposable income on beer and jeans. Yet you wouldn't
catch an urban bluesman wearing jeans, no matter how raw the
music. The late Muddy Waters may have roared 'I'm a maaaan,
I'm a rolling stone, I'm a man-child, I'm a hoochie coochie man,'
and sung dark songs of iodine in coffee, rat poison in bread, mean
red spiders, burying grounds, screaming and crying, rolling and
tumbling, but away from the microphone he was quiet, reserved
and professional. 'Grave even to the point of shyness,' was how
Alan Lomax described him. In photographs from the late forties
and early fifties he gazes straight into the camera lens, poised yet
almost transfixed. Around him others grin, affect nonchalence,
pursue their good times.

Paul Oliver recorded conversations with Muddy Waters during
his 'field trip' to America. Muddy talked about his poor childhood
in Rolling Fork, Mississippi – the story Europeans wanted to hear
about an authentic bluesman – and how he got that name. 'We
had a li'l – oh, two-room shack and there was a creek – Deer
Creek – come right up to the steps at the back porch. I was always
playin' in the creek and gettin' dirty and my sisters called me
Muddy Waters then.' No wonder those photographs snapped
three, four, even six decades later, captured a man in a conservative
grey suit with the jacket buttoned, a laundered white shirt fastened
at the collar, a slim tie with a mere touch of flamboyance in the
patterning. No more muddy water for Muddy Waters.

The sweaty exotic jungle of tough guys, hard drinking and
hard music portrayed in advertising may have been glossed with
the thin transparency of eighties style sheen but the fantasy still
drew from the 'noble savage' source that had sparked the first
blues boom. British television's treatment of blues in the mod era

was disgracefully *gauche* in this respect. Granada Televison's *Blues and Gospel Train*, transmitted in 1964, transported a train full of teenagers to a rural railway station. This device neatly mixed the theme of a current pop show, *6:5 Special*, with the romance of train blues and the metaphor of the gospel train, contemporaneously familiar from soul favourites like the Impressions' 'People Get Ready'. Muddy Waters was filmed walking along the railway track with a suitcase in his hand – the negro intinerant, the travelling man – singing 'You Can't Lose What You Ain't Never Had' while Sonny Terry and Brownie McGhee played their songs on a station platform, seated next to a tethered goat. Twenty-three years later, Brownie McGhee was still portraying the exotica, the Otherness, of black life as the murdered musician in Alan Parker's hoodoo movie, *Angel Heart*.

Paul Oliver, a British architect and academic, has been forthright about this European postcolonial attraction to primitivism, danger, Conrad's heart of darkness. As a teenager in 1942 he did 'harvest camp' in Suffolk. This was farm work done by teenagers who took the places of agricultural labourers who had been called up for Army service during World War II. In that period he was taken by a friend to eavesdrop on two newly arrived black American GIs singing as they dug trenches. 'We stayed behind the hedge,' he wrote in *Blues Off the Record*, 'getting cold. I was getting impatient, too, when suddenly the air seemed split by the most eerie sounds. The two men were singing, swooping undulating unintelligible words, and the back of my neck tingled. "They're singing a *blues*," Stan hissed. It was the strangest, most compelling singing I'd ever heard.'

I experienced a similar feeling myself in the sixties, seeing guitarist Freddie King at a small club in Battersea, the front-row seats full of blues luminaries like Alexis Korner and Peter Green. A week later King played at a less 'authentic' club above the Manor House pub in north London, where he added Chris Kenner's R&B/soul song, 'Something You've Got', to his set. It was the kind of gesture, ridiculously trivial now, that shocked the hard-core British blues fan's idea of purity. During the blues boom, blues musicians such as Little Walter, Howlin' Wolf, Arthur Crudup, Memphis Slim and Buddy Guy were fixtures on the

English club scene, many of them playing shows in obscure halls in small suburban towns. Growing up in one of these small towns in Hertfordshire, then a lower-middle-class suburb, now an execrable outpost of the north London sprawl, I remember Buddy Guy at Ware Corn Exchange, Howlin' Wolf at Welwyn Garden City (though illness forced him to cancel) and in Edmonton, Paul Butterfield's Blues Band, featuring Sammy Lay on drums, Mike Bloomfield and Elvin Bishop on guitars.

After hearing Butterfield's *East-West* psychedelic-raga blues, it came as no surprise to see the fiercely talented Chicago slide guitarist, Earl Hooker, play at the Royal Albert Hall in 1970. Like Ken dressed as Barbie, he wore a pink suit and pink socks with his pink shoes pumping a wah-wah pedal and his guitar held up behind his head. Could pink men sing the whites, or were they hypocrites? Young white males had devoted so much of their creativity to hi-heel sneakers, hoochie coochie men, mojo hands, John the Conquerer roots and other arcane phenomena of black spirituality and sartorialism; add a pink suit or a zebra-striped jacket and the notion of authenticity became impossibly convoluted.

In a 1986 issue of *Spin* magazine, journalist Bart Bull tackled the subject of the blues uniform head on. The white bluesman, he argued, would do anything to be like his black heroes except, *except*, wear the nylon polyblend socks, red polyester slacks and red dress shirts with wide-wingspan collars that ageing southern African-Americans often favoured. Levis? Nobody who came from Clarksdale or Rolling Fork, and made a little bit of cash, accrued a modicum of respect in the wider world, wanted to wear those working pants. The subject of Bart Bull's theory was John Lee Hooker, who retaliated, quick as a razor, on the *Spin* letters' page, accusing Bull of being, 'a little more concerned with socks and style than with the music and the message of the music I've played for 50 years'.

At the heart of all this was an incompatible dreaming: on the one hand, J.B. Lenoir's father scared away from the blues by a demon who talked in the human tongue; on the other hand, an elusive yet doggedly pursued dream about the capture and appropriation of a mythical essence, the 'realness' of Negritude.

With 'I Sing Um the Way I Feel', Lenoir seemed to be speaking for this quality, this capacity to reach down into the depths of experience and utter in a truthful voice.

But the song is not that straightforward. It burns with the unsaid, dancing around the chimera of authenticity with its own agendas of exoticism and strangeness that were beyond comprehension for a white suburbanite in England. 'Our inclination to interpret other societies through the filters of our classifications,' wrote Paul Oliver in *Shelter, Sign and Symbol*, 'is no more special than the perception of the alien from the west through the filters of their own language categorisations. However, in this one-way traffic where the curiosity of the west is focused on the cultures of others, our communication is heavily conditioned by our categorisation which threatens to draw distinctions in the structure of the cultures where, within the cultures themselves, none exists.'

Even now, more than thirty years after I first bought a copy of 'I Sing Um the Way I Feel', I can listen to this wisp of a song maybe four or five times in a row and be transfixed. Intrigued by that use of 'Um', a throwback to the 'darkie' speech of the black-face Minstrel Show era. Who wrote it in that way, particularly since Lenoir sings 'zem' rather than 'um'? Exhilarated yet left wanting by its concise, offhand perfection, puzzled by its stark originality, I hear it as a sound that was dreamed. I imagine J.B. waking with a start and for that dangerous moment when dreams can slip back into the underworld, struggling to keep the perfect strangeness intact until he can slip on his zebra-striped coat and convene the African Hunch Rhythm. I imagine if Charlie Keil had asked him where the track came from, he might have answered, 'Like through a dream.'

23

curios from the museum: part 2

◆◆◆◆◆◆◆◆◆◆◆◆◆◆◆◆◆◆◆

The second most exotic artefact, one that had lurked in the museum for years, was an easy listening Latin-Hawaiian album of music composed by His Majesty King Bhumibol Adulyadej of Thailand. I had first come across the Monarch's musical proclivities in Jeremy Marre's documentary film, *Two Faces of Thailand*. 'Once a week,' Marre wrote in *Beats of the Heart*, 'he would don shades and play clarinet with the palace band bopping away behind him. Every year he used to invite one of America's top jazzmen – like Dizzy Gillespie – to play and record in the palace with him. He built his own recording studio there, where his music could be mixed and then fed to local Thai stations.'

I like to think of the King in his 'bedroom' studio, recording the album I own. The front cover shows a faintly smiling young man, posed against a sky-blue background, wearing a brass-buttoned white jacket, his hair cut in casual post-Beatles style. This is Thanin Intarathep, heartthrob of yesteryear, a kind of Thai Cliff Richard. Open out the gatefold cover and we find a layout of King Bhumibol's musical scores for all twelve songs, written in Western notation with helpful chord symbols for guitarists. The lyrics, of course, are written in Thai. On the back cover, another photograph of Intarathep, this time wearing a black shirt and white tie. Thai features notwithstanding, he looks like a youthful gangster in a John Woo film.

As for the song titles and lyrics, I have to rely on the translations given by a Thai friend. Given the King's fragile health, the
military regimes he has seen come and go and his country's boom-
to-bust economic problems, it comes as no surprise to find that
the themes of the songs are nostalgic, exotic and escapist. The
album begins with a gentle Latin bolero, 'Dream', followed by
'Paradise Island' and 'Reminder of Love'. 'You're Always in My
Heart Forever', a bossa nova, bears an uncanny similarity to
'Our Day Will Come', recorded in the sixties by Ruby and the
Romantics. 'Starless' is not a cover version of a King Crimson
song but a Hawaiian number, orchestrated for Hawaiian slide
guitar, cocktail piano, vibraphone, flute and strings. Side one ends
with a slightly brighter bossa nova, 'Far From Worry'. Through
the mouthpiece of Thanin Intarathep, the King reveals details
of his seaside palace at Huahin. Listening to this tune with its
adventurous double-time piano and soaring strings, it is possible
to imagine the sea and sand that border this regal retreat in
paradise.

Side two begins with an ambient waltz called 'Rain Spray',
the rain evoked by chimes and piano trills. Heavily influenced by
George Shearing, 'Face Up to Problems with a Smile' is another
bossa nova. As the pathos of the title suggests, the King is one of
those composers incapable of writing cheerful music. Not even
the intrusion of flamboyant drum fills, maracas and double-time
piano can lift the hopelessly tragic mood. 'Twilight' is a Hawaiian
ballad that ends with Liberace flourishes. 'Star Filled Sky', yet
another 'Our Day Will Come'-style bossa, shows the King's debt
to Antonio Carlos Jobim's ambient bossa novas such as 'Wave'
and 'Mojave'.

According to the cover, 'Nighttime' is a slow rock. As with a
number of other tracks, the string section is not entirely in
tune. The song, I am told, paints a picture of that wee-small-
hours time when the woman has gone to bed and the man sits
alone, thinking about the mysteries of life. The album ends with
a Latin bolero called 'Sounds in the Air'. Poetically, this describes
the way in which sound can excite the imagination. Unhappily,
the string section and flute are not at one in the tuning depart-

ment, though their last chord is glorious. Extended by a few hours, it could have lifted King Bhumibol out of his melancholic hotel foyer genre and into the vanguard of international minimalism.

24

a rain dance

◆◆◆◆◆◆◆◆◆◆◆◆◆◆◆◆◆

A Friday evening, 8 June 1990. The location was Gunnersbury Park in west London. 'The setting for such an event is obviously crucial,' wrote Robert Atkins and Prakash Daswani in their brochure for the *Papua New Guinea Music Village European Tour 1990*. 'The "village" is not an attempt to recreate any actual village or traditional building. It is rather to create an environment, from impermanent structures and their natural surroundings, which seem on the right scale for the presentation. Certainly the location must not be too big and so much the better if it is a beautiful place with some indefinable "magic" about it.' They wrote about the acute problems of presenting the dance, music and ceremonies of so-called traditional societies (defined as pre-industrial) outside their local contexts. The intangible outdoor village was their answer. 'For climatic reasons here in the UK,' they added, 'reproducing such an experience is easier said than done.'

A marquee had been erected in Gunnersbury Park. Assembled here were dancers and musicians from the Sepik region of Papua New Guinea, Mount Hagen in the Western Highlands, the Eastern Highlands Asaro Valley, home of the famous Mud Men who smear their bodies with grey clay and dance in huge, ghostly head masks, and the Trobriand Islands, where Bronislaw Malinowski conducted his pioneering anthropological fieldwork.

As the first dance for a *Moka* exchange ceremony began, the dancers dressed in Bird of Paradise feathers and long striped aprons, the rain fell. Yodelling and bending their knees, the dancers carried on regardless, surrounded by a curious gaggle of park wanderers, pushing buggies, dressed for a cool English summer. The temperature plummeted, the sky darkened, the heavens opened.

With the rain now far too heavy for anybody to think about ceremonial exchange, the dancers retreated into the marquee. We huddled together like guests at a bizarre wedding reception: near-naked women, their faces painted red, crushed against the Mud Men, their masks looking more like an inconvenience than an apparition. The proximity was uncomfortable, as if Sun Ra and his Arkestra had been booked to play the tombola tent at a village fete. Overhead, a violent thunderstorm had broken, lightning adding anxiety to our feelings of discomfort and embarrassment. Some of the dancers looked as if they were running temperatures; other seemed to be teetering on the edge of hypothermia. Cigarettes were smoked. Tea was passed around in plastic cups. One man wrapped himself in an emergency blanket. For a passing second, nobody was exotic, though some of us were more suitably dressed for the environment than others.

25

the premature burial

◆◆◆◆◆◆◆◆◆◆◆◆◆◆◆◆◆

The memory resonated for a moment, inviting even more speculation. Finally, I closed the lid on my documents. The museum was hushed, dark, airless, sepulchral, as if demons had sucked out sound, light, then air, then life itself. My chest seemed to collapse. 'Ambivalance?' grated a voice behind me. I spun round. Mathers had crept in behind me on the silent soles of his wretched Hush Puppies. How long had he been spying on the final stages of my archaeology?

Yet suddenly I felt lifted. Of course, I knew I was implicated. Only a filthy exoticist such as myself could plunge, risking drowning, into this murky pool of fabulous misunderstandings and repellent exploitations. All of us are damaged by it, a catalogue of tortures, and yet there is the potential to experience a strange enrichment.

'Ambivalent, yes,' I answered. 'You've read Conrad, I suppose, soaked in whisky and the smell of your own decomposition?'

'Obligatory,' he replied. 'A racist, of course.'

'Of course,' I said, 'but a man of his time, immersed and distanced, ironic and compliant, for better and worse seeing new identities forged in hell or paradise, call it what you like.' From memory I quoted from Conrad's introduction to *An Outcast of the Islands*: 'The discovery of new values in life is a very chaotic experience; there is a tremendous amount of jostling and confusion and a momentary feeling of darkness. I let my spirit float supine over that chaos.'

I clicked shut the padlock on my box of documents, allowed that momentary feeling of darkness to expand and contract like a bellows. Full of chaos, the museum was empty.

afterword

The central section of this book – The Beast Within – is loosely based on a short article I wrote for *Collusion* magazine in 1982. Starting off by writing a straightforward article about Les Baxter, Martin Denny and Arthur Lyman, I found myself drawn into an exploration of the exotic fantasies that have generated so much creative work during the twentieth century. As I discovered during the writing of this book, the boundaries of these exotic fantasies expand.

The initial impetus to write that *Collusion* piece came from cassette tapes given to me by friends from Los Angeles, all of them long-term exotica fans: Tom Recchion, Fredrik Nilsen and Kevin Laffey. My thanks go to this trio, then, for their introduction to a genre of music that is so fascinating yet so stimulatingly problematic. Living at this distance from the exotic source, I have found Tom Recchion's continuing supply of 'unobtainable' albums invaluable.

During the writing of the book, Mike Cooper was particularly generous with ideas, facts and videos. I am grateful to Musa Kalamulah for his West African 'translations' in Pink Noir and to Kazuko Hohki for her collaborative work on the *Jungle-Da* sample from Tropical Dandies.

Some parts of the book were adapted from pieces previously published in *The Wire*, *The Face*, *Arena*, *The Times*, *GQ*, *Mojo*, *Womex 97* and *Andere Sinema*; my thanks to their respective commissioning editors. I would also like to thank Steve Knutson, Eiichi Azuma, Simon Hopkins, Clive Bell, Nikki Ratanapan, James Call, Chris Bohn, Tony Herrington, Ben Mandelson, Davie Allan, Talvin Singh, Charles Keil, Steven Feld, Werner Durand, Tom Paulus, Sue Steward and Andrew Brenner. All of them were helpful in various ways, big or small but always vital.

As was the case with *Ocean of Sound*, collaborating with Russell Mills has more to offer than just a design job. Russell can be depended on for his enthusiastic encouragement, not to mention obscure facts and corrections. Laurence O'Toole once again proved himself to be a skilled master of tactful severity in his editing. A certain amount of astonished gratitude is due to Pete Ayrton, who has taken a chance for the third time on music that has to be explained to be believed. As ever, my daughter Juliette has to put up with a lot, including hearing more Les Baxter than is good for her future development. *Exotica* is for her.

bibliography

Anger, Kenneth, *Hollywood Babylon*, Dell Publishing, New York, 1975.

Artaud, Antonin, *Collected Works volume 4*, Calder & Boyars, London, 1974.

Atkins, Robert, and Daswani, Prakash, *Papua New Guinea Music Village European Tour*, brochure, Cultural Co-operation, London, 1990.

Baby Boomer Collectibles, vol. 1, no. 5, February 1994, Waupaca, Wisconsin.

Balikci, Asen, 'Reconstructing Cultures on Film' (1975), in Paul Hockings (editor), *Principles of Visual Anthropology*, Mouton De Gruyter, Berlin and New York, 1995.

Beebe, William, *High Jungle*, The Bodley Head, London, 1950.

Behdad, Ali, *Belated Travelers: Orientalism in the Age of Colonial Dissolution*, Duke University Press, Durham and London, 1994.

Bell, Clive, 'Sayonara Cruel World: Haruomi Hosono', *The Wire*, Issue 162, August 1997, London.

Bell, Clive, 'Teiji Ito' review, *The Wire*, Issue 161, July 1997, London.

Betrock, Alan, *Rock 'n' Roll Movie Posters*, Shake Books, New York, 1979.

Bishop, Peter, *The Myth of Shangri-La: Tibet, Travel Writing and the Western Creation of Sacred Landscape*, Athlone Press, London, 1989.

Blades, James, *Percussion Instruments and Their History*, Faber & Faber, London, 1975.

Brain, Robert, *The Decorated Body*, Harper & Row, New York, 1979.

Brett, Philip, 'Eros and Orientalism in Britten's Operas', in Philip Brett, Elizabeth Wood and Gary C. Thomas (editors), *Queering the Pitch: The New Gay and Lesbian Musicology*, Routledge, New York and London, 1994.

Brunn, Ludwig von (editor), *The Amorous Drawings of the Marquis von Bayros*, Brandon House, North Hollywood, California, 1968.

Burroughs, William S., *My Education: A Book of Dreams*, Picador, London, 1995.

Burroughs, William S., *The Western Lands*, Viking Penguin, New York, 1987.

Burt, Rob, *Surf City, Drag City*, Blandford Press, Poole, Dorset, 1986.

Cabrera Infante, G., *Three Trapped Tigers*, Pan Books, London, 1980.

Call, James, and Huestis, Peter, 'Les Baxter: Godfather of Exotica' (*interview, 24 January 1995*), Parts 1 and 2, *Hypno*, spring issues, 1995.

Cantrill, Arthur and Corinne, Interview with Harry Smith, *Cantrills Filmnotes*, no. 19, 1974.

Chadavarkar, Bhaskar, 'The Man Who Went Beyond Stop', *Cinema Vision India*, vol. 1, no. 4, October 1980 (editor: Siddharth Kak), Bombay.

Clifford, James, *The Predicament of Culture: Twentieth-Century Ethnography, Literature, and Art*, Harvard University Press, Cambridge, Massachusetts, and London, 1988.

Clifford, James, *Routes: Travel and Translation in the Late Twentieth Century*, Harvard University Press, Cambridge, Massachusetts, 1997.

Clifford, James and Marcus, George E. (editors), *Writing Culture: The Poetics and Politics of Ethnography*, University of California Press, Berkeley, 1986.

Conrad, Joseph, *Almayer's Folly*, Oxford University Press, Oxford, England, 1992.

Conrad, Joseph, 'Freya of the Seven Isles', in *'Twixt Land and Sea*, Penguin Books, Harmondsworth, 1978.

Conrad, Joseph, *Heart of Darkness*, Penguin Books, Harmondsworth, 1973.

Conrad, Joseph, 'The Lagoon', in *The Lagoon and Other Stories*, Oxford University Press, Oxford and New York, 1997.

Conrad, Joseph, *An Outcast of the Islands*, Penguin Books, Harmondsworth, 1975.

Conrad, Joseph, 'An Outpost of Progress', in *Tales of Unrest*, Penguin Books, Harmondsworth, 1977.

Conrad, Joseph, *The Rescue*, Penguin Books, Harmondsworth, 1950.

Conrad, Joseph, *The Shadow-Line*, Oxford University Press, Oxford, England, 1985.

Conrad, Joseph, *Typhoon*, Penguin Books, Harmondsworth, 1963.

Conrad, Joseph, *Victory*, Penguin Books, Harmondsworth, 1985.

Conrad, Joseph, *Youth and The End of the Tether*, Penguin Books, Harmondsworth, 1975.

Cooper, Carol, 'Savannah Band: Only with Stony', *New York Rocker* 62, July/August 1982.

Cooper, Mike, 'A Man of Steel: The Extraordinary Times and Talents of Kealoha Life', *Folk Roots*, nos. 79–80, Jan/Feb, 1990.

Cotlow, Lewis, *Amazon Head-Hunters*, Robert Hale, London, 1954.

Crosby, David, with Gottlieb, Carl, *Long Time Gone*, Heinemann, London, 1989.

Currid, Brian, 'Finally, I Reach to Africa: Ryuichi Sakamoto and Sounding

Japan(ese)', in John Whittier Treat (editor), *Contemporary Japan and Popular Culture*, Curzon Press, Richmond, Surrey, 1996.

Densmore, Frances, *Nootka and Quileute Music*, Da Capo Press, New York, 1972.

Deren, Maya, *Divine Horsemen: The Voodoo Gods of Haiti*, Thames & Hudson, London, 1953.

Diolé, Philippe, *The Undersea Adventure*, Sidgwick & Jackson, London, 1954.

Dowidat, Willi, 'The Spotniks: The Complete History of Bo Windberg and His Groups', *Rumble: The Magazine for Collectors of Instrumental Records*, vol. 4, no. 1, Spring 1977.

Edwards, Gregory J., and Cross, Robin, *Worst Movie Posters of All Time*, Sphere Books, London, 1984.

Eliade, Mircea, *Shamanism: Archaic Techniques of Ecstasy*, Routledge & Kegan Paul, London, 1964.

Elliot, Brad, *Surf's Up: The Beach Boys on Record, 1961–1981*, Pierian Press, Ann Arbor, Michigan, 1982.

Fagg, William (editor), *The Raffles Gamelan: A Historical Note*, The Trustees of the British Museum, London, 1970.

Feld, Steven, 'Aesthetics as Iconicity of Style (uptown title); or, (downtown title) "Lift-up-over-sounding": Getting into the Kaluli Groove', in Charles Keil and Steven Feld (editors), *Music Grooves*, The University of Chicago Press, Chicago and London, 1994.

Fischer, Michael M.J., 'Ethnicity and the Post-Modern Arts of Memory', in James Clifford and George E. Marcus (editors), *Writing Culture: The Poetics and Politics of Ethnography*, University of California Press, Berkeley, 1986.

Fletcher, Alice Cunningham, *Omaha Music*, Peabody Museum, Cambridge, Massachusetts, 1893.

Flornoy, Bertrand, *Jívaro: Among the Head-Shrinkers of the Amazon*, Elek Books, London, 1953.

Frazer, James George, *The Golden Bough: A Study in Magic and Religion*, Oxford University Press, Oxford, 1994.

Freeman, Derek, *Margaret Mead and Samoa: The Making and Unmaking of an Anthropological Myth*, Penguin Books, Harmondsworth, 1984.

Freud, Sigmund, *Totem and Taboo*, translated by Abraham A. Brill, Random House, New York, 1960.

Gillespie, Dizzy, with Fraser, Al, *Dizzy: To Be Or Not To Bop*, Quartet Books, London, 1982.

Gillett, Charlie, *The Sound of the City: The Story of Rock and Roll*, Souvenir Press, London, 1983.

Green, Stanley, *The Rodgers and Hammerstein Story*, The John Day Company, New York, 1963.

Haney, Lynn, *Naked at the Feast*, Robson Books, London, 1981.

Harbison, Robert, *Eccentric Spaces*, 1977, Ecco Press, Hopewell, New Jersey, 1977.

Harich-Schneider, Eta, *A History of Japanese Music*, Oxford University Press, Oxford, 1973.

Harner, Michael J., *The Jívaro: People of the Sacred Waterfalls*, Robert Hale & Company, London, 1972.

Haskins, Jim, *The Cotton Club*, New American Library, New York, 1984.

Hearn, Lafcadio, *Writings from Japan*, edited by Francis King, Penguin Books, Harmondsworth, 1984.

Hess, Norbert, Screamin' Jay Hawkins interview, *Blues Unlimited*, no. 121, September/October 1976, London.

Heyerdahl, Thor, *Aku-Aku*, Allen & Unwin, London, 1958.

Hillman, James, *The Dream and the Underworld*, Harper & Row, New York, 1979.

Hobsbawm, E.J., *The Age of Empire: 1875–1914*, Sphere Books, London, 1989.

Holborn, Mark, *Beyond Japan*, Jonathan Cape, London, 1991.

Hooker, T. and Hooker, Barbara I., *Duetting*, in R.A. Hinde (editor), *Bird Vocalizations*, Cambridge University Press, London, 1969.

Hoskyns, Barney, *Waiting for the Sun: The Story of the Los Angeles Music Scene*, Viking, London, 1996.

Howarth, David, *Tahiti: A Paradise Lost*, Harvill Press, London, 1983.

Huggins, Nathan, *Harlem Renaissance*, Oxford University Press, Oxford, 1973.

Hughes, George, 'Entering Island Cultures: Synge, Hearn and the Irish Exotic', in Sukehiro Hirakawa (editor), *Rediscovering Lafcadio Hearn*, Global Oriental, Folkestone, 1997.

Isozaki, Arata, 'Ruins', introduction to Ryuji Miyamoto, *Architectural Apocalypse*, Heibonsha, Tokyo, 1988.

Jones, Leroi, *Blues People*, The Jazz Book Club, London, 1966.

Kanahele, George S., (editor), *Hawaiian Music and Musicians*, University Press of Hawaii, Honolulu, 1979.

Kawamura, Yosuke, *Exotica*, Parco Co. Ltd, Tokyo, Japan, 1981.

Kawamura, Yosuke, *La Tierra de la Salsa*, Hanashi-No-Tokushu, Tokyo, Japan, 1981.

Key, Wilson Bryan, *Subliminal Seduction*, Prentice-Hall, Englewood Cliffs, New Jersey, 1973.

Kiernan, Victor, *The Lords of Humankind*, Serif, London, 1995.

Kinsey, Alfred, *Sexual Behaviour in the Human Female*, Saunders, Philadelphia, 1953.

Kinsey, Alfred, *Sexual Behaviour in the Human Male*, Saunders, Philadelphia, 1948.

Knight, Alanna, *R.L.S. In the South Seas*, Mainstream Publishing, Edinburgh, 1986.

Kofsky, Frank, *Black Nationalism and the Revolution in Music*, Pathfinder Press, New York, 1970.

Kraft, David, and Bohn, Ronald, Les Baxter interview, *Soundtrack! The Collector's Quarterly*, Issue no. 26, Summer 1981.

Laing, Dave, Dallas, Karl, Denselow, Robin, and Shelton, Robert, *The Electric Muse*, Methuen, London, 1975.

Landis, Bill, *Anger: The Unauthorized Biography of Kenneth Anger*, HarperCollins, New York, 1995.

Langdon, Philip, *Orange Roofs, Golden Arches: The Architecture of American Chain Restaurants*, Michael Joseph, London, 1986.

Lanza, Joseph, *Elevator Music*, St Martin's Press, New York, 1994.

Legeza, Laszlo, *Tao Magic: The Secret Diagrams and Calligraphy*, Thames & Hudson, London, 1975.

Leiris, Michel, *Manhood*, Jonathan Cape, London, 1968.

Leiris, Michel, *Nights as Day, Days as Night*, Eridanos Press, Colorado, 1987.

Loti, Pierre, *The Desert*, translated by Jay Paul Minn, University of Utah Press, Salt Lake City, 1993. (*Le Désert* originally published 1895.)

Loti, Pierre, *The Marriage of Loti*, T. Werner Laurie, London, 1927.

MacKenzie, John M., *Propaganda and Empire*, Manchester University Press, Manchester, 1984.

Mangin, Arthur, *The Desert World*, T. Nelson, London, 1872.

Marcus, Greil, *Invisible Republic*, Picador, London, 1997.

Marre, Jeremy and Charlton, Hannah, *Beats of the Heart*, Pluto Press, London, 1985.

Martin, Andy, *Walking on Water*, Minerva, London, 1992.

McPhee, Colin, *A House in Bali*, Oxford University Press, Singapore, Oxford and New York, 1986.

McPhee, Colin, *Music in Bali*, Yale University Press, New Haven, Connecticut, 1966.

Melville, Herman, *Moby Dick*, New American Library, New York, 1961.

Melville, Herman, *Typee*, New American Library, New York, 1964.

Michener, James, *Tales of the South Pacific*, Fawcett Books, New York, 1989.

Miles, Barry, *Ginsberg: A Biography*, Harper Perennial, New York, 1989.

Miller, Russell, *Bunny: The Real Story of Playboy*, Michael Joseph, London, 1984.

Mishima, Yukio, *Confessions of a Mask*, Panther, London, 1972.

Mondo Music, issues 1 and 2, Libro Port, Japan, 1995.

Morgan, Ted, *Literary Outlaw: The Life and Times of William Burroughs*, The Bodley Head, London, 1991.

Morton, Jim, 'Sexploitation Films', in V. Vale and Andrea Juno (editors), *Incredibly Strange Films*, Re/Search Publications, San Francisco, 1986.

Naha, Ed, *The Films of Roger Corman*, Arco Publishing, New York, 1982.

Nochlin, L, 'The Imaginary Orient', *Art in America*, May 1983.

Ochs, Michael, *Rock Archives*, Blandford Press, Poole, Dorset, 1985.

Oja, Carol J., *Colin McPhee: Composer in Two Worlds*, Smithsonian Institution Press, Washington and London, 1990.

Oliver, Paul, *Blues Off the Record*, Baton Press, Tunbridge Wells, Kent, 1984.

Oliver, Paul, *Conversation with the Blues*, Jazz Book Club, London, 1967.

Oliver, Paul (editor), *Shelter, Sign and Symbol*, Barrie & Jenkins, London, 1975.

Oliver, Paul, *The Story of the Blues*, Penguin, Harmondsworth, 1972.

Partch, Harry, *Genesis of a Music*, Da Capo Press, New York, 1974.

Pelletier, P.M., *Sue Record Catalogue*, Record Information Services, Bromley, Kent, 1976.

Perloff, Nancy, *Art and the Everyday: Popular Entertainment and the Circle of Erik Satie*, Clarendon Press, Oxford, 1993.

Peterson, Elsa, 'On the Trail of Red Sky Lady and Other Scholars', published in *Heresies #10: Women and Music*, vol. 3, no. 2, issue 10. New York, 1980.

Poe, Edgar Allan, *The Poems of Edgar Allan Poe*, George Bell & Sons, London, 1970.

Poe, Edgar Allan, *Poe's Tales of Mystery and Imagination*, J.M. Dent & Sons, London, 1908.

Purl, Mara, *Watermill: A Historical Perspective*, http://www.nycballet.com.

Reed, Ishmael, *Mumbo Jumbo*, Allison & Busby, London, 1988.

Renan, Sheldon, *An Introduction to the American Underground Film*, E.P. Dutton, New York, 1967.

Rhodes, Colin, *Primitivism and Modern Art*, Thames & Hudson, London, 1994.

Rice, Boyd, 'Mondo Films', in V. Vale and Andrea Juno (editors), *Incredibly Strange Films*, Re/Search Publications, San Francisco, 1986.

Rieff, David, *Los Angeles: Capital of the Third World*, Jonathan Cape, London, 1992.

Ritvo, Harriet, *The Animal Estate: The English and Other Creatures in the Victorian Age*, Penguin Books, London, 1990.

Roberts, John Storm, *The Latin Tinge*, Oxford University Press, New York and Oxford, 1979.

Rothenberg, Jerome, *Ritual: A Book of Primitive Rites and Events*, A Great Bear Pamphlet, Something Else Press, New York, 1966.

Rothenberg, Jerome (editor), *Shaking the Pumpkin: Traditional Poetry of the Indian North Americas*, Doubleday Anchor, New York, 1972.

Rothenberg, Jerome, *Technicians of the Sacred: A Range of Poetries from Africa, America, Asia, Europe and Oceania*, 2nd edition, University of California Press, Berkeley, California, 1985.

Rudorff, Raymond, *Belle Epoque: Paris in the Nineties*, Hamish Hamilton, London, 1972.

Said, Edward, Introduction to Rudyard Kipling, *Kim*, Penguin Books, London, 1987.

Said, Edward, *Orientalism*, Penguin Books, London, 1985.

Sakolsky, Ron, and Koehnline, James, *Gone to Croatan*, Autonomedia/ AK Press, New York/Edinburgh, 1993.

Sammon, Paul M., *Future Noir: The Making of Blade Runner*, Orion Media, London, 1996.

Schmalenbach, Werner, 'Gauguin's Encounter with the World of Primitive Peoples', in *World Cultures and Modern Art*.

Schneckenburger, Manfred, 'Idol, Totem and Fetish in Modern Art', in *World Cultures and Modern Art*.

Sergeant, Jack, *Naked Lens*, Creation Press, London, 1997.

Shephard, Ben, 'Showbiz Imperialism: The Case of Peter Lobengula', in John M. MacKenzie (editor), *Imperialism and Popular Culture*, Manchester University Press, Manchester, 1986.

Shoemaker, Greg, 'The Toho Legacy', in *The Japanese Fantasy Film Journal*, no. 13, 1981, Toledo, Ohio.

Simmons, Steven, 'Man Without a Country', *The Movies*, November 1983, New York.

Sitney, P. Adams, *Visionary Film: The American Avant-Garde*, Oxford University Press, New York, 1974.

Sprawson, Charles, *Haunts of the Black Masseur: The Swimmer as Hero*, Jonathan Cape, London, 1992.

Stapleton, Chris, and May, Chris, *African All-Stars: The Pop Music of a Continent*, Quartet Books, London and New York, 1987.

Steiner, Franz, *Taboo*, Penguin Books, Harmondsworth, 1967.

Stewart, Charles, and Shaw, Rosalind, *Syncretism/Anti-Syncretism: The Politics of Religious Synthesis*, Routledge, London, 1994.

Sweetman, David, *Paul Gauguin: A Complete Life*, Hodder & Stoughton, London, 1995.

Swinglehurst, Edmund, *The Romantic Journey: The Story of Thomas Cook and Victorian Travel*, Pica Editions, London, 1974.

Szwed, John F., *Space Is the Place: The Lives and Times of Sun Ra*, Pantheon Books, New York, 1997.

Teraoka, Masami, with Hess, Lynda, 'Monitoring Our Times', in *Paintings by Masami Teraoka*, Arthur M. Sackler Gallery / Smithsonian Institution, Washington DC, 1996.

Thompson, Hunter S., *Hell's Angels: A Strange and Terrible Saga*, Ballantyne Books, New York, 1990.

Toop, David, *Ocean of Sound: Aether Talk, Ambient Sound and Imaginary Worlds*, Serpent's Tail, London and New York, 1995.

Torgovnick, Marianna, *Gone Primitive: Savage Intellects, Modern Lives*, University of Chicago Press, Chicago and London, 1990.

Tormé, Mel, *Wynner*, Stein & Day, New York, 1978.

Vale, V., 'Jello Biafra', in V. Vale and Andrea Juno (editors), *Incredibly Strange Music*, Volume II, Re/Search Publications, San Francisco, 1994.

Vale, V., 'Martin Denny', in V. Vale and Andrea Juno (editors), *Incredibly Strange Music*, Volume I, Re/Search Publications, San Francisco, 1993.

Who Put The Bomp!, Issue 14, Fall 1975, Burbank, California.

Wilson, Brian, with Gold, Todd, *Wouldn't It Be Nice*, Bloomsbury, London, 1992.

Wolfe, Tom, *The Bonfire of the Vanities*, Bantam Books, New York, 1988.

Wolfe, Tom, *The Kandy-Kolored Tangerine-Flake Streamline Baby*, Picador, London, 1981.

Wolfe, Tom, *The Purple Decades*, Jonathan Cape, London, 1983.

Wolfe, Tom, *Radical Chic & Mau-Mauing the Flak Catchers*, Farrar, Straus & Giroux, New York, 1970.

World Cultures and Modern Art: The Encounter of 19th and 20th Century European Art and Music with Asia, Africa, Oceania, Afro- and Indo-America, XXth Olympiad exhibition catalogue, Bruckmann Publishers, Munich, Germany, 1972.

Wright, Lawrence, 'Sympathy for the Devil', *Rolling Stone* 612, September 5, 1991, New York.

Yokoo, Tadanori, *Paintings, Prints and Drawings by Tadanori Yokoo*, Bujitsu Shuppan-sha, Tokyo, Japan, 1981.

Young, Jordan R., *Spike Jones and his City Slickers – The Untold Story*, Disharmony Books, Beverley Hills, California, 1982.

discography

This is not a 'proper' discography or guide to best recordings, nor is it a list of recommendations; simply a discography for this book, relating to the text and mixing vinyl, CD, singles and albums, deletions, bootlegs and not-for-sale items. Everything below may be worth hearing, though not necessarily worth buying (or vice versa).

Ahbez, Eden, *Eden's Island*, Del-Fi CD 71211-2.

Allan, Davie (and the Arrows), *Fuzz Fest*, Jupiton TWIST 001.

Allan, Davie (and the Arrows), *Loud Loose and Savage*, Iloki ILCD 1017.

Antarctica, Saydisc SDX 219.

Bacharach, Burt, *The Best of Burt Bacharach*, A&M 452-2.

Bacharach, Burt, *The Look of Love: The Classic Songs of Burt Bacharach*, Polygram 535 190-2.

Bacharach, Burt, *Reach Out*, A&M 394 131-2.

Baxter, Les, *Baxter's Best*, Capitol SM-1388.

Baxter, Les, *Caribbean Moonlight*, Capitol T733.

Baxter, Les, *Continental*, Music For Pleasure MFP 1028.

Baxter, Les, *Cry of the Banshee*, Citadel CTV 7013.

Baxter, Les, *The Exotic Moods of Les Baxter*, Capitol Records 7243 8 37025 2 7.

Baxter, Les, *Jewels of the Sea*, Capitol ST 1537.

Baxter, Les, *The Lost Episode*, Dionysus Records BA07-2, 1995.

Baxter, Les, *Open End Disc Jockey Interview*, Reprise OE-DJ-3.

Baxter, Les, *The Passions*, Oriental Pacific OP-1920-2.

Baxter, Les, *Que Mango!*, Scamp SCP 9718-2.

Baxter, Les, *Ritual of the Savage (Le Sacre du Sauvage)*, Capitol M-11702.

Beach Boys, *Brian Wilson Rarities*, EMI Australia ST 26463.

Beach Boys, *Friends*, Capitol ST 2895.

Beach Boys, *Good Vibrations: Thirty Years of the Beach Boys*, Capitol C2 0777 7 81294 2 4.

Beach Boys, *Smile*, Brother ST 2580 (bootleg).

Beach Boys, *Stack o' Tracks*, EMI E-ST 24009.

Bey, Hakim, *T.A.Z.*, Axiom 314-524 014-2.

Blaine, Hal, *Psychedelic Percussion*, Innerspace Records IS 50019-2.

Boo-Yaa T.R.I.B.E., 'Coming Hard to America', Villain Records BYT-01, 12″ single.

Boo-Yaa T.R.I.B.E., *New Funky Nation*, Island BRLP 842 396-1.

The Byrds, *The Notorious Byrd Brothers*, Columbia/Legacy 486751 2.

Cohen, Ira, *The Poetry of Ira Cohen*, Sub Rosa SR62.

Cole, Nat 'King', *Unforgettable*, Capitol EMS 1100.

Coleman, Ornette (& Prime Time), *Tone Dialling*, Harmolodic/Verve 527 483-2.

Colón, Willie, 'Set Fire to Me', A&M AMY 330 12″ single.

Colón, Willie, *Solo*, Fania.

Coltrane, Alice, *Eternity*, Warner Bros. BS 2916.

Coltrane, Alice, *Huntington Ashram Monastery*, Impulse AS-9185.

Coltrane, Alice, *A Monastic Trio*, Impulse A-9156.

Coltrane, Alice, *Ptah the El Daoud*, Impulse IMP 12012.

Coltrane, Alice, *Transcendence*, Warner Bros. BS 3077.

Coltrane, Alice, *Turiya Sings*, Avatar Book Institute ABI-100.

Coltrane, Alice, *Universal Consciousness*, Impulse AS-9210.

Cowell, Henry, *Piano Music*, Smithsonian Folkways SF-40801.

Cymatic Scan, *Cymatic Scan*, Fax PS 08/50.

Dale, Dick, *Calling Up Spirits*, Beggars Banquet, BBQCD 184.

Dale, Dick, *Unknown Territory*, Hightone HCD 8055.

Denny, Martin, *Another Taste of Honey*, Liberty LRP-3277.

Denny, Martin, *Exotic Moog*, Electronic Vanguard EV-906-2.

Denny, Martin, *The Exotic Sounds of Martin Denny*, Capitol CDP 7243 8 38374 2 7.

Denny, Martin, *The Exotic Sounds of Martin Denny*, REV-OLA CREV039CD.

Denny, Martin, *Exotic Percussion*, Liberty LRP 3168.

Denny, Martin, *Exotica*, United Artists LM-1009.

Denny, Martin, *Latin Village*, Liberty LBY 1221.

Diddley, Bo, *Go Bo Diddley*, London HA-M 2230.

Diddley, Bo, *Have Guitar Will Travel*, Checker LP 2974.

Diddley, Bo, *Hey! Bo Diddley*, Pye GGL 0358.

Diddley, Bo, *Surfin' With Bo Diddley*, Pye MAL 751.

Dr. Buzzard's Original Savannah Band, *Dr. Buzzard's Original Savannah Band*, RCA APL1-1504.

Dr. Buzzard's Original Savannah Band, *Dr. Buzzard's Original Savannah Band Meets King Penett*, RCA AFL1-2402.

Dr. John, the night tripper, *Gris-gris*, Atco SD 33-234.

Dr. John, the night tripper, *Remedies*, Atco SD 33-316.

Dr. John, *The Dr. John Anthology*, Rhino 8122-71450-2.

Drasnin, Robert, *Voodoo!*, Dionysus BA09.

Drum + Space, *Calcutta Cyber Cafe*, Omni CD 001.

Ellington, Duke, *The Afro-Eurasian Eclipse*, Fantasy OJCCD-645-2.

Ellington, Duke, *The Blanton-Webster Band*, Bluebird 5659-1-RB.

Ellington, Duke, *A Portrait of Duke Ellington*, Gallerie GALE 405.

Ellis, Don (The Don Ellis Orchestra), *Electric Bath*, CBS 63230.

Esquivel, *Cabaret Mañana*, BMG 07863 66657 2.

Esquivel, *Latin-esque*, RCA INTS 1063.

Gershwin, George, *Cuban Overture*, Supraphon SUA 10470.

Ghania, Maleem Mahmoud (with Pharoah Sanders), *The Trance of Seven Colors*, Axiom 314-524 047-2.

Gibbs, Terry, *El Nutto*, Mercury 220 003 LMY.

Gillespie, Dizzy, *The Best of Dizzy Gillespie*, RCA CL 42787.

Gillespie, Dizzy, *Diz Delights*, RCA CL89804.

Gnawa Music of Marrakesh: Night Spirit Masters, Axiom 314-510 147-2.

Hawkins, Screamin' Jay, *I Put a Spell on You*, CBS 8-63481.

Hosono, Haruomi, *Bon Voyage co.*, Panam Crown GW-4109.

Hosono, Haruomi, *Medicine Compilation from the Quiet Lodge*, Epic/Sony ESCB 1302.

Hosono, Haruomi, *Naga: Music for Monsoon*, FOA FRCA-1001.

Hosono, Haruomi, 'Super Xevious', Pick Up Records TPU 9, 12″ single.

Hosono, Haruomi, *Tropical Dandy*, Panam Crown CRCP-136.

Hosono, Haruomi (producer), *Video Game Music*, Pick Up LPU-0005.

Hosono, Haruomi, and Laswell, Bill, *Interspecies Organisation*, Teich Ku Records, TECN-30336.

Intarathep, Thanin, *Music Composed by H.M. the King*, Metro Records MTS 189.

Ito, Teiji, *Meshes: Music for Films and Theatre*, ¿What Next? Recordings, WN 0020.

Jenkins, Johnny, *Ton-Ton Macoute!*, Atlantic K40105.

Jobim, Antonio Carlos, *Wave*, A&M AMLS 2002.

Johnson, Plas, *Rockin' With the Plas*, Pathi Marconi EMI 2 C 068-86529 M.

Jones, Spike (and his City Slickers), *Murders Them All*, RCA NL 89044(2).

Jones, Spike, *Showcase*, RCA NL 42730.

Khan, Nusrat Fateh Ali, *Mustt Mustt*, Real World CD RW 15.

Khan, Nusrat Fateh Ali, *Night Song*, Real World CD RW 50.

Koshi, Miharu and Hosono Jr., Harry, *Swing Slow*, Mercury PHCR-916.

Lasry-Baschet, *Chronophagie: Structures Sonores*, Arion 30 U 060.

Laswell, Bill/Namlook, Pete, *Psychonavigation*, Subharmonic SD 7005-2.

Lavoe, Hector, *Comedia*, Fania LPS-88992.

Lecuona Cuban Boys, *Lecuona Cuban Boys*, EMI Electrola 1C134-45 875/76M.

Lenoir, J.B., 'I Sing Um the Way I Feel', Sue WI-339 (7" single).

Lenoir, J.B., *Mama Watch Your Daughter*, Charly CD BM 47.

Lubin, Harry, *Music From One Step Beyond* (soundtrack), Varèse Sarabande STV 81120.

Lyman, Arthur, *Blowin' in the Wind*, HiFi Life SAV-H 8054.

Lyman, Arthur, *The Colourful Percussions of Arthur Lyman*, HiFi Life VA 160184.

Lyman, Arthur, *Cotton Fields*, HiFi Life L1010.

Lyman, Arthur, *Isle of Enchantment*, HiFi Life SAV-H 8033.

Lyman, Arthur, *Paradise*, GNP Crescendo GNP 606.

Lyman, Arthur, *Polynesia*, HiFi Life VA-H 8048.

Lyman, Arthur, *Tabou: Les Sons Exotiques d'Arthur Lyman*, Barclay 80.933 34.

McPartland, Marian, *Marian McPartland's Piano Jazz with guest Alice Coltrane*, The Jazz Alliance, TJA-12020.

McPhee, Colin, *Ô Bali Colin McPhee and His Legacy*, CBC M VCD 1057.

McPhee, Colin, *Tabuh-Tabuhan*, Argo 444 560-2.

Mancini, Henry, *Music of Hawaii*, RCA AYL1-3877.

The Master Musicians of Jajouka, *Apocalypse Across the Sky*, Axiom 314-510 857-2.

Material, *Seven Souls*, Virgin V2596.

Melle, Gil (Gil Melle Quartet), *Primitive Modern*, Prestige LP 7040.

Milhaud, Darius, *La Création du Monde*, EMI ASD 3444.

Miranda, Carmen, *South American Way*, MCA MCL 1703.

Modern Jazz Quartet, *The Sheriff*, London Atlantic HA-K 8161.

Morales, Noro, *Campanitas de Cristal*, RCA 07863 53357 2.

Mu, *End of an Era*, Reckless RECK 7.

Musique Mnong Gar du Vietnam, Ocora OCR 80.

Palmieri, Eddie, *Lucumi Macumba Voodoo*, Epic 35523.

Pandit, Korla, *Exotica 2000*, Sympathy For the Record Industry SFTRI 387.

Parks, Van Dyke, *Discover America*, Edsel ED 210.

Parks, Van Dyke, *Song Cycle*, Warner Bros. WB1727.

Parks, Van Dyke, *Tokyo Rose*, Warner Bros. 925 968-1.

Partch, Harry, *The World of Harry Partch*, CBS Masterworks MS 7207.

The Peanuts, *The Peanuts Hit Parade*, London Globe GLB 1015.

Pink Floyd, *The Piper at the Gates of Dawn*, EMI SCX 6157.

Pre-Columbian Instruments, Ethnic Folkways FE 4177.

The Pyramids, *Penetration: The Best of the Pyramids*, Sundazed SC 11023.

Ravel, Maurice, *Daphnis et Chloë*, Laserlight 14013.

Revel, Harry, *Theremin for the Musical Smart Set*, Request RR231-2.

Revell, Graeme, *Musique Brut Collection*, Mute Records, BRUT 1 CD.

Rhythm Devils, *The Apocalypse Now Sessions*, RYKODISC 10109.

Riddle, Nelson, *Love Tide*, Capitol T 1571.

Rothenberg, Jerome, *From a Shaman's Notebook: Primitive and Archaic Poetry*, Broadside BR 652.

Sakamoto, Ryuichi, *B-2 Unit*, Island ILPS 9656.

Sanders, Pharoah, *Tauhid*, Impulse A-9138.

Santo & Johnny, *The Best of Santo & Johnny*, Stardust CD-1027.

Sauter-Finegan Orchestra, *Directions In Music*, BMG ND86468.

The Shadows, *The Shadows Greatest Hits*, Columbia SCX 1522.

Shearing, George, *George Shearing's Greatest Hits*, EMI C 048-50 703.

Shore, Howard and Coleman, Ornette, *Naked Lunch*, Milan 262 732.

S-ken, *Jungle-Da . . . Not Primitive . . .* , CBS Sony 28AH 1846.

Smith, Harry (editor), *Anthology of American Folk Music*, Vols 1 to 3, Folkway FA2951/2952/2953 (1997 CD reissue by Smithsonian Folkways).

Smith, Harry (editor), *The Kiowa Peyote Meeting*, Ethnic Folkways Records FE 4601.

Snow White and the Seven Dwarfs (soundtrack), BBC REC 539.

Sound in the Sea, Marine Resources Inc., EMS-205.

Sounds of Medicine: Operation and Stethoscope Sounds, Folkways FX 6127.

Sounds of North American Frogs, Folkways Records FX 6166.

Street and Gangland Rhythms: Beats and Improvisations by Six Boys in Trouble, Folkways FD 5589.

Sumac, Yma, *Mambo!*, Capitol M-11892.

Sumac, Yma, *Voice of the Xtabay*, Capitol SM-684.

Sumac, Yma, *Voice of the Xtabay . . . and Other Exotic Delights*, Rev-Ola CREV034CD.

Sun Ra, *Angels and Demons at Play*, Saturn 9956-2-O/P.

Sun Ra, *Art Forms of Dimensions Tomorrow*, Saturn 9956.

Sun Ra, *Fate In a Pleasant Mood*, Saturn 9956-2/A/B.

Sun Ra, *The Nubians of Plutonia*, ABC Impulse AS-9242.

The Swamp In June, Droll Yankees DY 17.

Takemitsu, Toru, *Film Music by Toru Takemitsu, volume 4*, JVC VICG-5127.

Taylor, Creed, *Panic: The Son of Shock*, ABC-Paramount ABCS-314.

Taylor, Creed, *Shock: Music in Hi-Fi*, Fear F-203-2.

Throbbing Gristle, *20 Jazz Funk Greats*, Industrial Records TGCD 4.

Thunderstorm, Rykodisc RCD 50285.

Tjader, Cal, *Several Shades of Jade*, Verve 314 537 083-2.

Tjader, Cal, *Soul Sauce (Guacha Guaro)*, Verve VK-127 (7'' single).

Toop, David, *Pink Noir*, Virgin AMBT18.

Toop, David, *Spirit World*, Virgin AMBT 22.

Tracy, Don, *A Night With the Voodoo Family*, Columbia Two 106.

The Trip (soundtrack), Edsel ED211.

Various Artists, *Baubles: Down to Middle Earth*, Big Beat WIK 72.

Various Artists, *Felipe Luciano Presents Latin Roots*, Cariño DBM 1-5810.

Various Artists, *Jungle Exotica*, Strip CD005.

Various Artists, *Jungle Exotica Volume 2*, Strip ST-076.

Various Artists, *Mondo for Space Age*, TOCP-8971.

Various Artists, *Paris after Dark*, EMI EMS 1296.

Various Artists, *Rock 'n' Roll at the Capitol Tower*, Pathé Marconi/EMI 2 C 184-81970/1.

Various Artists, *Savage Pencil Presents Angel Dust: Music for Movie Bikers*, Blast First FU 3 LP.

Various Artists, *Surf City Drag City*, Capitol EMS 1180.

Various Artists, *White Elephants & Golden Ducks*, Shanachie 64087.

The Ventures, *Another Smash*, London HA-G 2376.

The Ventures, *(The) Ventures In Space*, Dolton BLP-2027.

Voices of the Rainforest (recorded by Steven Feld), Rykodisc RCD 10173.

Waldo, Elisabeth, *Rites of the Pagan*, GNP Crescendo GNPS 601.

Warwick, Dionne, *Dionne Warwick's Golden Hits – Part One*, Scepter SPS 565.

Warwick, Dionne, *Dionne Warwick's Golden Hits – Part Two*, Scepter SPS 577.

Waters, Muddy, *Chess Masters*, Stylus SMR 850.

Waters, Muddy, *Rare & Unissued*, PRT CXMP 2057.

Watson, Johnny 'Guitar', *I Heard That*, Charly CRB1101.

West, Speedy, and Bryant, Jimmy, *Flaming Guitars*, Bear Family Records, BCD 15926 DI.

Wray, Link, *There's Good Rockin' Tonite*, Union Pacific UP002.

Yellow Magic Orchestra, *Yellow Magic Orchestra*, A&M AMLH 68506.

index